Keeping Your Head in the Game

Gary Bloom is a leading clinical sports psychotherapist who works with elite athletes. He also hosts the award-winning *On the Sporting Couch*, a talkSPORT radio show in which he speaks with athletes about difficulties they have had during their careers, and he has commentated for over twenty years – notably on Channel 4's iconic *Football Italia*. Registered with both the BACP and the UKCP, psychotherapy's governing bodies in the UK, he is one of the few sports psychotherapists working within a football league club. This is his first book.

Keeping Your Head
in the Game

*Untold Stories of the Highs and Lows
of a Life in Sport*

GARY BLOOM

PENGUIN LIFE
AN IMPRINT OF
PENGUIN BOOKS

PENGUIN LIFE

UK | USA | Canada | Ireland | Australia
India | New Zealand | South Africa

Penguin Life is part of the Penguin Random House group of companies
whose addresses can be found at global.penguinrandomhouse.com.

First published 2021
001

Copyright © Gary Bloom, 2021

The moral right of the author has been asserted

Set in 13.5/16pt Garamond MT Std
Typeset by Jouve (UK), Milton Keynes
Printed and bound in Great Britain by Clays Ltd, Elcograf S.p.A.

The authorized representative in the EEA is Penguin Random House Ireland,
Morrison Chambers, 32 Nassau Street, Dublin D02 YH68

A CIP catalogue record for this book is available from the British Library

ISBN: 978–0–241–45131–1

www.greenpenguin.co.uk

Contents

CONTENTS

Fear

Jealousy and Envy

CONTENTS

CONTENTS

Author's Note

The events described in this book are based on the life, experiences and recollections of the author. Client confidentiality and the privacy of others have been taken very seriously. All names and identifying features have been changed and the stories told are not based on any one specific client or individual but are rather a selection of composite characters drawn from various encounters. Any similarities are purely coincidental.

Introduction

On a freezing February night at the Kassam Stadium, Oxford United were playing Premier League Newcastle United in an FA Cup fourth-round replay. The match was being shown live on the BBC's *Match of the Day*.

With League One Oxford United on the verge of a narrow defeat, the TV cameras picked me out in the crowd. Former broadcast colleague and match commentator Steve Wilson said this into his microphone as my image flashed up on the nation's screens, 'Well, there's a fellow commentator of mine, Gary Bloom. You may know the name. He's also the only psychotherapist in professional football and might be busy tomorrow depending on what happens in the next couple of minutes. He is one of a rare breed of football commentators with a brain large enough to do a "proper job".'

Ex-Arsenal and England defender Martin Keown, who was the expert co-commentator, quipped, '*Is* that a proper job?'

That's one question I hope *Keeping Your Head in the Game* will answer. At its very core, this book is about helping people to better understand the strains that our elite sportsmen and women go through. I tell stories about sportspeople and what can happen when they confront all the problems that you or I might face, but with the added pressure of doing so in the glare of public life.

Psychotherapy is about understanding ourselves. I focus on an individual's overall emotional well-being, including looking at their personal relationships and, most importantly, how they feel about themselves. Put simply, the objective of sports psychotherapy is to produce happier players who play better. Because, as in everyday life, if people are happier they perform better.

I examine sportspeople's key relationships and challenge their thinking, identifying the changes that take place when they decide to alter their behaviour and what happens to their form as a result. My aim is to help individuals accept who they are and be happy in their own skin, which usually involves repairing and improving relationships with themselves and others.

Despite what their lives might look like from the outside, our sports stars are remarkably human. They have failed relationships, abusive parents and suffer all the insecurities that you and I have. I hear their desperation to please a parent, a wife or husband or lover. But I also hear their fears about being unceremoniously dumped by the sport they love, being rejected and ridiculed by so-called fans. I hear about their loss of form, non-selection and slipping scores and track times, as much as I hear about missed promotions, toxic working relationships and fear for the future.

After working for twenty-five years within the sports broadcasting industry, my psychotherapy journey began with five years of training and then gaining a position with one of the leading sports clinics based in London and specializing in player care. I was shocked to learn about the high levels of male suicide between the ages of twenty-five and fifty, and discovered that many men were reluctant to talk to a therapist because they were afraid of looking weak. I thought that if I could normalize these 'chats' and broadcast them, maybe I could break down the stigma around talking about your feelings to a complete stranger. I took this idea to talkSPORT and began the radio show called *On the Sporting Couch*. I hoped that if listeners heard well-known sports stars discuss their struggles, it might trigger one or two of them with their own challenges to ask themselves, 'If they can talk about their problems, why can't I?'

We all have a relationship with our own mental health. If you look back at your life there will have been times when you felt good about what was going on and other times when you were maybe less confident about what you were doing. The difficulty is how we measure these feelings. How do we know if we're OK?

When we are feeling physically ill, the right thing to do is see a GP, but how do we know when we are not mentally well? This is a question that even mental health professionals find hard to evaluate, but I find it helpful to follow 'the rule of three' when I am working with clients. It works like this: if you are feeling depressed or anxious more than three times in a week and this period goes on for more than three weeks in a month, it's time to consider seeking help.

Of course, this is not a hard and fast rule. In the way that you wouldn't rush to your doctor for every slight ailment or minor injury, it's the same with mental health. So, just as I might look after a bad back or creaking ankle, I look after my mental health on the odd day when I'm feeling slightly anxious or depressed. You know when something's not right.

But mental health is not binary: that is, we're neither completely well nor completely sick. All of us have a relationship with mental health somewhere between the two and we will have good days and bad days.

It's quite common now to hear about mental health in sport being an issue, with high-profile sportspeople (Frank

Bruno, Dame Kelly Holmes, Marcus Trescothick, Freddie Flintoff and so on) speaking out about their own experiences. These people have shown bravery to go public about their very personal problems, but the vast majority of those 'owning up' only do so once their sports careers have come to an end.

Keyboard warriors on social media will sometimes criticize sportspeople who have their every need catered for (one radio presenter once said, 'Anyone on fifty grand a week has no right to feel depressed'). But along with the everyday problems that we all face – regardless of salary – high-profile sportspeople have to deal with a whole host of additional pressures, such as a sudden career-ending/shortening injury, simple deselection or a loss of form that sees their whole career put in jeopardy.

This book will explore some of these issues and the ways I help my clients. Take the young footballer who came to me with career-damaging anger issues that were preventing him breaking into the first team. Every time he was given coaching he would react negatively. Through techniques that I'll explain later, I helped him learn to control his fiery temper, listen to the coaches and implement their suggestions on the pitch. He's now a first-team regular.

To say there is a stigma about seeking mental health support in sport is an understatement. On the one hand we want our players to have the freedom to speak about their personal problems so we can help them, but on the other hand when players do this they can be ridiculed and stigmatized by coaching staff and fellow players. The emphasis on coping and self-control is the misguided basis of what we understand to be 'mental toughness'. Number-one culprit: football.

My belief is that having *therapeutic* mental health support should be so everyday and low key that the stigma around it just melts away. It should be normal to simply have a 'chat' with a practitioner at the training ground or in the cafeteria. Many of the players I work with probably don't even realize they are seeking out mental health support when they come to talk to me, but they are. They would probably scoff at the idea that their distress or unhappiness is even close to being a mental health issue, given how quickly and easily things can be resolved, but it is. And the fact that everyone in any of the clubs I work in chats to me about all kinds of things means that anyone can, there's nothing special about it, and so the stigma goes away.

Ultimately, though, psychotherapy is about change, and crucially it has to be an active choice to make the necessary changes. As the joke goes:

Question: How many psychotherapists does it need to change a light bulb?
Answer: None. The light bulb has to *want* to change!

I'm trained as a humanistic integrative psychotherapist, which means I use many different techniques depending on the client's needs. Sometimes they just want to start playing or performing better; at other times they want to examine a long-standing relationship with a parent or loved one.

As you'll see in this book, I always let clients set their own agenda for every session – it's their therapy time after all – but I might offer suggestions or teach them about psychology and psychotherapy. My objective is to enable my clients to be open about things it is very difficult to speak about, and to understand why they're unhappy or anxious, or underperforming. It's important that each client leaves their work with me knowing what's going on and why.

For a client to share some very confidential details, they need to trust me, and establishing trust is no easy task, as there will always be times when I need to say things they won't like but need to hear: truths they have maybe been avoiding or denying. The art of good psychotherapy is the creation of trust, which can be difficult when sportspeople are pushed in my direction by managers or others – as some of these stories reveal – and arrive angry and resentful, in total denial that anything's the matter. Sports psychotherapy is no picnic.

This book is a combination of accounts of therapy sessions, psychological insights and reflections based on some of the elite sportspeople who have been guests on my radio show and clients in my private practice. To protect identities (and the trust I mentioned), names and details have necessarily been fictionalized, but the issues presented, and the therapeutic solutions discussed, are anything but.

The book is structured around the main primary emotions we all experience on a daily basis: Shame, Anger, Fear, Jealousy and Envy, and Love. Starting with the clinical case notes I would usually take during their first session, I track ten sports stars as each of their stories weaves through some of those emotions, and show how easy it is for people to end up struggling with these forces – and how therapeutic intervention helps.

People often mistake me for a sports psychologist. Sports psychology looks at how changes to environment, thinking and training can improve sporting performance. It has been around since the early 1890s, when the work of Norman Triplett demonstrated that cyclists would cycle faster with a pacemaker, or competitor.* Historically, sports psychology was

---

* Not a heart pacemaker, by the way. They wouldn't be around for another sixty or so years.

about treating the athlete and their thought processes with mental skills training, but in recent years the fields of psychology and psychotherapy seem to have moved closer together, accepting the need to treat an athlete more holistically.

However, it's impossible to give a sportsperson any sort of confidence playing their sport when their personal life is falling apart, and that's where sports psychotherapy really comes into its own. Some will shy away from reaching out for help, while others will put it in non-psychotherapeutic terms: 'Gaz, me head's gone, mate. I'm playing shite!'

Our sportsmen and women are just like us, with all the same flaws and insecurities. Everyone I meet, in or outside sport, wants to change, but they are often too frightened to do so. Paralysed into inaction by fear of moving out of their current predicament, but also what will happen if they don't change, they are compromising their mental health. And that goes for all of us.

There is no such thing as good health without good mental health.

Shame

My grandfather died of shame. He was married with two young daughters and had a successful property business in pre-war Berlin in 1931. Life was good. When his brother-in-law was accused of fraud, my grandfather stood by him and posted bail for 40,000 Reichsmarks (around quarter of a million pounds in today's money). But his brother-in-law absconded and my grandfather was financially ruined. The shame of being in penury was too much for him and, at the age of forty-five, he took his own life.

Shame is the withering of our own sense of who we are, our worth in the world, our validity, and being exposed to humiliation often leads to an individual withdrawing and hiding from the world. Taken to its worst conclusion, the shame-filled individual might feel that life is no longer worth living and hide from the world permanently. Many psychologists believe that shame is the strongest motivator of all the human emotions, so maybe it's no coincidence that the biggest killer of men aged between twenty-five and fifty in the UK is suicide.

Feelings of shame can come in many forms and can be a force for both good and bad.

Shame can promote social cohesion. Social behaviours that have evolved over many thousands of years depend heavily on living interdependently with other members of tribes and communities. Therefore 'good' shame is about understanding the expectations of those communities and learning to 'do the right thing', or face the shame of social exclusion.

Guilt and shame are not the same thing. Guilt is feeling bad about what we have *done*, whereas shame is feeling bad about *who we are*. In my experience, it is easier to work with feelings of guilt, because I encourage the client to work out what sort of reparations they might make to the person they wronged. It also helps to differentiate between someone being a 'bad person' and a person who has done bad things. Clients often mix up the two. I've heard many a player moan about a particular coach using words like 'lazy' and 'useless', and I would always encourage such a coach to see these descriptions as potentially harmful. A 'lazy' player might be demotivated because he or she might be anxious or depressed, and it is way more helpful to separate the behaviour from the person.

Shame in sport can often find its starting point with the fans of the team. Their expectations and disappointment can be a huge burden for a player to bear and can often orchestrate a public shaming after a poor result or performance. When the team or individual fulfils the need to win, they are praised for their actions and rewarded, and the players feel good about themselves. This acts as motivation for future performances. But no one wants to have to face the wrath of the manager, coaches or fans.

David Beckham was public enemy number one when he was sent off in a crucial World Cup match playing for England against Argentina in 1998. But he made positive use of that public shaming to inspire him and a year later led his team, Manchester United, to Champions League success against Bayern Munich. I couldn't say whether Beckham sought psychological help with his demons, but psychotherapy can help detoxify shame, especially when a client begins to understand where it comes from.

Bad shame is toxic and generates negative feelings about

who we are. These feelings have often been given to us initially by parents or carers, who were themselves not aware of what they were doing as they told us off when we were little. Later on, these negative feelings can easily be brought back to life by a situation or by another individual who makes us feel we are not good enough.

Sport is laced through with 'not good enough's. I once worked with a professional footballer whose father stood on the touchline and screamed negative comments at him as a young boy every time he had a bad touch of the ball. Dad was desperate for his son to become a professional footballer. In fact, Dad had had a burning ambition to do this himself but wasn't good enough, and his frustration at his own failings and then seeing his son making similar mistakes was just too much for him. The footballer felt shame every time his father screamed at him, and that feeling was triggered every time he made a mistake on the ball as an adult professional. Which is why he contacted me and explained, 'If I have a bad first touch in a game, the match is ruined for me.'

Sportspeople are regularly exposed to shaming moments both on and off the pitch when they fail to live up to the expectations of others. In this section, we'll meet a number of them who are struggling with feelings of shame, from a jockey who can't live up to his family's demands to a rugby player whose masculinity is being challenged.

Good shame can be the motivator for some extraordinary achievements in our sports stadiums. It can produce world champions and successful sports teams. But bad shame attacks an individual's sense of self-worth, as my grandfather discovered.

That's why this work is so valuable.

Richard Davies

CLINICAL NOTES: FIRST SESSION

RICHARD DAVIES — AGED 26

Profession: Client is a successful jump jockey and is leading the race to be crowned champion jockey for the year. He comes from a long line of racing jockeys, with both his grandfather and father being champion jockeys in their day.

Referral: Client has contacted me through the Riders Union suffering from anxiety.

He has negative thoughts about the Grand National at Aintree, and has an anxiety that he will fall or not be placed in next year's race. He has decided to see if he can address his negative beliefs about Aintree in the intervening time. He's ridden at the course eight times and only finished twice. His grandfather and father had similar stories.

Appearance: Client is blond, slightly built and about 5ft 8in tall. He speaks quickly with a slight West Country accent. He often pushes several sentences together, which means he talks for maybe two or three minutes without eye contact and then will stop suddenly and stare at me, waiting for my response.

There is no history of use of psychological medication, he is physically fit and exercises regularly. He does sometimes have an issue with his weight, which is common with jockeys.

Presenting Issues: He is convinced that he's jinxed as he fell at Aintree in the most recent race. The horse he was due to ride took ill just before the race, so he ended up riding an unfamiliar horse and it fell early. He is now keen to look at his negative thinking about this racecourse and try to turn things around when the Grand National takes place next year.

He wants to look at his so-called bad luck and investigate the superstition. Is it real or is it just in his mind?

His mother and father are still together. He has two brothers and two sisters. He has been dating his current girlfriend for some time. She comes from a successful racing family who are financially successful and secure, although does not ride herself.

He claims he sleeps well and has never sought psychological help before. He expresses cynicism about psychological well-being and the effectiveness of therapy, and has been persuaded to come to our first session by his girlfriend, who is fed up with him obsessing about his so-called 'Aintree hoodoo'.

He is articulate, bright and claims to have had a happy childhood, most of which has been involved in some shape or form with the racing industry.

He says he has good relationships with his siblings and has never suffered from anxiety before. In fact he finds racing to be relatively stress-free and apart from his anxiety around one particular racecourse he is happy in (if not sometimes slightly bored by) the industry. I feel he is asking me to come up with a solution or equation to help rid him of his superstition or negative belief about the next Grand National.

Therapeutic Thinking: Who is this a problem for? His family? His girlfriend? Or for the client? Richard seemed genuinely disappointed that our first session would not be the last, as he hoped for a quick resolution to his problem.

I feel this isn't necessarily about success at Aintree. This is a young man who is struggling to fulfil the historical wishes of his family and win a race which I am not entirely convinced really matters to him.

Painting Horses

Richard arrived twenty minutes early for his next session and texted me to let me know he was waiting outside in his car. When clients arrive early or late, it's normally a sign that they are testing the boundaries of our relationship. This is particularly the case in early sessions, so it was necessary to make clear to Richard how some aspects of the therapy process work. Timing is an important aspect of boundary-making and holding, both of which are necessary for a number of reasons, not least to allow the previous client sufficient time to leave, thus avoiding the embarrassment of bumping into the next client arriving.

I texted Richard back to say that I would be ready at the specified time of 11 a.m. and with thirty seconds to go my doorbell sounded. Opening the door, I was surprised to find Richard standing on my doorstep with heavy bruising to his right cheek and cuts about his face. I also noticed as he crossed the threshold that he was hobbling.

He saw my face and explained ruefully, 'I had a fall yesterday. To be honest I wasn't sure whether or not to come today, but I thought I'd better. The hospital gave me the all clear – nothing's broken, thankfully.'

He shuffled into my clinic space and I motioned for him to sit down in the chair opposite mine. Just as I expected him to sit down, he swerved at the last moment and walked a few paces to his left to inspect a painting on my wall, all hint of the hobble gone.

'Not bad, not bad. I like the brushwork on this one – it's quite unusual. I'm guessing this wasn't painted here in the UK?'

Richard was correct and I thought immediately this might be his way of guiding me away from enquiring about his injuries, although he was clearly drawn by the few pieces of foreign art I had collected over the years. I confirmed his assessment.

My mind was flitting between starting options – should I go with the topic of art or his bruising after the previous day's racing? I quickly weighed up the alternatives as he hobbled back across the room and sat down in my blue armchair with a heavy sigh. I wondered how much of this hobbling was for my benefit.

I encouraged him to start. He scanned the room and began to smile, a small, tight smile which missed his eyes.

'My girlfriend thinks I look a right bloody mess. She's not far wrong of course. Funny thing is, none of this was my fault. Simon Sharp pulled up in front of me as we went into the sixth from home and I didn't stand a chance. Anyway, I'm shit on left-handed courses [where riders gallop anticlockwise].'

As I sat and listened to Richard's unfolding story, I had the strong feeling that fence after fence was actually being erected in front of me. The question was, what were the obstacles meant to prevent me reaching?

'Anyway, I've been signed off for the next three weeks, when I'll have another medical assessment to see whether I'm fit to ride. I'm gutted, I really am. I wanted to ride tomorrow but now I'm at the beck and call of the racing authorities and they've told me to take it easy until the end of the week.'

I noticed the slight smile still playing on Richard's lips,

but it now looked more genuine. He certainly didn't look like a man who was 'gutted' to be out of the saddle for the next few weeks.

'I have to say, you don't look too gutted, Richard.'

He looked taken aback by my words. 'Sorry, I'm a bit confused. My girlfriend told me that therapy is about you just listening to me. Not telling me I'm lying!'

I explained that while his words were saying one thing, his facial expressions were saying something quite different. I am always on the lookout for a client's body language, facial expressions, change of tone or language, or the lack of eye contact – those unconscious reactions that tell you so much more than words about how a client is really thinking and feeling. Richard resembled a little boy hiding something, but I wasn't sure what.

I reassured him that if he felt uncomfortable continuing the session and would rather see another therapist who did 'just listen', then I could give him some details of my colleagues and we could stop right now. I felt it only fair that he understood that's not how I work. I will challenge clients when they make statements that are at odds with their body language. I try to be as honest as I can with clients, while taking into account their emotional temperature at that moment.

He nodded to continue, looking slightly more wary of me as I moved us on to safer ground.

'I can imagine your family and girlfriend were quite worried when they heard what had happened during the race?'

'My dad was absolutely furious and the first thing he did was ask if I'd be fit to ride at Cheltenham next month. I thought it a bit odd that all he could worry about was my next race rather than whether or not I was in one piece. Mum was really upset and she spent the night over at our house making sure I was OK.'

I felt this was the time to ask Richard a little more about what had happened the previous day during the race. Something just didn't feel right in his glossing over of the actual incident.

'Well, everything was going to plan and I was about three [fences] from home. My horse wanted to go, but I held him back thinking he might tire in the last few furlongs. That's when things went a bit wrong.'

'What happened? Can you say more?'

He nodded and continued more slowly. 'As sometimes happens during a race, a rider and horse can be out of sync and at that point the rider is at his most vulnerable to falling, mainly because you're travelling at around thirty to thirty-five miles per hour and neither of us is sure who's in control. The horse wants to do one thing and I another – in that split moment we are not riding as one.

'The next thing I knew another horse cut across me and I'm out of my saddle in a flash and straight under a couple of horses, getting kicked and bumped all over the place. I think in total three or four horses came over the top of me before I was dragged to safety by a paramedic.'

He said this in such a matter-of-fact voice it was obviously something that happened relatively frequently, an occupational hazard apparently.

Still struggling with the image of being trampled by charging horses, I was surprised that he didn't end up even more battered after such an accident, and asked if this kind of fall was typical.

He quite casually told me that he can fall two to three times in a bad month, but the falls don't amount to much damage for him or the horse as jockeys learn from an early age how to fall off safely to avoid major injuries.

'You roll yourself up into a ball to avoid breaking anything when you land and to protect yourself from hoof strikes,' he explained.

Even with his blasé tone, I couldn't help wondering to myself how *any* jockey managed to get back on a horse, or even why! The words 'hoof strikes' kept repeating in my mind.

'So, what went wrong? How come you still got a battering?' I asked him.

Silence. Richard broke my gaze and looked back at the paintings he was studying when he first entered the room.

'I don't know why but I didn't.' He kept staring dreamily at the painting.

'Didn't what?'

He looked down and started fidgeting with his hands, then said, 'I didn't tuck and roll, and to be honest I've no idea why. When I came off, my mind went blank.'

'Really? Why?'

He just shook his head and shrugged.

Every athlete involved in contact sport knows that they are one incident away from a career-ending injury. Most of us would still be able to turn up to work with the odd broken bone, but for many athletes a significant injury would mean a considerable amount of time on the touchline or out of action. I often think about what this does to them psychologically, knowing they could be moments away from such a catastrophic injury, with either temporary or permanent repercussions.

Once again, I let the room fall silent leaving my 'Why?' hanging in the air.

I needed him to really think about my question, because it

sounded like he had deliberately endangered his own life by not protecting himself after the fall, which could be considered an act of self-harm. Even if he couldn't yet understand why he hadn't protected himself when he fell, he needed to recognize that he had overridden an instinctive (and learned in his case) reaction for self-preservation. Things had now moved well away from a simple issue around riding at Aintree.

I watched Richard's eyes scan the room as if he was looking for something. He was wearing a frown now, and I waited, willing him to get to the same conclusion. He suddenly stopped scanning the room and looked at me.

'Hang on! You think I deliberately injured myself by not rolling into a ball. That's what you're thinking, isn't it?' His tone was defiant.

'It's not important what I'm thinking right now, Richard. It's about looking at your thought processes when you fell. But there was something going on that you seem to be un-aware of, guiding your decisions, and we need to find out what that was.'

Richard looked down for a moment, as if he was scram-bling for something to say. He then jumped neatly over that disturbing self-revelation and admitted to being secretly a bit pleased that he didn't have to ride for a couple of weeks, as the pressure of winning races would be off him. He went on to describe how he knew that his dad would be really pissed off with him for falling and damaging himself, and that his chances of riding his next big race at Cheltenham were now only fifty-fifty.

Ordinarily, I would bring the client back to examine an aspect more closely after dodging away from such a pro-found disclosure, but I felt Richard needed to take some time to process the issues. To confront them too soon would create anguish that maybe he wasn't able to manage at this point.

That allowed a conversation to open up between us about his relationship with his dad, who had always wanted Richard to be a jockey. Richard had been a decent A-level artist at school and wanted to go on to study fine art at Goldsmiths College in London. While Richard had dreamed of pursuing a career in art, his dad wanted him to spend more and more time in the stables, mucking out and riding out the horses.

'Dad used to ride for a leading trainer and every school holiday or free weekend I'd have to go with him to the stables and help. When I was old enough the trainer would allow me to exercise the horses on my own and Dad was always making jokes to the trainer that one day I'd be a successful jockey. I preferred to play football and rugby at school. I was a decent fly half at rugby and played right wing at football. If you had told me then that I might be a professional jockey, I would've laughed my arse off.'

Richard was eighteen and finishing his A levels when his dad organized an apprenticeship at a leading trainer's yard, convincing Richard that he would always be able to study art another time, but racing was in his blood and he might never get a chance like this again.

Whether it was fear of failure or wanting to please his father, Richard decided to give up on his dreams of art college and follow his dad's advice. Suddenly he had an income of his own.

'It wasn't much, but for the first time I had money. I lived and worked at the stables and while my friends were broke at university, I was out on the lash, dating girls, enjoying nights out and meals and just beginning to get the odd ride in a professional race. I didn't really miss university. Soon, I forgot what I really wanted to do. Dad played his "told you so" card and the more I rode the better I got. Dad gave me loads of advice early on and every ride I had would be examined in minute detail if we had access to the footage.

'The more I rode the luckier I got too, and eventually began to win some decent races. Dad started using his contacts with agents to get me better and better rides. People don't realize that the jockey's strike rate [rides to wins] is essentially dictated by the quality of horses they're riding. I'm not saying that anybody can ride and be successful, but being on a bloody good horse doesn't half improve your chances. Dad has been brilliant, but the truth is the industry was very different when he was riding. There weren't so many races and there was more time between the racing seasons. Now the industry is virtually 365 days a year. It's non-stop.'

Richard stopped talking and stared at me, then started again.

'Blimey, we've been talking for ages and we haven't even mentioned Aintree. That's why I'm here, isn't it? I have this hoodoo which I suppose has struck again, but I'm not sure I'm even going to need much therapy – feeling much better already.' This last bit was said with smugness.

I smiled to myself. If I had a pound for every client who thought we had solved their issues after one or two sessions . . .

'Look, Richard, we're coming to the end of the session now, but I think we need to recognize that I can't help you have a good ride in the Grand National after just a few sessions, but in time I can help you feel differently about racing there. What I would say is this seems to go much deeper than getting round the Liverpool course. Anyway, if you agree, I'd like to see you again next week and we can look in more depth at some of the things we've been talking about today.'

He looked a little surprised but agreed and we arranged another session. However, just as he was leaving, I was curious and said, 'Richard, can I ask you a question? If you weren't a professional jockey what would you be doing right now?'

His hand was on the door handle as he stopped and turned. 'Painting,' he said in an instant. 'Painting horses.'

Mark Silver

CLINICAL NOTES: FIRST SESSION

MARK SILVER – AGED 31

Profession: Professional snooker player

Referral: Client was referred by his agent, who was worried about his deteriorating form and had convinced Mark that I could help.

Appearance: About 5ft 7in and rather overweight, he was sweating and slightly breathless when he came into my clinic room. This client is balding and mentioned he was considering whether or not to shave his head completely, and be done with the whole hair 'thing'.

He was dressed in designer clothes which he self-consciously adjusted frequently, but none of them seemed to match or look particularly good on him, almost as if they were someone else's clothes. He wore a large gold ring on his little finger. He has an

Essex accent, with a surprisingly strong, confident way of speaking, and quite a quirky self-deprecating humour.

Presenting Issues: Anxieties around his relationship with his girlfriend and worried that his snooker career will be compromised by his deteriorating performance.

Says he drinks alcohol to excess sometimes, especially when anxious, and admitted that when drunk he can be quite aggressive. He claimed he is shy and only uses alcohol to boost his confidence, but accepts that his drinking may be adding to his weight.

Felt he was not getting enough sleep and is increasingly anxious about where his fiancée is when he's not with her, and feels unsure about her commitment to their relationship.

Client is close to his father and regularly enjoys spending time with him at their local pub.

Mark met his girlfriend, Jasmine, a former Miss England, two years earlier. At this point he was enjoying the trappings of a mid-ranking professional snooker player and on course for bigger success. Even with his keen sense of humour that usually helped with gaining female company, he was surprised at her interest and after a short courtship Mark asked her to move in. Things had started to become difficult from that point onwards.

It seemed that Jasmine had a strong desire to be seen out in public with her new famous partner, and the frequency with which she wanted to socialize has seen the relationship struggle and the client's form dip. As he has recently not been earning as much prize money, he's beginning to gamble his earnings to gain extra funds to keep up with the lifestyle, and is now in considerable debt.

This, he said, is one of the issues that has motivated him to come to see a therapist. He has not discussed this with Jasmine, nor does she know he is here. The client was recently involved in a drunken brawl in a nightclub after he believed Jasmine was getting too friendly with a male actor from a TV sitcom. This brawl generated negative media publicity for him, adding to his stress.

Therapeutic Thinking: It seems to me that the client has to work out if he needs Jasmine and her public persona to feel good about himself.

There also appears to be an overemphasis on how he thinks other people see him (overweight, balding).

I'm picking up a sense of latent aggression from Mark. This usually arises in a client as a defence mechanism to conceal fear about what's going to happen in the therapy session, but I don't feel threatened. His understanding of what's involved in working psychotherapeutically with me isn't clear. Maybe he was looking for me to simply help him 'fix' his relationship.

There seem to be some confidence issues at play about his being with a highly desirable partner, as he feels he is 'punching well above his not inconsiderable weight'. There is certainly something worth exploring about his possessiveness of Jasmine.

There is evidence that Mark is increasingly compensating for his anxiety with the gambling and drinking, and there could be other addictive behaviours.

I feel the client cannot rediscover his snooker form until he deals with his obsession with Jasmine and his need to please her, which may well be unachievable.

In Over His Head

I was due to see Mark Silver again the next day, but that
evening I noticed that he was playing in a big snooker championship match live on TV. I considered whether it was
ethical for me to watch the game, or whether that would
compromise my work with him and influence my thinking at
our next session.

Unless your client is someone famous, you have no idea
before you meet them who they are or what their personal
pressures might be. This is often different with sportspeople,
as their exploits are captured in minute detail in the media, so
it can be difficult to avoid gaining background knowledge
about a client that you might not normally have. This can colour your thinking around the issues that the client presents.

A good example would be if Jürgen Klopp booked in as a
client. There would be many preconceived ideas about how
he has become such a successful football manager because
of his fame and public image. Working with non-celebrity
clients who can operate freely outside of the glare of the
media, I would have none of that information and would
have only that client's version of events to work from.

It's a real dilemma, but therapists are humans – and often
downright nosy too! – so I tuned in to watch what turned out
to be an important quarter-final match. When I started watching, the game was nearing its completion and Mark wasn't

doing very well. The TV commentator seemed to suck and tut every time Mark approached the table.

'The tide of the match is going against Silver,' he intoned gravely. 'He really should be doing better against a much less experienced operator. I wonder if he feels a sense of humiliation losing to a man six years his junior.'

Ouch!

The narrative was certainly all about the young gun out-foxing the older man and the TV coverage was going to town on this. I felt a sense of uneasy voyeurism after little more than twenty minutes watching Mark's humiliation, so decided to switch the game off. It just felt too uncomfortable to see.

Looking at the now-blank screen, it struck me how emotionless most snooker matches are. Each player has to wait patiently for their chance to take back control of the frame in the focus of the cameras, while they watch their chances slowly being deconstructed. If they do manage to take back control, they have to deal with their stress to such a degree that most players appear emotionless. If Mark could suppress his feelings so well in a professional match, I wondered whether he did the same on a personal level when things got tough. Most sports involve extreme physical activity, which helps burn off many of the stress hormones generated, but not snooker. So how did Mark deal with this stress?

When my client is winning and doing well there's a huge feel-good factor that I recognize that I enjoy. I own this enjoyment, and also recognize that somehow the client's success is bound up in the work we are doing together. But when a client or a team I am working with loses, I feel the loss personally and, if I'm not careful, I blame myself for a missed goal, misplaced conversion kick or missed red over the pocket. This is one of the key drawbacks of being a sports psychotherapist.

Mark arrived slightly late for our therapy session the next day. After he had settled into the chair and taken a long drink of water, I asked him how he was.

'Fine,' he replied sullenly.

Fine . . . There was a joke when I was training that the word was an acronym for 'fucked off, insecure, neurotic and emotional'. I wondered how many of these words applied to Mark right now.

I could see Mark's discomfort with the silence I allowed to fall. It was becoming fairly obvious that he was not keen to be here today. I decided to tackle this head on.

'It feels like you don't want to be here today,' I told him.

'Give me a break. I just got marmalized by that twat last night.' He was becoming slightly more animated.

'If I'm honest, I watched the match last night and you didn't look very happy. But I didn't watch till the end.'

'For fuck's sake, how many years of training did it take to realize I was unhappy?' he snorted. 'That flash git took the piss out of me for the entire match and I couldn't concentrate. I nearly reported him to the organizers. He completely put me off my game.'

I could see the emotion from the match last night was now bubbling out, and it occurred to me that maybe Mark needed to vent the emotions after a major loss.

I asked him, 'What would you usually do after a loss like last night's?'

'What do you think I fucking do? I go and get pissed, usually with my dad. Am I seriously paying for this?'

I wasn't going to react to his insults, as that was what he

was expecting me to do, and I suspected this was how he usually pushed difficult people away.

Mark couldn't see whatever it was that was going on for him. He couldn't hold on to his shame, disappointment or anger, so each of them had to be fired in another direction. He'd turned his fire on the guy who beat him and was now turning it on me. I also noted that his opponent last night was labelled a 'flash git' and that led me to reflect if there was an element of masculine rivalry going on between them. His opponent was younger, taller and, by classical standards, would probably be judged more handsome.

Mark seemed to be calming down a little now. He'd blown the froth off the top of his coffee and we were now getting down to the hot, dark, juicy stuff.

'I couldn't concentrate to be honest,' Mark added. 'The harder I tried, the worse it got.'

'What were your thoughts when you were playing last night, Mark?'

Mark took a deep breath and let it out like a slowly deflating balloon. 'Look, I know I'm a better player than him, but I was getting more and more irritated because I couldn't focus. All I was thinking about was how things haven't been great between me and Jasmine for the last few weeks.'

I asked him what 'not great' actually meant. He explained there had been frequent arguments and Jasmine had even made him sleep on the sofa on a few occasions. They had managed to patch things up enough to keep going, but the relationship was on his mind most of the time – and he knew that wasn't helping.

'I keep thinking, "I wonder what she's doing right now. Is she watching this match on TV? Or is she out somewhere with her mates?" I know when she's out she can attract male attention pretty quickly. I know it sounds pathetic, but I worry about what's going on when I'm playing snooker. Is she safe?'

Mark had inadvertently put his finger on the essence of what sports psychotherapy is all about. He was unhappy and therefore couldn't play well. Happier players play better.

I asked him what he meant by 'safe'?

He was quiet for a while before responding, 'She's hardly safe lying under fifteen stones of another man!'

I asked him if that was likely to happen, to which he said, 'You tell me?'

I could see his insecurities were getting the better of him, so decided to explore another avenue.

'How did you guys get together?'

Mark told me that he'd been away in Germany, playing in a summer tournament, and there had been a mistake with the accommodation arrangements, which meant him having to travel half an hour away to a hotel in the countryside. When he got to the hotel late, he found he was the only one there from the tournament and, hitting the bar out of sheer boredom, he bumped into Jasmine, looking particularly 'delicious' with her waist-long fiery red hair, who was also staying at the same hotel on her own, while visiting friends nearby.

'We hit it off immediately. I mean, it was magic.' He grinned for the first time in the session. 'We chatted shitloads and flirted outrageously, and then we moved away from the bar and close to the hotel swimming pool. I said I was hot after travelling and would love a dip to cool off – shame the pool was closed for the evening. Then she suggests skinny-dipping. I thought she was kidding, but thirty minutes after meeting her I'm in a swimming pool naked, and we're splashing around and giggling like two little kids. There was plenty of kissing and touching going on but, to be honest, nothing seriously naughty happened. Afterwards she came back to my room, and when I woke in the morning, I couldn't believe it. There was this beautiful girl in the bed next to me surrounded by all this gorgeous red hair, just grinning up at me.'

As he went on with his story, his face changed. 'So we go down to breakfast and when we enter the breakfast hall we notice that we are the youngest hotel guests there by about twenty years. There was obviously an old folks' coach tour or something filling up the hotel.'

He described how they went into the breakfast room together, giggling and focused entirely on each other, oblivious to the other guests pointing, smiling and whispering, until they gradually noticed every head was turned towards them. Then a small round of applause began and gathered in intensity. Mark and Jasmine were both confused and Mark thought, What the hell? But then he noticed there was a blue shimmering light reflected on the breakfast tables. Slowly looking up, he realized that the ceiling of the breakfast room just so happened to be the bottom of the swimming pool. 'Some dirty bastards had been watching us snogging in the pool last night. They must have recognized Jasmine because of her hair and told the rest of the guests this morning.'

I thought it sounded like something out of a movie.

Mark and Jasmine ran straight out of the breakfast room, and all Mark could think of was that those old people had seen him naked. 'I can still hear their laughter.'

I was trying not to break into a smile.

'Everyone in the fucking hotel knew what we were doing and I was terrified my bare arse would be splashed over the tabloids the next day because some old git had whipped out their phone and taken a picture.'

36

Thankfully for Mark, it appeared that the elderly guests' reaction times were too slow, so none of them had managed to capture the moment.

That was eighteen months ago and it seemed that the relationship had been a bit of a whirlwind since then. According to Mark, Jasmine loved the limelight and getting public attention, but while it might have been fun at first, it was fast becoming problematic for him, or, as he described it, it was 'doing my head in'.

If Mark fancied staying in for a fish and chip supper, she wanted to go out to the most famous expensive restaurant in town, hoping some 'arsehole' of a photographer would be there to take her photograph. Mark then revealed the main reason he was unhappy with the attention: his focus was on what the photographers were most probably thinking – 'some fat lard arse with a gorgeous Miss UK!' If they went anywhere – surprise, surprise – some bloke with a camera showed up, and while it was now aggravating Mark, he was so keen to please Jasmine, he just smiled and kept quiet.

As Mark was talking, I realized that he seemed to think Jasmine had something to do with the media presence when they were out, maybe even setting it up herself.

He drew breath and began again.

'With a snooker cue in my hand, up to this point I'd been able to block out all those nasty thoughts about what she might be doing and who she could be flirting with, but for the past six months I've just been feeling fat and bald and that she is bound to find somebody else. A fortnight ago we had a holiday in Tenerife and some bastard photographer takes a snap of me and Jasmine by the hotel swimming pool. I'm looking a right lard lizard and she's looking gorgeous – it's doing my swede in!'

He shook his head as if trying to dislodge his thoughts.

Mark was clearly going to be no easy fix. He valued himself by being seen in public with Jasmine, yet hated the public exposure it brought – every camera flash highlighted his insecurities. He knew his spending on expensive restaurants was mounting up and financially this was becoming untenable, but didn't feel he could share this concern with Jasmine.

I was struck by his lack of trust in Jasmine, and wondered if he was blaming her for the worsening financial situation he now found himself in, even though she appeared unaware of his debts. I asked him why he didn't feel he could share his financial situation with Jasmine.

He looked up at me with red-rimmed eyes as he blurted out, 'Because I think she'd leave me if she knew.'

He held his head in his hands and I could sense his internal struggle for control was reaching a crescendo. When it came to Jasmine, he wasn't able to regulate his emotions and even during a snooker match it was now becoming increasingly difficult. There were the issues of not being attractive enough and not having sufficient funds to please her, and the shame he felt about being out of Jasmine's league and not trusting her. I really didn't know at this stage whether Mark could keep both his career and his partner, and be happy at the same time.

I felt snookered.

Jane Lovell

CLINICAL NOTES: FIRST SESSION

JANE LOVELL – AGED 38

Profession: Former Olympic heptathlete who represented her country at the Commonwealth Games in the 2000s and is now modelling/TV presenting.

Referral: Self-referral, having researched a therapist with experience of dealing with elite sportsmen and women.

Appearance: Slight build, 5ft 8in tall, well dressed with dark brown hair, has clearly taken care with her appearance, and has come to the first session dressed as if she was attending a job interview. She has a slight Essex accent, her choice of language is good and she has obviously had a good education. She appears confident, without seeming brash, but there is an obvious attempt to hide the nerves she is feeling as the unconscious fidgeting with her wedding ring reveals.

There is a slight playfulness about her that gradually becomes apparent as she gets more comfortable in my company.

Presenting Issues: She is very upset by the difficult relationships she has had historically with her parents and is now struggling in her marriage. Jane is feeling regret about her career. Could she have gone further as both an athlete and a model? Should she have instead decided to pursue solely a career in modelling? She is now suffering from issues of low self-esteem in her relationships and has hinted that she is considering leaving her husband.

Jane was forced to stop competing in 2012 due to an injury and has tried to forge her career in TV punditry, but is struggling due to her lack of confidence. She is clear she wants to work on her self-belief.

In her athletic career, she was initially coached by her father, who, she claims, was very demanding, and as a young woman she was torn between her father's wishes for her to pursue a career in athletics and her mother's encouragement to go into modelling.

She has been married for ten years and claims the relationship has been failing for the last eighteen months as she has tried to find her own identity. She has one daughter. She is worried about the effect it will have on her daughter if she decides to leave the marriage.

Therapeutic Thinking: Jane has talked in her first session about the control imposed on her by both her father and her husband. She has acquiesced historically to her father's wishes to become an athlete, but feels she has been manipulated by him and her injury in 2012 was somehow a sign that she made the wrong choice. She feels that she married somebody very similar to her father, a controlling man who at times has suppressed his jealousy at her outgoing and bubbly nature. She feels torn about staying in this airless relationship, held back by the shame of abandoning it with the ensuing effect it will have on her daughter. She is riddled with 'bad shame' around how her father manipulated her early life and career, and how this has affected her subsequent life.

Overall, this might be seen as an 'existential crisis'. Jane is asking who she is and what she wants to do with the rest of her life.

To Bee or Not to Bee

Jane arrived at my office promptly and immediately took me aback by asking whether she could have a cup of coffee. I don't normally offer my clients coffee and I thought this might be a boundary challenge, but I surprised myself by agreeing. Maybe I didn't want to deny her in case that made her not like me. Maybe I felt she needed a little kindness. But when she tried to follow me into the small kitchen, I hurriedly ushered her out, quickly regretting my impulsive decision.

Jane was carrying a small briefcase and, as when she arrived for the initial session, she looked as if she'd come to a business meeting. Her brown, shoulder-length hair was neatly coiffured and her make-up seemed a little on the heavy side for a therapy session, sporting bright red lipstick that seemed incongruous in this setting.

'It's lovely to see you,' she said, 'and you have such a lovely place here. I like the furniture. Great paintings too.'

I recognized that I was being flattered as she sipped her coffee and kept her gaze on me. I wondered what this flattery was for. Often it's a defence mechanism for a client when things get too emotionally difficult in a session. The earlier session was littered with comments like 'I wanted to see an experienced therapist' and 'I really like your radio show.' The same comments were beginning to punctuate our conversation now.

My supervisor used to say, 'Gary, once is an accident, twice a coincidence, three times a signal.' I decided I needed to tackle this.

'Jane, thank you for your compliments and I'm flattered by them, but I really think they are distracting us from the real reason you're here. Has anything happened in the week since we last met?'

She looked flustered for a moment, then began to describe how things had started pretty well. She had met up with her former colleagues from the Commonwealth Games team at a reunion and was especially pleased to meet an old boy-friend, Alan. He was now a human rights lawyer from Belfast who had recently moved to England to make a new start after the breakdown of a long-term relationship. Since the reunion, they had happily been catching up on old times, but Jane insisted there was no wish to rekindle their relationship, from either side. However, her chats with him had begun to open up emotional issues for Jane, and Alan had encouraged her to see a therapist.

Jane had found herself confiding in Alan about the unhappy state of her marriage and how she suspected she had moved from the influence of a controlling father to that of a controlling husband. The conversation between them had clearly been intimate, but apparently neither of them had wanted to take it further – not at this stage anyway.

'It was just nice that somebody was willing to listen to me. I've no desire to be unfaithful to my husband, but having that freedom to speak, it was just lovely. Alan and I remin-isced about old times and, for the first time in years, I was able to be honest about what was going on for me.'

It all came pouring out about how the relationship with her husband, Tony, was struggling, and how the ever more frequent rows often resulted in him saying really rather childish things, such as 'Why are you always criticizing me?', and somehow making her feel like his angry mum. After these flare-ups, Jane described often being confused about what had just happened, unable to understand why she was left feeling as if she'd acted so unfairly towards him.

'My husband and I haven't had sex in months – I have no desire to, to be honest. His "little boy" act is just such a huge turn-off. All I feel at the moment is that I am his mum – but at the same time somehow his property.' As she said this, I could see her eyes start to well up with tears, and I pushed a box of tissues towards her.

Her relationship with her husband made me think of a model of psychotherapy called transactional analysis. On a very basic level, the theory goes that whenever we interact with someone else, we are in one of three 'ego states': parent, adult or child. In a healthy relationship we will engage with another person adult to adult: that is, we will listen to what the other person has to say, consider their views and adapt our thinking and responses to that.

But many people, unable to do this, leave 'adult mode' and shift into acting like a parent or a child. By entering either the child or parent mode, the other person may respond to us in the opposite mode. So, acting like a parent may result in the other person responding in a childlike manner.

As an example, I recently went to pick up my elderly mother from a mainline London railway station. It had not been an easy journey: the traffic was dreadful, I was worried about getting there on time and it took an age to park. Eventually I got to the platform, where I waited patiently for her train to arrive. I made sure she got down on to the platform safely and I took her bags from her. The moment she was

safely off the train, she commented, 'What an awful haircut!'
I immediately felt angry and was instantly transported back
to feeling like a child being criticized by a parent. My immediate thought was, 'Carry your own fucking bags then' – not
exactly adult, I accept. Even with all my years of training and
insight, I found it supremely difficult to overcome the very
strong instinctive feelings her words had generated and to
drag myself back to actually responding like an adult. In fact,
I remember it taking a l-o-n-g count to ten.

Looking over at Jane, I found myself wondering what 'ego
state' she was in now. I sensed something childlike in the
way she had just spoken. I waited for a few seconds before
resuming.

'Jane, how old do you feel right now?'

The tears increased and her shoulders shook for a few
moments.

'Bloody hell! I feel I'm like a stupid thirteen-year-old girl.'

I asked her if there was anything significant she remembered happening when she was thirteen.

She seemed to mentally shake herself, then, gathering her
composure, she nodded. 'I do remember being invited to
one of Jenny Harrington's parties. You know the type –
contraband cider and spin-the-bottle. Only the most popular
people in school ever went and it was *the* party to go to. I hadn't
been invited to any of her previous parties, mainly because I
very rarely had anything to do with Jenny. Not that it mattered,
as I was never allowed out anyway – too busy training. But one
of the popular boys who was going quite fancied me and must
have asked Jenny to invite me. I was beyond excited about
being invited. The only downside was the party was meant to
take place on a Saturday night, and the following day I had an
important meet and was due to compete early in the morning.'

Jane went on to say she'd never been to a teenage party before and confided in her mum, who took her out to buy a new outfit. When her dad found out, though, he went 'nuts' and insisted she couldn't go because she needed to be in bed by 9 p.m. that evening to get a full night's rest in preparation for the next day. It turned into a 'bloody awful row' – Mum and Dad yelling at each other, and Jane in tears begging to be allowed to go. Her dad finally conceded and Jane went to the party – but she had an awful time. The boy who fancied her had apparently changed his mind and spent the evening chatting up another girl, and, just before leaving for home, some spotty boy tried to kiss her in front of everyone, to the great entertainment of the gathered crowd. Feeling foolish and humiliated, Jane left the party to the sounds of laughter.

While her mum was deeply sympathetic about the horrific party experience, Jane recalled that her dad wouldn't talk to her as they drove to the athletics meet the next morning. She came fifth in the event and, on the drive back home, her dad kept up an unrelenting tirade about the need to not be distracted by silly parties and dressing up – either she wanted to be a medal-winning athlete or she didn't. She sat on the back seat of the car with silent tears streaming down her face, feeling so angry at the unfairness of it all. How was she to know the party would end up like that, and all she ever did was train, so obviously she wanted to win, couldn't he see that?

The unfairness Jane felt aged thirteen was being dredged back up by her husband's behaviour.

Children who have been manipulated by parents often grow up feeling great shame that they were unable to do anything about it. This is particularly true in cases of abuse. As an adult the client knows intellectually that they could have done nothing about what was going on, but they are sometimes left with a great deal of shame that they didn't stand up to a bully-ing influence or manipulative force as a child.

Jane continued, saying, 'The meeting with Alan just woke something up in me. He treated me like an adult – two adults together, just chatting normally.' She had a wistful smile on her face as she was transported back to her encounters with him.

I asked why the relationship didn't work out with Alan when they were together years ago.

'It was exciting, but things weren't perfect with Alan when we were together. He was so dedicated to being a top athlete that he didn't really have any actual time for me. He was a bit selfish that way.'

So here she was, seeing a therapist as Alan had suggested. I asked her what she was seeking from therapy.

'I want the ability to be me, to know who I really am, because all I've ever lived before is somebody else's version of me – some man's version of me – an athlete, a model, a television presenter. It's all bullshit and I've got to the stage in my life where I want to decide what I'm going to do. Not allow somebody else to decide for me again.'

I pondered over what the reconnection with Alan really meant. I wasn't convinced it had the makings of an affair. It was more like a reawakening of Jane's intellect and spirit, which had lain dormant for some time. In my experience, people are sometimes prompted to go into therapy when they have – maybe for the first time for ages – a reason to reflect on their life and their difficulties. In Jane's situation, it's clear that Alan had triggered that thinking.

The truth is that we often repeat relationships from our childhood, and Jane's description of her controlling father made it likely she might end up with a controlling husband. What made this seem more acceptable was that her father's

controlling had a tangible positive outcome, her athletic success, and so it was OK to go along with it.

Later in the session, Jane described how conflicted she felt
about really enjoying her time with Alan, and the shame of not
disclosing to her husband that she had met an ex-partner.

'I really felt bad not telling him, but it would open a can of
worms I'm just not ready to open yet.' She paused to consider
her words, a troubled look on her face as she gazed unsee-
ingly at the floor, going through in her head what telling her
husband would be like.

I kept silent, giving her space to think.

She eventually said, 'I think I'm frightened that if I told
him I'd met Alan, I'd want to tell him the rest.'

I asked her what 'the rest' was.

'That I'm unhappy in the marriage and want to leave him!'

She said this with a defiant tilt of her head, looking me
directly in the eye. I got the sense that the desire to defy her
husband was a profound one, long held deep within. But I
also guessed that she had never really had a good enough
reason to allow the defiance to erupt, knowing the upheaval
it would cause and the strength she would need to deal with
the aftermath.

Jane went on to describe how things had become worse in
the last couple of days. She had done a modelling job some
months ago and had eventually been paid this week. She told
me how she'd been planning to use the money to convert the
garage into a gym, and she and her husband had discussed
this and agreed that's how they would use the money. But
yesterday, he'd suddenly announced he wanted to use the
money for a beekeeping project he'd never mentioned
previously.

'God knows where beekeeping came from. There have

been so many of his hare-brained schemes like this, I've lost count. And all financed with my money. I just snapped.'

I asked what happened then.

'I told him I'm not financing any more of his money-wasting ideas.' There was a defiant tilt of the head again before she quickly looked down. 'He went absolutely potty and then, out of nowhere, accused me of having an affair.' She was clenching and unclenching her fists.

I could feel the anger and frustration sparking off her. I was not surprised to hear that her husband had launched an attack on Jane when he was made to feel under pressure, as this is a common response when controlling people are criticized. A controlling person is often very skilled at making their partner feel that they've done something wrong even when they haven't. Why do they do this? To justify punishing their partner in some way for the 'indiscretion', or pre-emptively trying to keep them from making that 'error' again, controlling them to keep them acting in certain ways.

When she spoke again her words came thick and fast. 'I did feel ashamed about meeting Alan and not telling Tony, but now I'm left with his accusations and anger and none of the fun of actually having had an affair. I just don't know what to do any more. It's my money, after all, and I feel that he is using the money as a stick to beat me with.'

I gave her a moment to recover her emotions before asking what she was going to do next. She shook her head. There was no sign of the defiance now – only rounded shoulders and downcast eyes looking at hands clasped in her lap.

'I just feel like running away.'

I wondered if that's something she's been doing all her life – and at great speed.

Kwasi Adepodji

CLINICAL NOTES: FIRST SESSION

KWASI ADEPODJI — AGED 22

Profession: Kwasi (which means 'Born on a Sunday') is a professional footballer. A striker, he is currently on loan with an English club, having been signed on a one-year deal from a club in Belgium. His form is patchy and he has not scored a goal in several weeks.

Referral: A nearby club has invited me in to counsel Kwasi as he is obviously very upset, having been seen on social media at a sex party in London which he was attending with his Ghanaian friends (he comes from Ghana, where his father and mother are pastors in a church in Accra, the capital).

The football club (unsurprisingly) wants to make sure that their player is not emotionally affected and is able to play at the weekend in a vital league match, and has given me access to all areas of their facilities.

Appearance: Tall and powerfully built. He speaks with a slight Ghanaian accent. He is obviously well educated and fully understands the implications of what has happened, but is terribly worried about what his teammates will say when they find out.

Presenting Issues: Football club striker is dealing with the fallout from the social media and press exposure, both in the UK and Ghana, after one of the girls attending the party posted photos clearly identifying Kwasi in sexually compromising positions. The press have run the story and now the club wants to protect their player.

Kwasi's father did not want him to become a professional footballer but instead to follow him into the Church. Kwasi, against his father's wishes, joined a football academy in Ghana and then went on to play professionally in Belgium.

It was apparent that he had been coerced into meeting me and, when I asked him, he said he'd never seen or worked with a therapist before, and explained that back in Accra the Church tended to sort out personal difficulties without recourse to professional help. He had two main issues:

1) The teasing of his teammates, which would begin in the next half-hour when they arrived at training, along with the taunting of away supporters, which he would have to face at the weekend.

2) The fallout back home in Accra when his parents found out that he had behaved in a manner that they felt was not appropriate for the son of a church minister.

Of these two I would guess that the fury of Kwasi's father was far more significant than the teasing he would get in the UK.

Therapeutic Thinking: There has been a major rift between what Kwasi wants to do in his career and what his father wanted him to do. In becoming a professional footballer, Kwasi has disobeyed his father, who no doubt feels hubris that this now seems to be going wrong in such a shame-inducing way. It seems to me that there are two separate objectives:

1) To help Kwasi deal with the initial fallout from teammates and opposing fans and get him ready to play at the weekend.

2) To help him think about his relationship with his parents and how he has separated from them in pursuing his career.

Kwasi cut short the session (which lasted fifteen minutes) as he had to go to a team meeting. We've arranged to meet later today away from the club in my clinic.

Born on a Sunday

Kwasi arrived later the same day at my clinic, on time. He was wearing a club tracksuit top with a white number nine over the club crest. He looked round the clinic space as if he was searching for something he'd lost. I wondered whether he simply didn't trust me and was checking out if I really was a therapist, or a journalist masquerading as a therapist ready to sell his story. Whatever he saw seemed to reassure him. He sat down heavily in one of my armchairs. His limbs looked too long for the piece of furniture and he seemed to squirm for a while before he got fully comfortable.

When I asked him if anything had changed since that morning, he said things were much as they were.

'I'm just wondering whether you have spoken to your parents, Kwasi. I know you were concerned about how it would go down back home.'

Kwasi explained that he had spoken to both his parents, who had made numerous telephone calls to him after the story had broken. The story had made the Ghanaian press, but strangely not as prominently as it did in a London tabloid. The club's PR manager had managed to do a deal with the Ghanaian papers, who agreed to stop running the story. Instead Kwasi did an interview for them about a decision he was going to have to make about representing Ghana or Belgium at international football. His father wasn't convinced by the smokescreen, was furious and demanded that Kwasi return back home to Accra and end his football career immediately.

I suspected that this was highly unlikely to happen.

I felt I needed to make it clear to Kwasi why he was here and what to expect, and also to gain his trust, which I could tell was a little thin at this point.

'Kwasi, do you know what psychotherapy is?'

He shook his head. 'I've heard of psychology but not psychotherapy.'

'OK. The basic premise of psychotherapy is that it will help you to understand yourself better, and when you do that, it will enable you to make better choices. One of the most important aspects is that anything you say to me is confidential, and that allows you to speak freely.'

He was looking at me rather sceptically. 'That all sounds great, but how do I know I can trust you?'

I explained to him that confidentiality is one of the key rules that regulate my profession. If I were to tell anyone else about what clients discuss with me, it would very soon get out and no one would want to work with me, so I'd be out of a job.

I asked him if he had any further questions about what I do. He just shook his head, but seemed a little less edgy with me.

'How did it go with the rest of the lads, Kwasi?'

'Oh, they took the piss of course, but what did I expect? Everything settled down pretty quickly, though, and apart from the odd silly comment it's been OK. To be honest, I got off lucky – it could have been a lot worse.'

I reflected on the many times I'd witnessed 'bants' (banter) in the dressing rooms and was inclined to agree with him. After working with many sportspeople over the years, I am still unsure at times when banter is actually good-natured teasing and when it's outright bullying, as the two seem to share similar characteristics: name-calling and personal insults. However, there is a clear distinction for me. If the person handing out the banter has power over the person the banter is aimed at, I'm pretty sure it's bullying. Banter can be the glue that holds a dressing room together, but when it morphs into bullying, it can be the acid that corrodes the cohesion.

'Kwasi, what do you really need right now?' I asked him.

He thought for a moment, then said, 'I think I could really do with my mum being over here. I know that if she was here, things might feel easier – at least for a few days.'

Kwasi went on to explain that after the incidents reported in the press, he had been walking past an evangelical church during the service and, for the first time since he left Accra, he felt the need to reconnect with a congregation.

'I guess I was looking for a sense of something familiar to soothe my soul. I know it sounds pretty stupid but just at that moment, when I heard a hymn we used to sing back home, I turned and went inside. That's when the usher – the security man who is on the door – spotted me. I didn't realize he was a big football fan, but he recognized me immediately. He took me to one side of the church reception and whispered to me, "Look, brother, we don't want any trouble and I think if you came in it might cause a bit of a problem. I know this is the House of the Lord, but maybe the Lord needs a break from you for a week or two."'

Kwasi bowed his head and sat in silence for a little while, before beginning again. 'It was as if my dad had been on reception at that church. I felt completely kicked in the nuts. I mean, these places are meant to be for everyone, including sinners. It felt like Mum and Dad were chucking me out as well. Maybe I deserved it.'

'Kwasi, I'm not sure what exactly you have done wrong. You haven't cheated on anybody or been dishonest about your actions. You're not in a full-time relationship right now and you are a young man with wants and needs.'

He shook his head, denying my comments. 'You don't understand. I've been trying to make a new life for myself ever since I left Accra. Dad didn't want me to break away. Didn't want me to leave Ghana. Didn't want me to leave the Church. I guess he was right. I'm just a screw-up.' He sat with his head in his hands, the shame palpable.

This mixture of wanting a mother figure for comfort in times of emotional challenge and needing to separate from her in order to forge an adult life is at the heart of many a struggle for young men. To put it more simply, we're not supposed to need our mums because we are grown men, but if we're honest we can't do without them.

I wondered about the relationship Kwasi had with the Church, and the shame he felt at being rejected by his family and the Church as well. Talk about a modern-day excommunication! Yet his other family – the football club – had stayed faithful, and now it was my job to make sure that at least that relationship remained secure.

I think the work with Kwasi was not only about trying to help him come to terms with what he'd done, but also about increasing his positive feelings in relation to breaking away from his mother and father. If he wanted Mum in the UK to comfort him and if she was willing to come, then why not? I certainly thought it would help him play at the weekend when the team had a home game with the top club in the division.

I decided to ask how he felt about playing in the crucial match.

'What do you think your form is like at the moment, Kwasi?'

'I think you know I'm not really on fire at the moment. The manager thinks I'm too soft when it comes to playing at centre forward. He says I'm too easily bullied by opposing centre halves. I'm desperate to find a goal, but I seem to seize up every time I get near the penalty area and then I usually can't get my shot away.'

I often teach my underperforming sports clients the difference between having a 'challenger' mindset and a 'threat' mindset while playing, a concept I've borrowed from sports psychology. The 'challenger' mindset can be summed up by having belief that you can overcome the opposition, no matter what the odds. The 'threat' mindset can be summed up as looking over your shoulder, worried that your nearest rival is about to overtake you. In Kwasi's case, this presented itself in the belief that he simply couldn't score. When this occurs, I give confidence drills and exercises to enable players to control their mindset when it matters, but in Kwasi's case there was no opportunity to really make much headway with exercises or drills as the manager wanted to name his squad for the weekend. Thankfully, if Kwasi's mum was on her way from Accra, that should at least give him a sense of security and provide some comfort.

Kwasi went on to explain about his time in the football academy in Accra when, as a promising eighteen-year-old, he was spotted by a Belgian first division club and offered the chance to play in Belgium with citizenship and a passport to sweeten the deal. His first years at the Belgian club weren't easy and he described the casual racism he experienced inside the club and from the terraces as well. While he enjoyed the cultural change and the different kind of football, he didn't settle easily and found it hard making friends, especially having to overcome the language barrier.

It appears that his potential was never quite fulfilled and, after three years battling to win a place in the first-team squad, the Belgian club decided to listen to offers for Kwasi. There weren't many – until the opportunity to play in the UK arose. But he had now been at the club six months without making a serious impression on the first team.

'The manager wants to know whether you are fit, and by that he means mentally and psychologically fit to play at the weekend against City. How do you feel about playing on Saturday?'

He held my stare for a few seconds.

'I feel sorry for the other team. I'm playing!'

I immediately thought, Kwasi: born on a Sunday? He must think I was born yesterday!

James Holmes

CLINICAL NOTES: FIRST SESSION

JAMES HOLMES — AGED 30

Profession: Professional cricket player (fast bowler)

Referral: The player has self-referred through his players' union.
He came home from a tour of India, where he had felt unwell
while away with the England team. At first, he was not sure if
he was suffering from some form of virus or dehydration, but he
admitted to the team psychologist that he was feeling anxious and
had lied to the medical staff that the reason he was returning
home was because his father was gravely ill with a heart
condition.

His anxiety on tour was not new, having occurred previously
when he was abroad for warm-weather training with his
county, and he said that he was tormented by images of
something catastrophic happening to his family back
home.

Appearance: James is tall (6ft plus) with distinctive blond curls and broad shoulders, presumably the result of upper-body exercise and gym work for fast-bowling. He is quietly spoken, without an accent and with good diction.

He appeared to find it difficult to engage with me on an emotional level, and most of his answers to my questions were very defensive. He often started a sentence with 'I think', and when asked about his feelings regarding anxiety around being away he said, 'I don't know . . . If I did, I wouldn't be sitting here.'

Presenting Issues: James appears to be suffering from some sort of anxiety brought on by being away from home. He has irrational fears that while he is away his girlfriend, mother, father and older sister might be vulnerable to some sort of terrible accident. This makes him unable to concentrate on his sport and he is experiencing psychosomatic illnesses (stomach aches and headaches) which often prevent him from training. Consequently, while in India he did not manage to play any competitive cricket and indeed his training schedule was severely curtailed.

Therapeutic Thinking: From what I've seen so far this looks like a case of general anxiety disorder (GAD), but the client is also struggling with feelings of guilt at having let his teammates down, and is feeling ashamed about his lack of honesty with the medical staff of the England team. He admitted that his father has been ill for many years and the excuse to come home was a convenient one.

What happened when he was a young man to make him anxious about the welfare of his mother and father, who are still alive, in good health for their age, and still together? He has an older sister with whom he gets on and a female partner of four years who is in full-time employment in the banking sector.

My suspicion is that it could well be the case that the client finds it difficult to be away from a maternal figure (this is reflected in his anxiety around safety and being away from a 'home base'), so this is an area I would like to examine with him. He claims that he had a very happy childhood and that Mum and Dad were involved in village cricket most of their lives, with Dad a decent wicketkeeper and Mum on the organizing committee of their small club in the south of England. There are no obvious fractures in his relationship with his partner, although there is evidence of obsessive thinking about her.

James said he needs to keep a daily diary, otherwise he gets very anxious about where he is meant to be and what he is meant to be doing.

He also has superstitious rituals around his bowling and a lucky mascot (a marble kept from his school days) that he keeps in his trouser pocket while he is bowling. He told me that once, when he couldn't find the marble, he was so anxious it was difficult for him to walk out on to the field of play.

I feel I need to help James understand better his desire to be close to his family, create strategies for being away from home and be more honest with those around him in a professional capacity about his anxiety and possible OCD tendencies.

Hard Boundaries

Working as a sports psychotherapist with high-profile clients, I sometimes find that events overtake the therapy, and this was one such case. The day before James was due to see me, I happened to notice on a news website a story concerning James and his father. James had told the England cricket medical team that he needed to return home to look after his seriously ill father, Harry, and while James had already admitted to me that his father had been chronically sick for some time but was not in any immediate danger, the public story hadn't changed.

In the previous week, an enterprising photo journalist had tracked down James's father, Harry Holmes, and snapped him walking out of his local Tesco carrying two heavy bags of shopping, showing no signs of being even slightly unwell. Under the headline 'England's fast bowler and his emotional baggage', the story went on to explain how James had not been entirely truthful about his reasons for returning home from India. It ridiculed him for complaining about the standard of the food out there and speculated on the likely recipient of the curry ready-meals which could clearly be seen peeking out from the top of the shopping bags.

In normal therapy work, you don't usually get a snapshot of a client's inner world and everything comes to you fresh in the session through the lens of the client. But with high-profile sports clients it's not like that, and while listening to *Test Match Special* I can find myself inadvertently hearing about a client I'm soon to work with and checking whether he's had a particularly good or bad game.

James arrived on time for the therapy session. I was impressed by the perfect creases in his chinos and the well-polished brown brogues. He sat down in the armchair in front of me and crossed his legs purposefully, interlocked his fingers in a steeple shape, resting his elbows on the arms of the chair, and immediately asked me whether I could produce a medical certificate for his anxiety and depression.

The way he was self-diagnosing his own condition rang immediate alarm bells with me, as in my experience this is usually done to mask a deeper issue. For instance, I once had a sports client who was diagnosed with insomnia, but when therapy began it emerged that he couldn't get to sleep because he felt guilt about an affair he was considering and found it hard to be at rest next to his partner.

I had hardly begun talking with James when I suddenly felt that he was running up to deliver one of his fast balls. He looked as if he was about to go into a high-stakes business deal. Having a client behave in this forceful way is not uncommon, and it's usually when they are initially afraid of engaging with therapy. I knew so little about this brooding young man who was clearly confused about where he should be right now: India or back home?

I told him I could write a medical report, but only after I had gained sufficient insight into the issues affecting the client. He was now insistent that he wanted a medical report, becoming quite agitated.

'So write me a medical report, then. I'm obviously depressed and anxious, so what's the problem?'

'The problem is I don't know yet if you are depressed. Just as you wouldn't presume to tell your GP what medication you need, I need to establish the underlying issues to be able to write a report about them. Why do you need the report?'

He didn't answer but jumped to his feet and began pacing the room, as he ran his hands through his hair in frustration.

'I can see how angry you are, James, but it would be more helpful if you could sit down and tell me what's going on for you right now.'

After a moment's more pacing, he reluctantly sat down and let out a long slow breath. He eventually said in a low voice, 'I can't go back out there.' His fear at the prospect of having to return to India and his anxiety around the safety of his family were now so great that he was becoming desperate.

My initial thinking was this was about adjustment anxiety disorder, a term used to describe the inability of a person to adjust to changes in their life, with the creation of anxiety around the possibility of having to face that change. Most of the clients I have treated with this are usually just coming out of a relationship – usually a long-term one – or leaving employment against their will. Neither of these applied to James.

Much of the remaining session seemed like a push and pull between me and James, as I tried to decide whether this was a mental health issue or he simply didn't like being in India. He had never been there before and was quick to tell me about the poor quality of Indian food, how stifling the weather was and how hard the pitches were, to the point where he couldn't get his bowling accurate enough. I was beginning to feel the stirrings of frustration about the lack of openness between us. One minute he was complaining about being in India, the next minute he was talking about depression. So, which was it?

I also thought that the press story about his dad had sharpened James's anxiety. Now he had the additional shame to contend with, having been exposed lying to the England medical staff. I decided to talk about James's family to try and work out why he had this overwhelming need to stay close to them and why touring was so difficult.

'James, are you closer to Mum or Dad?' I asked, knowing the answer before it came.

Somewhat impatiently, he replied, 'I suppose Mum. She was always there when I was growing up. Dad often spent a lot of time away from home.'

And then he looked at me expectantly, as if he'd done what I'd asked and now I should do the same and produce his medical report. I wasn't finished yet – nowhere near.

'So, what was life like at home when you were growing up?' I asked.

With a dawning sense of resignation, he realized that if he stood even the remotest chance of getting the report he'd come for, he'd have to be way more forthcoming.

With a deep sigh, he continued. 'Debbie, my sister, is quite a bit older than me, so when I was growing up I had two mums really. But when Debbie turned eighteen, she went to college and Mum and I were on our own a fair bit. When he was there, Dad was quite strict really. But Mum used to spoil me and get my favourite food and treats.' He smiled briefly.

I encouraged him to go on.

'To this day, Dad still says she spoiled me. I don't see it like that. I think she was just trying to protect me from the other kids.'

I wondered aloud why he might need protecting from other kids and he explained that they used to tease him about his mum and dad actually being divorced because his dad was away such a lot. I considered the impact of an absent father on the young James growing up and having to deal with the unkind teasing of his peers, and came to understand a little more about how the close relationship between James and his mum had developed. His dad's long absences would also have had a profound impact on his mum, so maybe there was a little smothering going on on her side – common in mother–son relationships where the father is absent.

If the relationship between James and his 'smothering' mother was one of close mutual dependency, I wondered if he'd come to feel responsible for his mother and her happiness. This can happen, and it's not usually emotionally healthy.

I asked James how he first got involved with cricket and he explained that it was through a friend at junior school whose father was a big cricket fan. Things developed from there and he was given his first professional contract with his county team at eighteen. After a few years he got his own flat a few roads away from where his parents lived, enlisting the help of Mum to do all the soft furnishings – curtains and the like – while Dad popped round at the weekends to do all the DIY to make sure the place was comfortable. Mum was always popping round with food, and if he was playing an away game for a few days, he would come back to find the fridge fully stocked.

When I asked if he felt this was rather intrusive, he told me that, on the contrary, he used to love his mum popping in.

When I asked if it interfered with his romantic relationships, he told me how his mum was very sensitive if he had a girl-friend, always checking it was OK before she came round. He did mention there were a couple of occasions when girl-friends he was dating thought it rather odd that he and his mum were so close. In one instance, it caused the end of the relationship.

'You know, I've not thought about this for a long time, but once when I was playing in a youth game, I really lost it with a batsman who was sledging me [verbal abuse between bats-man and bowler]. He said something horrible about Mum and how I was a "Mummy's boy". He insinuated that I was gay. The next ball I delivered was a bouncer, deliberately aimed at his head, and he was furious. My captain was not impressed and told me to "get a grip". There's been plenty of sledging in my career, and I've given as much as I've received, but I really wanted to hurt that arse.'

Therapists often see the process of a boy growing up as being about moving away from the initial caregiver (usually the mother) and beginning to identify with the father, with the boy sometimes mimicking his father as he learns how the world works. As his independence grows, a young man will clash with his father because he understands that his father's way is not the only way, and that challenge to paternal author-ity can sometimes make a father cross.

The best parents don't get angry with their children as they make the inevitable mistakes. In their own time chil-dren work out their own way of doing things, and create relationships in the world away from their mum and dad. But this process doesn't happen unless we can break away from the powerful orbit of a mother's love. As a teenager I remember my mum teasing me about every girlfriend I brought home for tea, and I wonder now whether this was actually about her anxiety around being 'abandoned' by me.

I felt that this was very likely a major issue for James – that he needed the closeness with his mum to feel safe. The three-day county games were doable for James as he returned to his flat and found his full fridge. Food can be a substitute for love and Mum might be reminding him that she loved him.

Towards the end of the session James returned to the issue of the medical report. He drew a deep breath and the volume of his voice increased as he said, 'Look, I need a medical certificate or report or something. The press are on my case and I need something to keep them at bay. Mum is really upset by all this nonsense. She feels she can't go out of the house now without some photographer following her. I need to protect her. This isn't fair on them. Can you help me or not?'

I told him that it was too early to assess whether he was depressed or not, and if he wanted a physical examination, he should go to see a GP.

'I'm sorry, James, but our work together has only just begun. Right now, I see a confused man who is in the glare of the media spotlight and is looking for a quick fix. I don't provide quick fixes here. However, I am happy to help you work out why you came back from the tour of India, why this has happened before and will probably happen again. It's important we understand this before we draw any conclusions.'

James inhaled deeply before speaking again. 'In that case, can you refer me to someone who can get me this bloody certificate?'

Edwin Thomas

CLINICAL NOTES: FIRST SESSION

EDWIN THOMAS — AGED 32

Profession: Professional rugby union player with a Welsh team and former Welsh international

Referral: I was contacted by the lead psychologist at a Welsh rugby union club who was concerned about Edwin following an incident in a pub the previous week.

He was arrested after a drunken brawl and spent the night in a police cell. This is the first time he has ever had any incident of this type and he confided in the club psychologist that 'maybe he needed to see someone'.

Appearance: Edwin is about 5ft 9in, bald (shaven head) and broad-chested and would be considered handsome. Met my gaze in a very direct way, almost defiantly, and was seemingly cheerful and open in his answers, although while engaging with me, the actual information shared was minimal. He was dressed in his club's tracksuit. He spoke with a slight Welsh lilt, with good diction, and was clearly well educated.

He had a small cut above his left eye, possibly the result of the drunken brawl (see above).

Presenting Issues: The club is concerned that one of its long-standing halfbacks is becoming increasingly demotivated about playing professional rugby, resulting in a dip in form. Fellow players have pointed out to the club psychologist that Edwin 'just doesn't seem himself'.

In our initial session, Edwin accepted that his form is below par at the moment, but he thought it was a passing phase related to the number of injuries he was now picking up on a regular basis.

He did allude to his inability to feel real enthusiasm for playing rugby any more and, when asked about his domestic situation, said that he and his wife have been arguing a little more recently, but he didn't think this was a real problem and they could usually sort out their issues by talking. He has been married to Cerys for four years and says up to this point their marriage has been stable, but he feels they are more than capable of sorting out their issues without help. They don't have any children.

He was dismissive of the brawl, seeing it as just a one-off and of little concern, but was open to using the sessions to help return to enjoying his rugby again, although was unsure if there was a connection between his recent arrest and his lack of enthusiasm for the game.

Therapeutic Thinking: There seem to be two presenting issues, which may be related:

1) His lack of club form and persistent injuries which are hampering his career. He seems to be working on the understanding that I can help his form with some performance hints and tips, rather than wanting to look at what might be lying deeper.

2) What caused the brawl and why he is reluctant to look at this. I need to understand the nature of the incident because this will give me a clue as to why Edwin reacted so violently and out of character.

Edwin seemed intent on talking about his rugby career, but there was very little willingness to look at other areas of his life. He will be coming to the end of his professional playing career in the next couple of years, so this could be a transitioning issue (when a player leaves a sport through retirement or injury), and maybe the real problem is uncertainty about what he is going to do after he finishes playing.

This client was unusual in the amount of control he wanted to exert in our initial session and I wondered if I would be able to work with him psychotherapeutically. I felt there was much he was concealing or unable to share.

He was clear that my role was to get him back into the first team, nothing else.

Deal or No Deal

When Edwin arrived at the third session he was wearing a blue V-neck sweater and casual trousers. The tracksuit he had worn previously had been dispensed with, so did that mean he was more likely to be open to talking about the brawl? I was pleased he had dressed in a more relaxed fashion, because I felt he was using the tracksuit as a barrier to addressing his personal issues. Maybe now we could start to make some real progress.

The previous sessions had produced frustratingly little: a bit about his family, his background, his education, but nothing that would give me any real clue as to what was really going on in the significant areas of his life. I'd heard about how his mum and dad were still together, that he'd been to a private school in Wales, that he had two successful siblings who were not involved in sport, how he'd enjoyed his time playing for his club in Wales, and a lot about the shoulder injury, but little about his feelings at being arrested following the beery brawl.

He talked proudly about his excellent disciplinary record and how he wasn't a big fan of going out drinking with his teammates, which was one of the reasons why the incident that led to his arrest was even more surprising, to him and everyone else. But still we didn't go into any depth about why it happened.

Beginning the third session, I wondered if I was ever going to get much further with him and was preparing to write back to the club psychologist with my thoughts, with a recommendation that he might want to try another therapist as I was struggling to make progress. I had determined to call an end to the therapy work after this one if I was still unable to break through his tightly controlled facade.

So, with a sense of frustration, I motioned for him to sit down in the chair in the therapy space. He looked intently at me as if he was expecting me to start the conversation and I had a strong feeling that he felt slightly triumphant because so far he'd managed to deny me any real insights. This therapy was only going where he wanted it to go. Almost as if our sessions were like a battle of wits between two protagonists, and he was winning. And he was enjoying the situation immensely.

I decided to try something different, so mentioned that we had only a few more sessions left out of his allocation and it would be worthwhile at this stage to review whether or not to continue.

This technique often changes the 'gear' in my therapy work and signals the beginning of the end of my time with a client. This was when he or she needed to decide whether to address the issues or stop wasting our time (and their money). Edwin looked almost disappointed that the fun would soon stop and indicated that he'd like to continue at least until the allocated sessions had been used up.

'So, Edwin, where would you like to start today?'

He sighed and settled into a long deconstruction of the game he'd played since our last meeting. Most of his chatter centred around the unfairness of the referee, the poor tactics of his coach, the weather conditions on the day, how the pack had not done their job, and more on how the opposition were blatantly flouting the rules without incurring the referee's disapproval. You might as well have written 'blame someone else' all the way through his thought processes. And yet, during his monologue, it felt like he was almost daring me to challenge his version of events.

I stepped away from the temptation to do just that and suggested it sounded like he'd had a pretty awful game, and then Edwin launched into a tirade about how awful his career was at present, the quality of the club coaching and how he simply just wasn't enjoying his rugby any more.

As I sat and listened to him, all I could hear was that Edwin was apportioning blame to everybody and everything. I was waiting for him to complain next that the rugby ball was too oval! But he still hadn't brought up the whole issue of being arrested after the drunken brawl. I realized that the conversation was going absolutely nowhere again and that an eavesdropper could be excused for mistaking it as a friendly chat between two blokes who like rugby, rather than a therapy session, so I decided to take the plunge.

'Edwin, for us to work effectively together we need total honesty between us. I know this might be a tough question, but can you give me a sense of how and why you ended up being arrested after a night on the town?'

I was expecting another expert fly half sidestep and was not disappointed.

'Why are we talking about this again? I thought we were discussing how to improve my performance.'

'We've done that, Edwin, but what I really want to explore is why your behaviour was so out of character that night.'

'OK, better get it out of the way. Well, just a bit of drunken nonsense really. I don't know what all the fuss is about. Some dickhead said something stupid to me and I guess I just over-reacted. It was a bit silly really. One minute we are having a few jars and next it's like a scene from a Wild West saloon bar and it's all kicking off.'

I asked him how it all kicked off.

'What's that got to do with anything?' I could see he was becoming rather irritated at my line of questioning.

'It's got everything to do with it, Edwin.'

He gave me a long, hard stare and, holding his gaze, I could see this might be the make or break moment of our work together. He shook his head in mock exasperation and then he started.

'God knows how it all kicked off. We're all having a laugh, like, and next thing Johners, a prop who's not played with us for long, announces to everybody that his missus is expect-ing and we should get a round in to congratulate the family. Fuck knows why, he's already got two kids, so what's the big deal? When I made a comment to that effect, he looked a bit surprised and then he says to me, "When are you ever gonna get your Cerys pregnant, then? I've heard that you're firing blanks!"'

Edwin started to shift in his seat, as if reliving his agita-tion during the altercation. He told me how the other lads exploded with laughter and how something in his head just 'went'.

I asked him what he meant by 'went' and was surprised by the violence of his response.

'Who the fuck is he to talk about my private life like? He's only been at the club for two minutes and he's lording it over me and my missus. Well, I wasn't having it and next thing we're swapping punches. I tell you, it went from zero to 100 in just a few seconds.'

I could see that as he spoke angry spit was coming out of his mouth like venom.

'Next thing I know, the other lads are dragging me out of the bar, then the police were there and I'm being bundled into a police car. I'd only had two or three pints, but they told me I needed to calm down.'

Fortunately for Edwin, the arresting officer happened to be a big rugby fan and recognized him immediately. He put him in a cell with a blanket and a glass of water, told him to cool off and kept his presence at the police station off the official records. The officer then phoned his friend, the rugby club secretary, and left it to him to make sure the papers didn't get hold of the story.

I reflected that the brawl seemed to be about Edwin's masculinity, which had obviously taken a knock from all the public taunting, but the topic of him and Cerys had not featured in any of our previous sessions. Edwin hadn't even mentioned previously that a family might be on the horizon, let alone touched on any possible problems with conception. I wondered why that was. Was it maybe because I'd mentioned that we were running out of sessions that he had finally decided to make use of our time together?

I recall a comment from one of my supervisors when talking about waiting for the client to open up and tell me what they needed to disclose: 'Gary, wait at the bus stop with the client. Don't shove them into a taxi and take them where they need to go.' I had well and truly waited at the bus stop with Edwin and now this big red bus had arrived with the words 'male virility' written in the destination plate. I waited a moment before starting again.

I asked if he and Cerys were currently trying for a baby.

I was surprised to see a look of anger cross his face. Was it directed at me for asking such a personal question or at someone else? I expected him to lash out at any moment in the way he had done at the pub, so when he suddenly lunged forward, sitting on the edge of his seat and clasping his hands together tightly, elbows on knees, it took all my effort not to flinch from his unexpected movement.

He didn't answer for a few minutes, just looked at the table in front of him and gripped his hands together. For some reason I got the strong sense that he was struggling to decide how much to divulge rather than how to express his feelings. When he eventually spoke, his voice was soft, low and slow, and cracked with the emotions he was desperately trying to hold in check.

'We are hoping to start a family at some time soon, but things are not quite right for us at the moment.'

I noticed his hands were so tightly clasped they appeared white. I felt I needed to handle the situation delicately. Edwin was on the verge of either a huge breakthrough or getting up and walking away (and possibly smashing some of the furniture on the way out), so I made some reassuring comments about how things had to be right between a couple and no one should rush into these things, and as my words flowed over him I could see his emotional temperature cooling down. I could work with that. And I wanted to buy myself some time to think of the best way forward – therapists don't always know exactly what to say.

Developments in neuroscience are well integrated within psychotherapeutic understanding and influence how we understand behaviour in particular states of emotion. When we get overwhelmed by our emotions, what's usually happening is the limbic part of our brain – the instinctive and strongest area, which controls emotions and memory – has become dominant and taken over control from the prefrontal cortex – the computer or rational part of the brain. The prefrontal cortex doesn't develop fully until we are around twenty-five years old, so it's easy to see why teenagers have an emotional roller coaster of a time going through puberty.

I could see the rational part of Edwin's brain was now trying to get back in control. I thought it was OK to ask again, but in a slightly different way.

'What does "not quite right" mean, Edwin?'

'I don't want to talk about this. End of.'

Edwin was attempting to snatch back control of our therapy session like snatching a ball from the back of a scrum. I had to decide whether to try and challenge him on this or run the risk of fracturing a fragile relationship. Unsure of which direction to choose, I decided to change tack slightly and return to the subject of the brawl.

'How did Cerys react when she heard about the fight?'

Edwin was tight-lipped as he told me how angry Cerys had been when she first heard about it, having been called by the club secretary later that night, but her anger soon changed to hurt when Edwin wouldn't discuss why the fight had started.

He confided that he was irritated about being goaded into fighting, but also at having to toast someone else's new arrival when he really didn't give a 'flying fuck' about their kids. His reaction at the pub surprised himself, let alone everyone else at the club.

'Why is having a family important to you?'

'What sort of a stupid question is that?'

I asked him if having a family was something they both wanted.

'It doesn't matter. What's the point of this conversation? Cerys is never going to get pregnant.'

'Why is that?'

I could see he was getting rattled again and knew this was when his control was at its weakest.

'Because we're not having sex, OK? Are you happy now?'

And there it was. Suddenly the door of frustration and resentment towards his wife had been kicked wide open. It had taken several sessions to get to this point and I didn't want to open the door only for it to slam shut with the wrong comment, as it could so easily do.

This was Edwin's shame, and he had allowed his control to slip to such a degree that his reactions got the better of him and left him feeling embarrassed and ashamed of his perceived failings.

'Well,' he began again, 'normal couples by this time would have children. That's what I had in mind for us – a nice house, good career and young family – and it was all happening as it should, apart from her not keeping her side of the bargain.'

I asked him what the 'bargain' between them was. He looked at me as if I was rather dim and for some reason I got the sense that he was disappointed in me for not understanding his position.

'I look after her, I've given her a nice house and she doesn't have to work, and all she has to do is behave whenever she's out and not make me look like a dick. She should be pregnant by now, but she's decided she's not sure she wants a family so we're not even having sex. She's not keeping her end of the deal.'

I remembered he'd mentioned previously that he'd had some sessions with the club psychologist and had said he'd found it impossible to talk with her when she tried to engage him in what had happened at the pub, but he felt slightly easier talking to another man. At that point, I had got a rather strong whiff of misogyny in his attitude, but with this latest revelation, that whiff had turned into a fully-fledged nasal assault.

At least he was now showing real emotion. A heavy silence extended between us. Normally, I am comfortable with letting the silence continue as this is a powerful tool. By encouraging a client to break the silence and resume dialogue, it puts pressure on him or her to pick up the baton and run with it. However, in this instance, I was unsure of where this session was going.

After a few moments Edwin looked down at his watch. We still had ten minutes to go when he suddenly stood up, saying that he had to go for a scan on his knee and would see me at the same time next week. He then calmly left the room – his emotions back in check.

Part of the therapist's training is to make sense of the feelings that clients generate within us as we work. These can sometimes take the form of negative feelings of revulsion, fear or even disgust. It's something we therapists constantly struggle with in trying to monitor ourselves to deal with our inner feelings. In this case, I was trying to manage feelings of physical intimidation, a vague sympathy for his inability to start a family, hostility around his attitude to his wife and plain old dislike. To put it bluntly, I wondered if I'd seen the last of him and, to be honest, I was half hoping I had.

Anger

'Anyone can become angry . . . That is easy. But to be angry with the right person, to the right degree, at the right time, for the right purpose and in the right way – now that's not easy.'
Aristotle, *Nichomachean Ethics* (c. 340 BC)

You would have thought that in the two and a half millennia since those words were written, mankind would have worked it out. But we haven't. If you've ever been to a football match, barring exceptional circumstances earlier on, towards the end of the second half you'll have seen some football manager losing it on the touchline, belting out expletives at the referee. Why the referee? And why don't these outbursts occur earlier on during the match?

The first answer is that anger needs an object of blame and the second is that anger is caused by excessive distress. Early on in a game that distress might exist, but the effects are cumulative and so it takes a while for irritation to fester to something darker. Anger is also contagious. Think of road rage and how the anger from someone who is honking their horn behind you triggers a similar response in you in a matter of seconds. Maybe unconsciously, the team manager is trying to make his team play with more aggression and by being angry on the touchline he's hoping his anger is transmittable. However, anger and aggression are not the same things. Aggression is controllable. Anger rarely is.

I have worked with a few managers who are often quite proud of their touchline antics. Some believe that it influences the match official, who might try to placate the angry manager by giving a decision later in the game in favour of his team.

We are all born with anger. Think of the emotion as already pre-installed in our software package; it is with us all our lives. Unfortunately, it's often misdirected and my job is to help clients understand their anger, direct it constructively and use the emotion as a tool for positive change.

One summer I travelled to visit my elderly parents. My father, who was very poorly with terminal cancer, was in a shocking mood when I arrived. I asked my mum what the problem was and she replied, 'He wants a diary for next year. I can't find one anywhere. He's furious. Even if he had a diary, he'd have nothing to write in it. He's too poorly to meet anyone and rarely leaves the house.'

My father was in his late eighties and had lived a full life, but he was furious that his illness was going to end his life. He understood he couldn't control the advancing cancer and wouldn't talk to anyone about it, so he focused on a diary. A tangible thing he could hold in his hand somehow represented a future for him. Sadly, he never did live long enough to use that diary.

Control is a key component in the anger process and this takes both skill and practice. Many young people often have anger issues as they haven't yet learned how to either control events or manoeuvre around the people they might come into conflict with. If they find it hard to control that anger, it can often be because of unresolved disagreements in their earlier life – for example, with a domineering or aggressive parent.

When we are very little, anger is a way of keeping us safe. Our rage lets our parents or caregivers know that there's a problem and the strength of our anger or yelling gives them a yardstick of how serious the problem is. If that baby's anger is met with parental anger – such as, 'WHY DOESN'T THAT FUCKING BABY SHUT THE FUCK UP?' – we will truly learn to shut up and we will absorb the sense that expressing our anger isn't safe. In later life those children often get involved in toxic or unfulfilling relationships because their 'anger software' is defective and they can't express their anger.

I've worked with plenty of ex-players who are still furious that their career is over or that modern-day players earn more money than they did. It's why so many of them turn to addictive behaviours to try to rid themselves of the pain. In this chapter we'll see what happens when anger turns inward, and we'll also examine how anger impacts on low self-esteem. We'll encounter those whose anger is directed outward – sometimes at me – and we'll hear stories from those who still don't understand what they're angry about . . . yet.

Tony Oldfield

CLINICAL NOTES: FIRST SESSION

TONY OLDFIELD — AGED 59

Profession: Tony is a former professional footballer now making a meagre living working in his former club's hospitality lounge on match days, meeting the fans and talking about his past career. He is a former TV pundit, but this work has now dried up. He stopped playing professional football in 1989 with an ACL injury.

Referral: Tony has self-referred. He claims that we met many years ago while we were both working on the television circuit, before my training as a psychotherapist. He asked whether I did 'mates' rates' as we have known each other in the past, but in truth I remember nothing of him. I did not offer him a discount.

Appearance: Tall (5ft 11in plus), with rugged good looks, Tony is slim and has a slight Lancastrian accent. His use of English is good although a little clichéd.

Presenting Issues: Tony appears to be suffering from depression. His various careers (which have all been associated with professional football) seem to be coming to an end. He said he was finding it very difficult some days to get out of bed when there was 'no reason', and when he was speaking at a Premier League club on a Saturday in the hospitality lounge, he found it more and more difficult as he was experiencing a complete lack of enthusiasm around meeting new people.

He found it increasingly difficult to accept that younger generations of football fans do not know who he is, or what he did as a player. He was also deeply unhappy about his relationship with a younger woman he was dating, and their relationship appeared to be struggling. He described her as 'cruel', and although he seems unable to break away from her, he is increasingly financially stretched as he is part-funding her lifestyle.

Therapeutic Thinking: Many of Tony's concerns focus on money. He finished playing just before the advent of the Premier League (and the beginning of huge salaries), and he never really invested the earnings he made from professional football. He seems clinically depressed although this may be mixed up with financial anxiety and his inability to break free from a difficult relationship which is financially onerous.

I wonder what stops Tony leaving his current girlfriend, and I need to investigate his relationship with his son, who is also a professional footballer, although Tony has little contact with him.

In our first session Tony talked about having a very strict mother who didn't have a lot of time for him and how his early football career was guided by an encouraging teacher. I'm interested in Tony's overly generous nature, and whether this is to 'buy' friendship, as his narrative suggests he has been easily manipulated in previous relationships. Was this something that also happened in his childhood? He said he found it very difficult to challenge authority figures, especially his parents, teachers, football coaches and bosses at the TV companies, and I feel Tony has poor boundaries (such as his request for mates' rates from me). My work with him will be to help him find his own voice to prevent him from being easily pushed around, and to set and maintain healthy boundaries.

The main part of the work will be to investigate his depression. Depression can arise from unexpressed (or frozen) anger, so I find myself wondering who he might _really_ be angry with.

The Pearl Necklace

When Tony Oldfield arrived for his next session with me, my first thought was he didn't look his fifty-nine years. He came dressed smartly and looked like a man ten years his junior who was ready to go out on a date. He wore an open-necked blue checked shirt, chinos and highly polished black shoes and his haircut (1940s style) was more befitting a man in his thirties. He had a cheeky grin and the terms 'pal' and 'mate' were littered all the way through his dialogue.

He seemed intent on reminding me that we'd met before and that we had been colleagues at a television station for a brief time some twenty years previously. All I remembered was watching old footage of a slight right winger with a good turn of pace, but I had no recollection of ever working with him. Did he think having some kind of previous connection meant I'd go easier on him out of sympathy for a fellow broadcaster?

Regardless of our previous connection (or lack of it), it struck me that he was likely to be uneasy at our different roles now, and in making the comparison between us, he might feel slightly uncomfortable now that he found himself in a position where he needed therapy.

The power dynamic of a therapist–client relationship is not equal. When the work is going well, a therapist will get to know an awful lot about a client, but a client often knows little or nothing about the therapist. I wondered whether Tony was struggling with this. Older clients who are new to therapy can initially find it difficult to understand the rules of a totally different kind of relationship. It can be hard for them to be open and trust a complete stranger when they have spent most of their lives building walls against people they've just met.

I felt I had to tread gently, because whatever was going on for Tony, it didn't seem likely he was going to divulge it easily and I could see his distress beneath the surface. He seemed a little awkward and unsure as to how to begin, so, to ease him in gently, I asked how he found the game these days. He grabbed the topic with both hands.

'You know,' he said, 'the game is completely changed these days. I don't recognize the young lads as proper football players, with all their social media stuff going on, and all that pandering to players when they get it wrong. In my day, the manager would have you up by your throat against the dressing-room wall and, after yelling in your face for a full five minutes, tell you to pull yourself together, then that would be the end of it. I probably wouldn't last two minutes inside a football club dressing room now, because if someone wasn't pulling their weight, I'd do the same. Now they have all this money they think they're in charge. When I was playing, I was thrilled to have a bog-standard Ford Cortina to drive, but look at all these jumped-up kids driving round in their 4x4s and supercars. What are they trying to prove?'

Tony fell silent and sat there glumly. Recognizing that the session had momentarily stalled, I asked what had happened in the last week.

He told me with rising anger that he had decided to surprise his girlfriend, Anna, with a present of a piece of jewellery. He'd sorted it out with a former teammate who had a friend in a jewellery shop in Hatton Garden in London. Apparently, a shipment of antique Tahitian black pearls had arrived and were being made up into single-stone necklaces. Tony was thrilled, had one made up and rushed round to see Anna as soon as he had the pearl in his possession. He'd thought this was a romantic gesture that even she would appreciate (and perhaps love him more for it?). But he didn't get quite the response he'd expected.

'When I showed her the necklace, her face was like curdled milk.' He flushed with anger as he recalled the moment. 'I wish I hadn't gone to the bother of buying the bloody thing.'

He went on to tell me she had called him a 'cheap bastard' because he'd done a deal through a friend rather than splashing out on something expensive for her, like a whole string of pearls instead of just the one, and then she launched into a whole angry rant about how she wanted 'white pearls rather than shitty black ones'.

'Black pearls ... I mean, these are some of the most expensive money can buy, but I said I'd try to get some white ones. I know a whole set is way out of my price range, but for some God-awful reason, I stupidly said I'd see what I can do. I can barely afford a necklace of plastic beads never mind a full pearl necklace.

'It's not easy for me to find work, so money is an issue, and if she appreciated that then maybe she'd realize this necklace is already more than I can afford. If it wasn't for my mate, there wouldn't be any present. Or maybe she just doesn't care.'

His head hung low and he paused for a moment as he considered that last comment.

'You know I pay for her car as well? Series 3 BMW no less,' he told me with some pride and a faraway look in his eyes. 'She never says thanks.'

He was quiet and I let him stay with his thoughts for a

moment or two. When he lifted his head, there was real fury in his eyes.

'I get so cross sometimes I can't cope with her. It's doing me in. When I took the necklace round, and she was getting all nasty with me about the black pearls, I got so angry I could hardly think straight. I remember that happening once before when I was playing in a game against Grimsby. Their centre half had just taken me out when I had a clear shot on goal and I just went up and chinned him. Straight red card.'

He told me of his embarrassment in wanting to do her physical harm, admitting that if he'd stayed at her place much longer, he thought he'd have done the same to her.

'Jeez. What a mess!'

He went on to tell me how, when he walked out of the house without saying a word, she started yelling at him, 'Where the hell are you going?' He just got in his car and left. On the drive home, he felt awful and wished he'd never bought the necklace. Her words calling him a cheap bastard kept replaying over and over in his mind.

'Story of my life really . . . Try to do something nice for somebody and they shit on you. The next day I hardly got out of bed I felt so low.'

I'd come across this many times before with ex-professional players from all areas of sport. They find it difficult to make the gear change from the lifestyle they enjoyed while playing to a less affluent one when not. I wondered whether Tony's 'lavish' persona was used in his courtship and now Anna was unimpressed with the reality of his financial situation. It was clear that Tony's increasingly untenable lifestyle was making him deeply unhappy as well as furious.

I felt sympathy for Tony. His anger was obviously at the perceived frailty of the modern footballer and yet they were earning sums of money that he could only ever have dreamed of. He couldn't see the irony that he was in a way competing with them, trying to present a semblance of success by lavishing money on an expensive woman, maintaining a standard of living well beyond his modest means. I use the word 'expensive' meaning not just financially expensive, but emotionally expensive too. How to get him to make the connection?

I also considered the connection between money and lack of love. In my work, clients who have a difficult relationship with money, sex and/or eating (and we all have relationships with how much of these we get) often have family backgrounds where love has been in short supply and find solace 'topping up' with one of the above.

I asked him to tell me a little about Anna and how they met. He described an attractive blonde woman in her late forties who worked as a medical secretary. She had been married in the past but hadn't wanted children. She seemed keen to enjoy the finer things in life and Tony was keen for her to have them, feeling that he was batting well above his average and was lucky to have her. They had met online through a free dating site and had been together about eighteen months now. Tony accepted that things weren't perfect but was happy being in a relationship, even though they lived apart and there were no plans to bring their lives closer together. He admitted that he enjoyed being seen with Anna as she drew a lot of male attention.

We all create an image of ourselves for other people to see. Our clothes, our hairstyle, our demeanour, who we socialize with – just about anything we present to the world is an attempt to be understood and seen as we would like to be. These days, social media gives us a way to finesse that image, providing a curated version of ourselves, and the disparity between the reality of our ordinary lives and the version we present grows ever wider. This leads to social anxiety and depression because we feel we have failed when we cannot achieve or maintain that reality.

At a fundamental level, we feel the need to be fully understood by one individual, which might be a throwback to when we were babies and our mums or caregivers understood what we needed at any given time. As we grow older and mature, we come to the disappointing realization that it is actually impossible for another individual to truly understand everything about us and, in that sense, we are truly alone.

Tony fell silent for a few moments and then, in a much quieter voice, began again.

'This is pretty shameful, but I need to tell you this. Last Saturday I had agreed to do the 100 Club gig at United. You know, walk round 100 half-pissed people in the hospitality lounge for twenty minutes' pre-match chatter along with another ex-player, five minutes at half-time and then a Q and A session afterwards, telling them what I thought about the match. It's 500 notes, easy money, and I've done it countless times before. Well, last Saturday was a big one. We were playing Chelsea and they'd sold the lounge to full capacity. Darren, from the commercial side, was well up for me doing my bit as I'd scored a famous goal against Chelsea many years before in an FA Cup tie.'

Tony bowed his head. He couldn't hold my gaze any longer and, speaking mainly to the floor, he told me how he was deeply ashamed to admit he called in sick the night before the match. He told them he'd eaten something dodgy. The truth was, he just couldn't cope with all those people asking who the hell he was, or had been.

After a long pause, Tony began again with a tortured look

on his face, telling me that the feelings of being a nobody seemed to bring on physical symptoms.

'It's like a pain in my chest. I try to do my best for Anna, for myself, for my ex-wife, a son I never hear from. I don't smoke, only drink now and then and don't gamble, and I try to be kind to people, but sometimes the pain is so much it's like having a clamp around my lungs and I just can't breathe. I can't go back to the hospitality suite and work there, having yet another spotty kid asking who I am, then turn away mid-conversation because they simply don't care.'

He lifted his chin defiantly.

'I'm not a nobody. I'm Tony fucking Oldfield.'

Richard Davies

Dreams and Streams

Richard Davies had recovered from his fall and was back racing again, but, sitting across from me in the clinic, he hardly looked like a man who was glad to be back in the saddle. He sat motionless and speechless at the start of our next session. He had this way of scanning the room before he delivered one of his word-crammed, meandering sentences. It reminded me of the tape going up at the start of a horse race. But not this week. He rubbed his hands together and licked his lips as if preparing to carefully craft his next sentence. I felt a bit wary. I wasn't expecting his next words.

'Do you do dreams?'

In truth, part of my training was to help clients interpret their dreams, maybe help decipher them or make more sense of where they'd come from. Before I could answer, Richard was asking again.

'You see, since I began racing again, I've had these odd dreams of late. And I thought, you know, you could give me a hand making sense of them. What are dreams for anyway?'

'Well, there are lots of theories, Richard, but here's one

that makes sense to me. Imagine all you experience – see, hear, smell, taste, touch – in one day, these pieces of data are processed by your conscious brain, but this part of your brain is only the tip of an iceberg. There's a load more we take in but don't really notice, and this is processed in the unconscious part of your brain. Think of this bit as a massive junk folder in your brain.

'During dreaming we sift through the junk folder and decide if there's anything that needs looking at again. We process an enormous amount of information during the day, more so these days than our brains have ever been used to. It's estimated we process twice the amount of information we did fifteen years ago, mainly due to our online activity.'

He looked rather bored, so I invited him to tell me about his dream.

Tape up. And we're off.

'Well, we were racing at Ayr – I just knew it was Ayr, I'm not even sure why – and the race starts and I'm ahead by several lengths. It's a bright day and suddenly I'm aware I'm so far ahead of the race that something doesn't feel right. Then I notice all the other horses have taken a different route from me and I'm no longer on the racecourse. The landscape had changed and I was approaching a riverbank. I'd clearly taken a wrong turn somehow and then I realized that my horse wasn't a racehorse after all. It was a small pony that wanted to munch the grass from the bank. People were approaching me, saying didn't I have a sweet pony to sit on, and I felt like I was a little boy again. They were feeding it handfuls of grass. Suddenly the people were yelling at me that I was too old to be on a kid's horse and I was arguing, trying to tell them I wasn't meant to be on this horse, it was a mistake, but no one believed me. Now what do you make of that?'

I sat still for a moment in reflection and a little trepidation, trying to process the information and detail that had just been fired at me. With a previous client I had got the next bit spectacularly wrong, succumbing to the temptation to play the brilliant Freudian therapist, interpreting a dream only for the client to say, 'Nah, you've got that completely wrong', and then trying to repair the damage done to the client–therapist relationship and my credibility.

In conscious everyday thought, we are often limited by our fears, so while awake we would most likely shy away from exploring anything too disturbing or uncomfortable. Our unconscious doesn't have those limitations and goes just where it pleases, regardless of how upsetting it might be – hence the phenomenon of nightmares. The truth is, we still do not understand the true purpose of dreams; there are only theories that try to attribute meanings, nothing that can be substantiated. I decided to play safe and find out a little more about what Richard's thoughts were, given that it was his mind creating the dream.

I proceeded to use the standard therapist's line: 'Interesting, Richard. What do *you* think the dream is about?'

Richard said he wasn't sure, but then went on to tell me that his first week back racing following his fall had been filled with anger and frustration. He'd been 'jocked off' a horse (when an owner or trainer decides to switch jockeys at the last moment) and wasn't in the least bit happy about it. The owner felt Richard wasn't fully fit after his injury lay-off.

'I was going to ride Rogue Rage – a lovely little horse – at Newbury, but at the last minute my trainer got a call from the owner and was instructed to put me on another horse, Serendipity, in the same race. But I believed Serendipity was carrying too much weight [there is a handicap system in horse racing with the faster horses carrying weights under the saddle to even up the odds and make the race less predictable]. He is a stroppy bugger at the best of times, and especially when the going is soft [when the ground at the racecourse is wet], and he hadn't been competitive racing for a while.*

'I begged the trainer to let me ride Rogue Rage, but he wouldn't listen. As I thought would happen, three quarters of the way through the race, Serendipity is blowing out of his arse, and I'd already used the crop the maximum eight times, so had no way to urge the horse on. He was finished. Turns out Rogue Rage won by three lengths.'

'Sounds like you were on the wrong horse, Richard. Like in your dream.'

'Yeah, I'd worked that bit out. I love Rogue Rage and have often painted pictures of him. Sometimes I can spend hours and hours painting horses. It's my way of relaxing – some people do DIY or play golf, but I like to paint. Last week I was nearly late for a race at Cheltenham because I'd lost track of time after getting lost in one of my paintings.'

'But not painting a racecourse?'

He looked up. 'How did you know that?'

'Well, if I was a gambling man, I'd guess there was a riverbank and water involved,' I suggested.

Richard ignored my clever-dick-therapist moment.

'I was so angry. I'd discussed tactics with my trainer before the race and he made it clear it was Rogue Rage who was meant to be the pacemaker. But I ended up losing to that prick riding Rogue Rage and it was all planned. Dad and I had a furious row and he accused me of behaving like a spoilt kid, not getting my own way, then my girlfriend wades in on

* This can cause stress in horses and classic equine distressed behaviour.

his side and we were still rowing the next day. Keira said I'm sabotaging my career and told me in no uncertain terms that I was wasting my time as a painter.'

'Back to your dream, Richard. Tell me how you felt during the dream rather than what happened.'

Dream theory suggests that the best way to access the unconscious meaning of a dream is to concentrate on the feelings that it leaves behind. Our memories are much better at remembering emotions than facts. That's why two people experiencing the same event might have very different recollections of what occurred. I don't remember much of the detail of the time the football team I support won the FA Cup, but I recall vividly the excitement, joy and relief at the final whistle. Likewise, the unfathomable despair is fresh in my memory from the following year when they lost in the final.

Richard stroked his chin and said, 'I felt calmness during the dream when I was on the pony by the riverbank. I couldn't give a toss about all the people who'd be angry with me for not winning. I just wanted to stay and really enjoy the peace of the countryside and the warmth of the horse's back underneath me. I was truly happy, till all those tossers came along and wanted to know what a grown man was doing on a pony's back.'

'Richard, are you happy being a jockey, or do you really want to take a different path like you did in the dream?'

He thought about my question for a moment, then replied, 'Sometimes I feel like I'm living Dad's version of my life. This is what he wanted. To win at Aintree one day. Now I'm gonna have to wait another year. Maybe it's what I want too, but I've never discovered that. Rogue Rage was *my* pick and I couldn't have it. Maybe I came back from injury too soon. The trainer, Dad, Keira, they all seem to know what's best for me.'

'Was the defeat on Serendipity avoidable? Looking back with twenty-twenty vision, could you have done anything differently?'

Richard looked agitated.

'You know what, I'm really not sure. The trainer, Dad and Keira . . . They don't help.'

Instead of agreeing to ride Serendipity as instructed, Richard might have offered some push-back to his trainer and indirectly to the owner, but instead he allowed himself to be directed to ride a horse he didn't want to. This mirrored the way his father directed him into becoming a jockey when maybe his heart wasn't entirely in it.

Complaining about both circumstances, Richard was prepared to blame everyone else for his misfortune rather than look at his own inability to manage conflict. Playing the victim showed that he spoke from the 'child' ego state that transactional analysis identifies. Maybe it was easier for him to invent some 'hoodoo' at Aintree rather than accept that by competing in a high-profile steeplechase, he was simply acting out the wishes and whims of his family and trainer. Who would really be holding the reins when the race began at Liverpool?

Richard's dreams were now telling him something. Through them, could I help him access his real anger and channel it in a positive way rather than acting it out in a childlike way?

Eddie Stamp

CLINICAL NOTES: FIRST SESSION

EDDIE STAMP – AGED 43

Profession: Assistant manager at a Championship football club in the north of England. He is a former professional footballer who played briefly at Premier League level before retiring in 2013 with an ankle injury.

Referral: I was approached by Jack Braithwaite, the manager of a northern football club, after giving a talk to a group of football managers. Jack spoke of an incident at the club's training ground that involved Eddie Stamp.

He was concerned that Stamp displayed a level of violence far above what was warranted in a training session. Stamp had apparently lost his temper and tackled a first-team player violently, resulting in an injury to the player.

It should be noted that the client had not requested psychological help, but the manager said he would like me to 'have a chat with Stamp' if Stamp agreed. I approached him and he accepted my invitation.*

Appearance: Eddie is about 5ft 9in, has grey hair and a stocky frame, and is physically very fit. Born in the North-East, he still has a slight but noticeable accent. When I saw Eddie, he was in a club tracksuit and had come straight from a training session. He was evasive and unwilling to engage with me and, although not rude, was confrontational.

Presenting Issues: Eddie had a reputation as a highly aggressive midfielder who was regularly in trouble with referees and managers. Jack Braithwaite told me that since Eddie had been in his new role as assistant manager, there had been incidents when he had picked on younger players, on one occasion grabbing a player by the throat, pushing him up against a wall and threatening him because he wasn't trying hard enough. Eddie had a reputation for binge-drinking and this led to the sorts of antisocial episodes that affected him throughout his playing career.

Therapeutic Thinking: I am concerned about the welfare of the first-team players after the incident in training. Eddie had clearly taken out his frustrations on a player and this had caused an injury. It meant the player in question would not be available to play at the weekend. My other concern was for the morale of

---

* It's important to understand that the basis of psychotherapy depends on the client reaching a point in his or her life when they realize that they need some form of therapeutic help. If they haven't yet reached that point, their engagement is harder to achieve.

the group. Despite the obvious respect they all had for Eddie, how could they train alongside him when he could be reckless in his tackling? There is a clear power imbalance between the footballers and their coach, and his behaviours could be construed as bullying.

In theory Eddie is a responsible adult at the club and so he should be looking out for vulnerable individuals. However, on this occasion, as he had failed in his duty, my worry was that the club might be liable at some point in the future if an injury was caused by a member of the training staff who had not been offered psychological help.

There were several questions that needed to be answered:

1) Was his anger solely concentrated in the football club?

2) Did he have some addictive behaviours that he was hiding and was the anger a defence against these?

3) Was he finding it difficult to properly transition from being a player to a coach?

In our first meeting, Eddie was forthright, complaining about the lack of commitment from several of the younger players. He felt they needed to be taught a lesson and 'toughened up', that the players involved were 'soft as shit'. He explained to me that he had been brought to the club to help the manager, Jack Braithwaite, bring some old-school discipline to the first-team squad.

Eddie reluctantly agreed to see me for a few therapy sessions to discuss some of the anger issues, accepting that he was bringing these into the club. But he added that he thought 'the gaffer', Jack Braithwaite, was 'making a mountain out of a molehill', and the training-ground incident was 'ten a penny at any football club up and down the country'.

Sacked in the Morning

I'd arrived at the training ground ten minutes early and was now waiting in the small quiet office the club had allocated for my second meeting with Eddie Stamp. The train from my home to the North-West had been on time and I was congratulating myself that everything had gone like clockwork, so far.

Jack Braithwaite had arranged for me to meet Eddie here, well away from the dressing rooms. 'No one will know who you are,' he said, 'so there'll be no tongues wagging that Eddie needs to see a shrink. If anyone asks, tell them you're an agent.'

Five minutes late for our appointment, Eddie burst through the door, without knocking or saying a word, and settled into the chair opposite me.

His grey hair, which had once been raven black, had now receded to the point where frequent shaving to a short and spiky bristle was his only sensible option, and it seemed to echo his stature and his manner. His eyes were an unexpected deep blue – somehow at odds with his long-cultivated hardman image. He looked and smelled sweaty, and it was obvious he'd come straight from the training pitch. He had his mobile phone in his hand and put it down on the table in front of him, face up, then started spinning it around as he looked at me with a sense of defiance.

'How long's this gonna take?' he said. 'I've only got a few

minutes. Gotta get away. My lad's been in trouble again at school, so I need to get there and sort him out. Second time this week.' Eddie grimaced comically but with an underlying sense of pride. 'He's a bit of a lad.'

I felt uneasy at Eddie's impatience given that I was here for his benefit because the manager had expressed concern that he might injure one of the first-team players with his overenthusiastic tackling. While Jack was happy for me to have a discreet conversation with Eddie, he wasn't overly optimistic I'd make much headway, having known Eddie for a good many years.

I could tell this was going to be an uncomfortable few minutes, if it lasted that long. Impatience was pouring out of Eddie along with his sweat as he fixed me with a glare. I opened with my concerns, and asked if he realized just how brutal he was being on the field with the players. He started to shake his head, smiling before I'd even finished.

'This is all bollocks, mate, and to be honest I don't know what I'm doing sitting here talking to you. Like I said at our first meeting, those lads need a bit of toughening up and to understand what it's like playing against real players. That's what Jack brought me in for and it's what they need!'

He then looked at me directly, as if to say *he* knew what the players needed, not me.

I asked if he was worried about really injuring one of them and spoiling their chances of playing at the weekend (or maybe for even longer). I could see he was starting to get rather rattled and his mood was rapidly deteriorating, as he saw my questioning of his methods as a challenge to his authority.

His eyes narrowed as he responded. 'I am preparing them for the weekend, and they'll thank me for being a bit harder on them now, so they can take it when it matters.' He shook his head as if dismissing my words, before deciding on a different tack. 'No offence, mate, but to be honest, if I was your gaffer, I wouldn't have you there. The young 'uns these days need a kick up the arse, not a bleeding nanny.'

Eddie leaned back on his chair and crossed his arms in front of him. He was unshaven and his stubble and the short hair on his head were roughly the same length. If I was being unkind, I'd have described his appearance as 'thuggish'.

'We conceded a soft goal against City last Saturday. We've got this Portuguese lad, Pablo – all silky skills and hair gel. Well, the lazy bastard didn't pick up their number eight about fifteen seconds before they scored. It's quite simple. He doesn't give it 100 per cent, he drops us in it.' Eddie's voice was getting louder and his face redder as he spoke. 'After the game, me and Pabs had a little chat in the dressing room.'

The way he said 'chat' made it sound quite chilling, and I doubted if many pleasantries were exchanged. I'd heard about Eddie's 'chats', which, I understood from Jack Braithwaite, usually revolved around being pinned by the neck against the lockers and verbally blasted.

'He won't be letting anyone run past him again like that. You wouldn't catch me not trying while I was playing. I might not have been the best player, but I tell you what, nobody ran past me and lived to tell the tale.'

Aggression is a vital element in most sports, but how it's controlled is key. Sports psychology distinguishes between being under-aroused (scared, anxious, worried about the outcome of a sporting fixture) and over-aroused (blood pumping, raw aggression unchecked emotions – the stuff red cards are made of). Research has shown that the ideal point for an athlete in competitive sport is midway between the two. There's a fine line between positive sporting aggression and uncontained violence, and it appeared that Eddie's handle on his own emotions was at times rather lacking. Maybe his aggression towards me was his defence mechanism to make sure he didn't have to look at this too closely. I was determined not to take Eddie's rant against me personally.

As I mentioned in the introduction to this section, anger is part of our survival mechanism. As babies, if we don't cry or yell, we won't get the attention we need for feeding, soothing or to be cleaned and changed. If our caregivers meet that baby anger with adult anger, we become frightened of getting angry and that leads to fear of conflict in adult life. Conversely, if our caregivers ignore our anger, it can go unchecked. In some circumstances, parents who've never challenged their toddlers' anger end up fearful of their own children when they grow into bigger, stronger and potentially more dangerous adolescents. Those kids learn to use anger as a manipulative tool to get what they want.

Eddie spun his mobile phone on the desk once again, as if by so doing he'd won the argument with me. I was beginning to doubt the value of travelling so far for this session, as Jack, the manager, had predicted. I assumed that Eddie would probably need to get showered and changed before leaving the club, and therefore he saw any time spent with me as delaying him from something much more important.

Eddie looked at his watch again, then said, 'Five more minutes and I'm off, mate.'

I tried another approach, to see if I could salvage anything useful from our time, and asked Eddie about his son, who had been accepted to play in a football academy close by, wondering if the 'trouble' he was in was a worry for Eddie.

He started smiling. 'Nah, he's a chip off the old block. Just like me, he's in trouble at school, starting fights and so on. My missus gets furious with him, but I tell him he has to stand up for himself, otherwise the bigger kids will think they've won, and that ain't right.'

I asked him if his son was difficult at home, to which Eddie replied not when he was around. What about when it was just him and his mum, did he behave then?

'My missus hasn't been great for a long time and she finds it hard to deal with him. He just needs a good clip round the ear every now and then, but she doesn't like doing that. She suffers with her nerves and takes those pills.'

He seemed to be talking about antidepressants, and there was a clear sense of contempt when he talked about her and her need for 'those pills'.

'She's another one who's as soft as shit and guess who has to clean that up when she can't cope. Last week I asked her to pick me up from Wigan when I'd been looking at an academy kid. But no, she can't drive at night on the motorways. Apparently, it's too scary. Can you believe that!' He shook his head dismissively.

I explained to Eddie that my role was to help players and coaching staff talk about their feelings, get stuff off their chest and make sure that their emotional lives do not interfere negatively with their sporting ones. I then grasped the nettle and asked him if he'd ever had the chance to talk about his anger with his wife, or his son's problems to anyone else. I kept my voice low and unemotional and told him I would be a support for him if he wanted to use it.

Eddie broke into a sarcastic laugh that sounded more like a shout. 'Look, mate . . .'

I felt anything but Eddie's 'mate' at this moment and the use of that word seemed highly ironic. Had we met anywhere else I would be concerned about my physical safety at this moment, as Eddie had a reputation for starting fights in the blink of an eye.

'Me talk to you? Ha! I don't think so. I'm only here because the gaffer told me to come and as far as I'm concerned we're done.' He paused. 'You know what, if I'd met you twenty years ago and you'd started with your psychological shit I'd have probably chinned you. To be honest, I'm insulted that the gaffer even wants me to talk to you.'

His voice was getting louder and I could see him getting seriously agitated. He stood abruptly and grabbed his mobile phone off the table.

'I'm not sitting here listening to this shit! I don't see what good you're doing here, and just so we are clear, I'm going to tell the gaffer this is the last time we're seeing each other. Now get your poxy train back home. You and I are done!'

Jane Lovell

Charity Jane

Before my next therapy session with Jane, my attention was drawn to a post on Twitter. A former broadcast colleague of mine had retweeted one of Jane's posts. It was a short video that contained a news report of her winning the 100-metre hurdles event of the women's heptathlon at the Commonwealth Games in the 2000s, when she shot to prominence. Jane looked remarkably young, but the footage of her race revealed a raw power. With fifty metres to go, she unleashed a blistering turn of pace, as if someone his just ignited a rocket she was strapped to. Diving at the finishing line, she took first place ahead of a Canadian and a Jamaican athlete. Cut to a cheesy trackside interview:

Interviewer: You looked like you were having great fun.
Jane: I was. I'm loving it here.
Interviewer (*with slight innuendo in his voice*): And how are you faring in the athletes' village? I hear the men outnumber the women three to one.

Jane (*grinning*): I'm not complaining. (*She winks at the interviewer.*)

I was struck not only by the outdated approach of the interviewer, but also by Jane's confidence and how all that seemed to have been lost in the intervening years. What had happened to transform that cheeky, confident, 'don't mess with me' athlete into a woman in her thirties suffering from low self-esteem and mired in an unhappy marriage? If my maths was correct, she'd have been dating Alan, the old flame she'd recently reconnected with, during the period of the Games.

Given the dominating influence of her father that we'd discussed, I wondered where he was during this trackside interview, and if he was with her at the Games. It struck me that maybe the domestic strife she now faced was a replaying of an older struggle to get away from his influence. We all have a tendency to replay relationships from an earlier part of our life and maybe her early relationship struggles had already begun at the time of the Games.

At puberty, girls can feel rejected by their fathers if the two clash about the girl's burgeoning sexuality (Dad: 'Where are you going dressed like that with such a short skirt on?' etc., etc.). Many teenage girls I've worked with find this rejection painful and confusing. The story where her dad hadn't wanted Jane to attend the teenage 'cider and spin-the-bottle' party suggested that this father–daughter struggle was already there, and as Dad was her coach, that control may have been suffocating. Indeed, maybe Dad was her coach as an unconscious way to control her.

At our next session, Jane had barely taken off her coat when she said, 'I'm so angry right now I can hardly speak.'

My first therapeutic thought was to wonder who had shut her up in the past when she was angry. When children display anger, often parents respond with their own anger, which has the effect of frightening the child, effectively shutting them up for evermore.

Then for the second time I watched Jane Lovell cry. I wondered how long it had been since she'd really cried like this. Eventually, the sobs subsided and she was able to vent some of her fury.

Alan had asked her to become an ambassador for a charity supporting underprivileged children who wanted to develop their sporting careers. Jane had been invited to speak at some posh do in a west London hotel and was due to stay overnight. When Jane discussed the arrangements with her husband he flew into a rage, accusing her of abandoning their child and claiming that the speaking arrangement was a ruse to spend a night away from him. To make matters worse, Jane's husband had contacted his father-in-law and had brought him onside to criticize Jane's plans to speak in London.

What followed was a full-on row between Jane and her father. She told him how controlling he was, and always had been, and even blamed him for ending her career because he had pushed her to train when she was injured.

'If I'd realized the extent of my injury at the time, I'd never have done what my dad was asking me to. I remember one day the pain in my ankle was so bad I couldn't get out of bed. Dad told me I was just being lazy and I'd never become an Olympic champion. I was furious. I was in tears, in so much pain and so angry at him.'

We expect our parents to protect us, look after us, keep an eye on us. Jane was getting close to the realization that *her* success was essentially a manifestation of *his*, and they were inextricably linked. If Jane Lovell's dad was such a great athletics coach, why hadn't he been able to create another equally great athlete?

My hunch was that no other athlete would put up with the level of control Jane endured. It is unusual in my experience that a parent continues to coach a son or daughter past the early part of his or her career. Often at some stage the young athlete and parent will realize that to get to the next level of athletic excellence, a professional and more experienced coach is required. Mum or Dad might have some issues about 'letting go' and I suspected this was the case with Jane's dad.

Bizarrely, I never knew the name of Jane's father, and she rarely used the first name of her husband either (Tony), referring to them simply as 'Dad' or 'my husband' and revealing (possibly) an emotional distance between herself and these men.

Jane told me she was meeting Alan about once a month now and was very interested in taking up his offer to be an ambassador for his sporting charity. There were two things holding her back. The first was that she didn't know if she wanted to run the gauntlet of her husband's anger and the second was that she was acutely aware of her own lack of self-esteem.

'How can I be a role model to the sports kids of tomorrow when I'm such a bloody wreck? I want to go to this charity dinner in London and support Alan's work, but is it worth all the fuss it's going to cause?'

Silence.

'Jane, who is Alan to you?'

'I don't understand the question.'

'Well, when we meet someone, they remind us of someone else. They kind of fit a template of someone we've met before. If we have good feelings about the original template, we're often inclined to transfer those good feelings on to the new person.'

Jane looked puzzled. 'Nope, I'm still not getting this.'

'Well, Jane, what are Alan's qualities? Why do you like him?'

Jane sighed. 'Well, he's kind, funny, generous, and really listens to what I have to say. That's it. He listens, no one has ever really listened to me!'

'And who does that remind you of?'

Jane stared into space and then her face changed, just gradually at the start but then like a cloud blotting out the sun on a summer's day and the sobs began again.

It is not unusual for clients to cry in my presence and I never try to stop their tears. So many have told me that their tears were stopped by parents who might say, 'Big boys don't cry' or 'Stop now, that's enough.' My favourite from my own childhood was, 'If you don't stop crying, I'll give you something to cry about.' I often think that this is to do with a parent's discomfort around tears, that maybe the parent feels they have failed if their child cries.

Jane began slowly. 'It's my grandpa. My mum's dad. I loved him so, so much. He was kind and fun and used to read to me. He died when I was about nine. He bought me my first pair of spikes and joked that when I put them on, he was with me. I've only just thought of this now. Every time I put spikes on, I used to think of him. Just for a nanosecond, but I did.'

Jane's anger returned. 'I'm so angry with all these men. Dad, Tony, even Alan.'

'Why Alan?'

'Well, I feel he's putting me under pressure to accept this ambassadorial role and speak at this event in London. But it's causing such trouble at home, and now Dad's got involved. I just feel so controlled.'

Jane reminded me of a hammer thrower who is twirling round and round wanting to release the shot but cannot find the right opening, whichever way she turns. Jane couldn't release the steel ball.

I felt my work was to support Jane in developing the skills she needed to be able to withstand this pressure and decide for herself what *she* really wanted. But that's easier said than done. Imagine trying to throw that hammer. With every spin the steel ball feels heavier. If and when you do throw it, it's not going to go very far. Her dad and husband still had a huge influence on her. Could I help Jane find the opening she needed to release the hammer, to find her path to freedom?

Ben Phillips

CLINICAL NOTES: FIRST SESSION

BEN PHILLIPS – AGED 15

Profession: Academy goalkeeper with a local EFL League One team, still at school studying for GCSEs

Referral: I have been contacted by Ben's mother, who has exhausted all the medical reasons for her son's lower-back injury. She has sent me a file of notes from the NHS explaining that there is no reason for her son to suffer the pain he does, and she has been advised to seek psychological help for him.

Appearance: Ben is unusually tall for his age (6ft plus), with long gangly limbs, and his mother has indicated that he has always been more physically mature than his peers. However, when I asked about his back pain, he looked at the ground. But what struck me about Ben was his sense of calm — he never fidgeted, which is unusual in one so young, especially in an uncomfortable and unfamiliar environment.

He also has unusually large hands.

Presenting Issues: Ben is unable to train or play football due to a lower-back injury that has kept him out for the last month and he is becoming increasingly depressed about the pain, which has been ongoing for several months. He has had X-rays, scans and MRI imaging and all have indicated there is no clinical reason why he still has a problem. Ben's mother has taken him to regular physio massage but every morning he wakes up with the same complaint.

Therapeutic Thinking: Ben is worried that others don't believe him that he has an injury and is in pain. His football academy is sympathetic and has funded several private medical checks but so far there is no medical explanation.

Ben has an older brother, Keiron, an outfield player at another professional club academy, who lives mainly with his dad and his dad's new partner, close to the academy, and sees Ben every weekend. Ben is academically bright, although not outstanding, and his desire to do PE is severely hampered by his back injury. The pain is limiting more and more of his normal activities.

I am interested in Ben's relationship with his brother, of whom he speaks in glowing terms, and whether or not there could be any sibling rivalry. Ben's mum seems very protective of her son, and so far there has been little mention of Ben's dad, who hasn't lived in the family home for many years.

One possibility is that Ben's back pain is a way of attracting attention in a family that seems largely focused on the footballing success of his older brother.

While I firmly believe Ben is in pain, I also believe this could be a psychosomatic reaction (pain caused by unresolved psychological anxiety) to other events in his life.

It is possible that Ben's inability to play football on medical grounds spares him from any chance of failing as an academy goalkeeper. When I questioned the club about Ben's likely success in making it professionally, they said, 'Fifty-fifty,' with Ben's lack of training being a concern. He has never had a girlfriend and doesn't have a wide friendship group.

His relationship with his mum, brother, teammates and school friends, I believe, will be the clue to treating Ben.

Don't Look Black in Anger

Ben's mum brought her son to my door and stood there looking expectantly at me as I invited Ben in. I think she was expecting to sit in on the session, as she had done the first time I saw Ben, but this would have broken the client–therapist boundary. Ben was my client, not her, and I suspected Ben's close relationship with his mum might be contributing in no small part to the problem. I asked her to return in fifty minutes and gently but firmly closed the door in her obviously disappointed face. I did wonder whether Ben would feel comfortable, as this was the first time we'd been on our own together. He looked shy and unsure and a lot younger than his fifteen years.

When he sat down in the chair opposite me, I could see his unease. He wasn't sure where to look so was looking everywhere. I noted that he was playing with the chestnut curls within his fringe – obviously he'd inherited his hair colour and curls from his mum.

I initially found it hard to get any sort of conversation going with Ben, so I asked him what he'd been doing at the weekend. I could have predicted his monotone teenage response: 'Nothing much.' He was sat looking down at his long, slender fingers as he played with them in his lap, as if he didn't know what to do with his hands without the obligatory mobile phone in them.

I tried again, asking him if he enjoyed school. This elicited a little more response, but only to say he'd rather not have to do RE, but he enjoyed seeing his friends. I continued trying to coax more information out of Ben, getting him to relax in my company and feel comfortable sharing personal details he'd probably never spoken to anyone else about in his life.

Ben slowly opened up in his quiet, soft voice, showing himself to be quite articulate and insightful at times, which made me optimistic we could make progress together. It turned out there had been quite a lot going on recently in his life and slowly, as the session unfolded, he began to talk about going over to his dad's for the weekend and spending time with his father and his father's new girlfriend, Jenny.

Apparently, Jenny was a nurse and had been living with Dad for roughly the last six months. When I asked Ben how he got on with Jenny, he replied that at first she seemed a really friendly, fun person, but recently she seemed to have changed and now she was beginning to be quite critical of Ben, especially when it came to his back pain.

I asked what she had said.

'Well,' he replied slowly and cautiously, 'she asks me all the time whether I'm OK, but it's as if she doesn't really mean it.'

He was looking at me earnestly, hoping I wouldn't tell him he was just being 'silly', and it made me wonder if his father had already heard this and told him exactly that.

'What does Jenny do or say that makes you think she doesn't really mean it?' I asked, not sure if he would be able to come up with a clear answer, but I should have given him more credit.

Again, he answered slowly and cautiously. 'She looks at

me as if she already knows what I'm going to say when she asks how I am, and then turns away when I answer as if she doesn't care what my answer is.'

He was looking at me hopefully, I guessed wanting some sort of validation to show my understanding of the situation. I told him it did sound like she wasn't being very sincere, and asked how that made Ben feel.

'Really angry,' he replies, and for the first time I saw a hint of steel behind the soft, vulnerable-looking teenager's face.

I asked if he'd mentioned any of this to his dad and he said he had, but his dad had told him that of course Jenny cared and was just expressing her concern. So, no support there. Ben told me he had overheard Jenny telling his dad that maybe Ben needed surgery, and if the scans didn't show anything, either there was nothing wrong with him or only surgery would reveal what was really going on.

I could sense Ben's fear at the prospect of surgery, and the anger again at Jenny's interference, and I suspected that wasn't the only thing Ben had overheard Jenny say about him.

Many athletes have surgery to cure pain that is most likely caused by psychological issues and end up in a worse state than before due to scar-tissue problems.

We talked a little bit about Ben's relationship with his dad and how they get on, and Ben said he had spent a lot of time in his room at his dad's house in recent weeks. When I asked why that was, he told me in a very quiet voice, almost as if he didn't want his dad to hear, that he thought Jenny was turning his dad against him. Ben looked sad and a little teary at the idea of his dad believing Jenny and not him.

I felt it was important for Ben to feel that at least one adult other than his mum believed him about his back pain. I explained to him that I certainly had no doubt that he was in pain but, if I was honest, I had no real clue as to what was causing it and that was what we were going to try to find out together.

If my hunch was correct, he was suffering from some psychosomatic episode which, it appeared, had been going on for several months now. What I wasn't going tell him was that aches and pains of this nature are rarely easy to treat because there are usually significant underlying emotional problems feeding the discomfort. I didn't think he could handle that detail just at this point in his treatment.

There's a saying in the sports therapy world: 'The issues are in the tissues.' Treating the back injury as a musculoskeletal issue was, in my opinion – and also in that of the variety of specialists in this field that he'd seen already – probably heading down the wrong path. If my work with Ben was going to be successful, we were going to have to create a therapeutic alliance (trust each other enough for the therapy to work) and that might mean some tough conversations. But I was encouraged that Ben was at least opening up about Jenny, although I suspected Jenny was not the real problem. She was simply a bullseye for Ben to chuck his angry darts at, and maybe this was the first time he'd been allowed to do that. I certainly wasn't going to stop him.

He went on to tell me about the rest of the weekend, and how he, his dad and Jenny had gone to see Kieron play for City's under-eighteens. Kieron was a decent player according to Ben, and popular with the other boys, and as he spoke, it became obvious there was more than a little hero-worshipping going on for his big brother. Then Ben's face clouded and he told me how Jenny was talking to the other mums and dads on the touchline, as if Keiron was her son, calling him 'my

Keiron' and telling them how close she and Keiron were. Ben told me Keiron didn't like Jenny either.

I asked if Ben enjoyed watching Keiron play football, especially as Ben couldn't play at the moment. He told me he'd been watching Keiron play for as long as he could remember, and the family all believed that Kieron was going to make it as a footballer. He used to score loads of goals for the school team, so it was only a matter of time before he got scouted.

I asked what life was like for him growing up and he said it was mostly all about watching Keiron. He told me his evenings and weekends were a constant round of travelling to training sessions or games, going to buy Keiron new boots or other kit, and all his parents seemed to talk about was Keiron and whether or not he was in the team. When Ben was old enough, he was put in a makeshift goal in their back garden so Keiron could practise shooting.

He smiled a gentle, warm smile. 'Mum and Dad bought me this really cool goalkeeping strip for my seventh birthday – black jersey, black shorts and black socks. I thought I was some sort of superhero. At first, I wanted to be Kieron – you know, scoring the goals. But Keiron needed the shooting practice so I stayed in goal, and I spent that many hours practising with Keiron, I got quite good at it.'

Good enough that he was soon being offered trials for the local football club academy as a goalkeeper. But around this time his world suddenly changed for ever, as his mum and dad announced out of the blue that they were splitting up.

Our session was going reasonably well, so I tried to push Ben about his feelings around the break-up. He was reluctant to talk about his dad, but did say he missed him and wished he was back at home. When he was telling me this it looked like the tears weren't very far away, so I decided to back off that topic for now as it was obviously something that was quite painful for Ben to think about. At this early stage of the therapeutic process, I didn't think it would be wise to push Ben past the point of tears because I feared he wouldn't want to continue with therapy after what he might see as the shame of crying so early on.

I gave him a moment to gather his thoughts, then I asked him about his mum, if she was seeing anyone or even dating. He looked embarrassed and mumbled that he didn't think so. It was obviously something he felt uncomfortable talking about, and from the look of it, the thought of his mum with a new partner was not a very appealing one.

Many young men find it hard to see their parents as sexual objects of desire for new partners. Sexuality between their own parents is difficult enough for kids to get their heads around, so a new partner can be troubling.

Ben couldn't look at me directly, instead hiding behind his fringe, but he asked me quietly, 'Don't you want to talk about my back pain?'

He seemed to be steeling himself to talk about it, yet again. However, I'd avoided even mentioning it, wanting to get a much clearer picture of Ben's life and his feelings about the key people in it before we went on to the subject of his pain, so I could understand his confusion. I told him that we would pick that up in the next session, but for now I just wanted him to relax and feel comfortable talking openly with me about anything he wanted to.

He responded with a beaming, innocent smile and said, 'Thank God for that.'

Edwin Thomas

I Can't Get No . . .

At the beginning of our next session, I told Edwin I was interested in what had happened last time when I mentioned him and Cerys starting a family. I was trying to work out why he had been so abrupt in his response. Other than the outburst about his wife, there had been no further cracks in Edwin's well-constructed facade. Despite my trying to find a way in during the last session, he was once again back in supreme control of his emotions and reverting to playing his game of cat and mouse, with me very much the mouse.

He looked away in the distance to my right. Some psychological theories, including neuro-linguistic programming, suggest that the direction of a person's gaze when contemplating and answering a question indicates the area of the brain they are accessing to form their response. Looking to the right is a sign that they are accessing the artistic area of the brain, which invents or creates thoughts. In short, they could be preparing a lie. Deception seemed very much Edwin's forte, as both a player and, I suspected, a person.

I'm often fascinated by the position a player plays in a team. As a rugby halfback, Edwin could go in any direction, and there was a flavour of that in our therapy. Just as I thought we were going in one direction, I'd notice that he'd sidestepped what we were discussing and had darted off elsewhere. It felt at times as if I was desperately trying to follow him all over the pitch.

Edwin came up with another expert sidestep, mumbling about the psychological stress it was putting him and Cerys under, and dismissed my line of questioning. I felt exasperated.

He began again. 'Look, I accept things with me and Cerys aren't that great right now, but once I get a chance to sort it out with her, we'll have things back on track in no time.'

'What do you mean, once you "get a chance to sort it out with her"?' I asked.

He looked at me with what could only be described as disdain, then said, 'Once she comes back home from staying at her mum and dad's for a few days.'

I asked how well Cerys got on with her parents and Edwin replied with a measure of impatience, 'She's really close to them, but she has to learn to stand up for herself with them. She lets them tell her what to do and I can't help thinking they are a major reason things aren't going so well between us just now.'

I asked Edwin what his relationship was like with his in-laws. He suddenly had what could only be described as a 'shifty' look as he said, 'Good enough.'

'So do you think they influence Cerys?'

He seemed irritated by my question, but spoke about Cerys's relationship with her parents, drawing a picture of interference around money, with them saying she needed her own income and interests. Edwin disagreed with them, claiming he made enough for the both of them and she simply didn't need to work. Cerys had had to leave her previous position when he relocated from a London club to the Welsh one he now played for, and Edwin believed there was a high likelihood that she could only get a rather low-paid job, something neither of them wanted.

I asked him what job Cerys had had before they met and if she wanted to go back to work.

Apparently, Cerys had recently raised the possibility of going back to work with Edwin. She used to be an events manager at the London club's stadium, but he had been against her returning to work. Besides, he told me, she'd only have to give it up again when they eventually started a family, so what was the point? Once again he neatly sidestepped the second question.

I asked how long they had been trying for a family and there was a look of annoyance on his face. I wondered if it was frustration at how long it was taking him to impregnate his wife compared to Johners, or something else. Edwin told me they'd only been trying for a few months so it was really early days yet, but the way he couldn't look directly at me seemed to indicate this response was designed to cloak more than just the minor details he was willing to share. I decided to investigate.

'I'm surprised at such an early stage, things have already started to get difficult for the two of you. Couples don't usually reach the stressed-out stage for at least a year of trying to get pregnant. Any thoughts as to why you and Cerys might be hitting problems already, and have things changed in the last week?' He looked directly at me and again I got the sense he was assessing how much he was willing to divulge.

'Starting a family has always been high on our agenda. It's the natural progression when we are established as a couple.'

I was struck by the strong sense of control that came out of that statement. Edwin had a clear path he thought their relationship should follow, and I wondered if Cerys was in total agreement with the direction of that path. He went on to present a picture in which Cerys was no longer interested in having sex – she seemed to be going through the motions, rather than actively engaging in the act of lovemaking. This had been the case since before the pub brawl, to a point where intimacy had now ended and things hadn't changed since our last session.

Edwin's inability to see their situation as anything other than a 'Cerys problem' made me think that Cerys did indeed have a different path in mind, but had not yet found her voice to make her thoughts and feelings clear to Edwin, so had resorted to withdrawing from him physically.

'I told her that if she really wanted a proper marriage with me, then staying *in* my house was the best way to make things right, not keep running back to her mum and dad, which isn't going to achieve anything.' His fists were clenched tight, as if trying to hold on to her. He took a deep breath, and I could see the naked anger he was trying to control. 'She decided to go anyway, but at least it's only temporary.'

'Your house, Edwin? Don't you mean yours *and* Cerys's house?'

'Actually no, it's not "our" house. You see, I've done well from playing rugby and that house was bought with my earnings, so it belongs to me, not her. She knew what the score was when she married me.'

Edwin's single-mindedness was at times chilling. It wasn't the first time I'd come across this attitude working with professional sportspeople, and I'd noted that sometimes the determination to succeed as an athlete made them quite self-ish in their personal relationships. One F1 driver once said to me in our work together, 'Don't take away my competitive edge.' That competitive edge was part of the reason he was so successful at his sport, but it was also deeply damaging to his personal life.

I began to get a flavour of Edwin's control of Cerys and how this had played out down the years in their relationship. It appeared that the only way she could get any power was to move out of his orbit and return to planet Mum and Dad.

The conversation flowed back to his rugby club.

'The rugby is going nowhere, to be honest. I've told the physio that he needs to up his game if he's going to get a match out of me soon. They're bloody useless – the physios, strength and conditioning people, coaches, everybody! I can't get a game of rugby and I can't even get a shag!'

Edwin snorted and there was an uncomfortable silence. He then went on to tell me that he had received a text from Cerys the day before. He'd just returned home, having had to eat out because when he arrived back from training he found the fridge was completely empty. Cerys's text was to tell him that she was going to be staying with her parents for a bit longer. He rang her immediately to ask whether the marriage was over and she said she didn't know. Edwin was furious, barking down the phone that he'd provided her with every-thing, and she'd even taken the car he bought her.

I wondered what might have stopped him going over to see his in-laws and talking to Cerys in person about the prob-lems they evidently had in their marriage, but clearly this was not part of his current agenda. I didn't believe his self-imposed exile was bringing him any great happiness, but it might have been his way of punishing Cerys for moving out.

I was pretty sure that their marriage was heading south right now. Unless Edwin decided to face reality and do something about it, there wouldn't be a marriage left in a few months. There was nothing wrong with deciding the marriage was over, but Edwin couldn't or wouldn't deal with the situation as it was.

We were getting to the end of the session so I had to deal with the matter of what Edwin wanted to do about continuing therapy with me.

'I'm actually beginning to enjoy these chats,' he said cheerfully. 'I think we should carry on and I'm happy to pay you. Just send me the bill.'

That last 'Just send me the bill' was said so dismissively that I suspected I knew what Cerys felt like living under his roof.

As the session ended, I shared with Edwin my concerns about the future of his marriage, saying, 'I'm worried that by not talking to Cerys face to face about how your relationship is going at the moment, things will be even harder to fix further down the line.'

'Her bloody fault, pissing off back to her mum and dad. I'm so angry with her right now. Running away when things get a bit tough is hardly a grown-up way of behaving, is it? She needs to know what side her bread is buttered on.'

And with that he stood up and walked out, leaving me with a feeling of real revulsion.

Madison King

CLINICAL NOTES: FIRST SESSION

MADISON KING – AGED 32

Profession: Established Scottish international women's footballer currently playing in London at a women's Premier League club. Has been out of the game for four months having sustained a head injury after being hit by a car while out walking.

Referral: Through a senior psychiatrist via her players' union, in consultation with the football club's doctor, after the client had repeatedly failed the 'return to play' protocols due to the continued symptoms of the head injury.

Appearance: Tall, with a strong physique, Madison has been involved in women's football for a decade. Her shoulder-length black hair and make-up-free face accentuated her youthful-looking features. She was wearing a plain white shirt and jeans, which looked both feminine and smart, without being too formal.

She was softly spoken with a gentle Scottish (possibly Edinburgh) burr, with little or no humour about her, but while her demeanour was quite sombre, she was articulate and expressive in her choice of language, using gestures to help add emphasis to what she said.

Presenting Issues: Madison was involved in an RTC while walking in which she was hit by a car and sustained a serious head injury.

She was concussed and taken to a nearby hospital, where doctors were concerned enough to keep her in overnight. She has not been able to play competitive football since.

Every time Madison attempts to return to training, she suffers symptoms aligned to a possible ongoing brain injury. These include vestibular problems (dizziness), double vision, severe headaches and slight stumbling. The symptoms seem to settle down when she doesn't train or play, but even when she's inactive, she experiences mood swings and is seeking psychological help to deal with anger issues. She described this as 'going from zero to 100 in seconds — one minute I'm calm and the next I'm screaming with rage'.

Madison has been advised to retire from football as another head injury might result in long-lasting damage. She could be dealing with transition issues (possibly leaving football permanently).

Therapeutic Thinking: There is no hard and fast rule about head injuries, but Madison is getting increasingly angry and depressed about having to give up the game. Any medical advice to stop playing is inevitably cautious, rather than scientifically certain. The only way to examine the brain damage properly would have to be done post-mortem!

The work is to help Madison recognize the triggers that cause her anger and learn how to deal with them.

Then there is the realization that her career is possibly at an end, so I need to help her think about leaving the sport, and how this might affect her life (financial, personal, time management, future career, etc.).

Added to this is the question of how Madison will deal with the sudden and possibly catastrophic effects of the loss of the social aspects of playing football. Her flatmate and old school friend has been very supportive to date, but there seem to be signs of friction between the two of them, possibly due to Madison's mood swings.

At present Madison says she feels 'cut off' from her teammates and her life is now 'one long round of medical appointment after medical appointment'. She also admits to having increased her alcohol consumption — approximately one bottle of gin a week.

The True Cost of a Galaxy

With much of psychotherapy subjective – Am I more down than usual? Is it normal to feel this way? Am I being reasonable to expect my mum/partner to . . . ? – a client who presents with an indisputable physical injury poses an entirely different set of challenges.

Madison played centre half at a professional football club and would possibly head the ball between five and eight times a game, plus many more times in training, so factors like neck strength and genetic considerations often make women more susceptible than men to head and neck injuries. Women can also be susceptible to more cranial and neck injuries during their menstrual cycle due to ligament laxity that is brought on by hormonal changes. So head injuries in women's football aren't uncommon.

Madison's CT scans suggested some minor irregularities, but it was unclear whether the long-term significance of the injury warranted the curtailment of her career. That said, the signs weren't positive as it had now been four months since the initial injury and every time Madison trained she complained of related symptoms in the subsequent forty-eight hours. As the risk of future injury – and all the severe consequences that would flow from it – was considerable, this made for a compelling argument that she might have to give up the game permanently.

The topic of transitioning (leaving the sport) comes up a lot in my work. From success-desperate young players who are heartbroken to be told they are being released by their club to the experienced pros who'd play for nothing rather than accept their playing days are behind them, all find it extremely tough. But in both of those groups, the individual usually has a sense of what's coming. Young academy players are constantly being informed of their progress or lack of it by their coaches or academy management. Likewise, the thirty-something player will know that sooner rather than later they are going to be fortunate to eke out a new contract. Then there are the athletes whose gently increasing times are now pushing them further and further down the pecking order. Age comes to us all, but while most ordinary humans can continue with most careers even when their bodies no longer perform at their peak, for elite athletes that is not possible. Things are made worse by the gunslinger theory – that there will always be someone younger, faster and more deadly wanting to take your title. But the sudden career-ending injury is the cruellest cut of all. The best way to describe it is as a sudden bereavement.

In our session Madison was going through the stages of the Kübler-Ross grief cycle, coming to terms with the fact that her career was almost certainly over. This widely known theory suggests that bereavement is a process with specific stages. Madison was in denial, thinking that she could probably play again, but then she was also showing signs of anger, depression and bargaining (wondering if she should forfeit her long-term health for her short-term career). It was clear she was far from the final desired stage of acceptance.

I have usually found that this grief cycle doesn't proceed smoothly from one stage to the next, and often a client can be at the end of the cycle only for events or comments to suddenly loop them back to an earlier stage. Madison seemed to be firmly locked into her cycle, on a roundabout with no exits. When I next saw her, she was predominantly in the anger stage, and this anger was largely directed inwardly towards herself.

'I'm still trying to work out just why I had to go to the shop that day. Of all the stupid things to take me out – all for a fucking bar of chocolate.'

She was highly animated and her arms were flailing around, gesticulating wildly with her emotions.

'I couldn't get the thought of biting into a bar of Galaxy out of my head and was nipping to the shop. I didn't look when I dashed across the road and simply didn't see the car. Next thing I know, I wake up in hospital. Couldn't remember a thing.'

She looked pensive, as if replaying the events of the accident through her mind, then shook her head gently, at a loss for an answer. Her face clouded again and the strength of her anger caused her to clench her fists.

'I'm so angry with myself for being so bloody stupid. I mean, even little kids know they have to be careful crossing the road, and all for a bar of Galaxy. Not worth this.'

Her usually soft Scottish lilt had been replaced by a more aggressive throaty and guttural sound as she was obviously fighting back tears.

'Maybe it's time to forgive yourself, Madison. It was an accident, nobody's fault.'

She fell silent and stared into another place that only she could see.

'What are you thinking right now, Madison?'

She shook herself out of her reverie and said, 'I'm thinking of my flatmate, Becky, and how I keep getting so angry.

Since the injury, things haven't been that good, not really. One minute we're great, the next we're at each other's throats. We were never like that before the injury.'

She paused a moment and looked around the room, and a small smile touched her lips. 'When we were at school together we were inseparable – got into loads of scrapes.'

I watched as a single tear escaped her left eye. She brushed it away impatiently.

'And I hate crying too. Hate all this. I can't seem to stop myself, even when I watch some shit romcom film now, I end up bawling. I never used to be like that.'

She fell silent again, then screwed up her face, as if to stop the sobs from coming back. She looked at me with pleading in her eyes, desperate for the normality she once took for granted.

'What's happening to me? I mope around the house, waiting for Becky to come back from work or from the gym to relieve the boredom. I've tried going with her to the gym, but I just end up dizzy for the next twenty-four hours. I've become bloody housebound. Me!' Her voice was rising again. 'I spiral out of control over the smallest things, and it ends up in a big row when she gets home. If she comes home and I've had a glass of wine – or two, or three – the same thing happens. I'm sick of it. I just wanna play football again without these fucking dizzy spells and headaches.'

The tears flowed once more. Madison's emotional gauge swung between fury and misery. It was like watching a slow metronome: the more she swung one way, the more violently she swung the other.

Silence. Then she raised her voice to its full throttle and shouted, 'I fucking hate being me!', looking at me with all the fury and hate that she'd been holding on to for a long time.

When a client puts me in their cross hairs it's often both unnerving and comforting. If I am counselling a larger person, there's sometimes an air of menace or violence, and that can be frightening, but I didn't feel any sense of threat in the room when I was with Madison. At the same time, she'd allowed her anger to be directed towards me and that meant I was able to work with it more efficiently. Anger directed inward by a client causes depression, and I'd rather work with an angry sportsperson than a depressed one. Sitting alone with a client who barely utters a word and is in a deep pit of despair is difficult for both therapist and client.

The following week Madison returned for her next session. She slumped down in the chair and it was clear that she wanted to unburden herself. After a deep breath and long, slow exhale, she began.

'God, I've had one seriously shitty week. It's all gone tits up.' She paused for a moment and then revealed with a break in her voice, 'Becky's threatened to move out.'

After a moment of heavy silence, I asked Madison if she wanted to tell me what had happened. She nodded, then went on to explain how the previous weekend Becky's parents had travelled south from Scotland to see them. Madison said she and Becky usually joked about these parental trips that they often felt like a 'royal visit'.

'We feel we have to clean the flat from top to bottom, then prepare an elaborate meal for all of us on the Sunday, before they get the early-afternoon train home. Anyway, I wasn't feeling 100 per cent on Friday and Becky was working late. On my bad days I can get exhausted really quickly, and Friday was one of the worst I've had recently. Maybe it was the stress of the visit, but regardless, all the cleaning and cooking was down to me.'

Madison told me she'd always felt that Becky's mum was never quite comfortable with her and Becky's close friendship, feeling that Madison's chosen career was inappropriate for a woman, and maybe she saw the situation as an opportunity for Becky to put this friendship behind her and to find herself some proper friends (ones her mother approved of).

It seems that Becky's parents arrived on the Friday night, and her mum, whom Madison described as 'a tad fierce', got stuck in as soon as they walked in. Becky's mum began asking Madison lots of questions. Had she thought about what she was going to do now? Had she started any therapy? What had she been doing to fill her time?

Becky and her dad just stayed silent, looking uncomfortable. It was at this point that Madison felt the anger rise like a hot roaring wave of magma, first in her chest, then in her neck, until she felt a burning in her throat like she needed to erupt. When Becky's mum made yet another 'sarky' remark, something about what exactly *was* Madison doing in the house all day, Madison found herself blurting out, 'I wait in the house all day for Becky to get home, then we have glorious sex.' Madison told me that for a moment it was so satisfying to see the shock on Becky's mum's face, but she soon regretted her words as within a few minutes she found herself alone in the house after much screaming and shouting.

Becky went back with her parents to their hotel and decided to stay there, and Madison hadn't seen her since. She was still obviously very angry with Madison because there had been pretty much radio silence since.

'I got a single text from her late on Saturday. It just read "That was not cool! Sort yourself out."'

Madison looked down and began crying silently. This wasn't the hopeless racking sobs I'd seen from her previously,

more the residue from that, when there really is nothing else
left.

I had a strong desire to comfort her somehow, but therapists are never encouraged to have any physical contact with
their clients. For whom would the comfort have been – her
or me? I think it's one of the hardest things I have to do as a
therapist. To quote one of my instructors from way back in
my college days, 'You just have to sit with the discomfort.'

Madison eventually looked at me and said, with anger rising again in her voice, 'Sort myself out! How the hell am I
supposed to sort out a brain that's basically fucked?'

Fear

Fear keeps us alive. It's the vital emotion that throughout our evolution has helped us identify danger. If our ancestors hadn't experienced fear when facing a predator, they'd soon have been the predator's lunch. In today's society, we have eliminated many of those risks to our survival, yet we still have chronic anxieties and fears which saturate our lives. Without those fears, which might be real or imagined, I wouldn't have a job!

As babies we are born with only two 'pre-programmed' fears: the fear of loud noises and the fear of falling. The rest of our fears are taught to us by our caregivers, schools, friends and society in general. There's a theory that scary children's stories are a way of teaching our offspring to be wary of the real world. Maybe think of this as 'inoculation'. The Roald Dahl children's books are a psychologist's treasure trove, full of children being abducted and preyed upon by malevolent adults, but the children always triumph in the end.

Fear in sport stalks every training ground and dressing room. It's there in what I describe as 'the tyranny of success'. No one in a professional sports club will entertain the idea of defeat in the next match. That concept isn't allowed. No one ever wants to talk about the fear of a career-ending injury or the loneliness that might exist after a sporting career comes to an end. My presence in a football club can be a safe reposi-tory for most of the fears and anxieties swirling around, enabling people to carry on with their day-to-day lives, unburdened and carefree.

The fact that few coaches want a walking reminder of their vulnerability is possibly the reason why I am the only psychotherapist that I know of working in first-team professional football in the UK. Historically, many sports clubs have watched their highly paid employees self-implode under the weight of trying to achieve sporting excellence rather than deal with their crippling fears. If it becomes clear to the management that a player can't stand the pressure, they simply get rid of that player and find one who can.

This section on fear shares some of the aspects we've already looked at in the section on shame. Shame is fear's sly brother. Our football academies are full of young men and women who are too frightened to say 'I don't know what I'm doing' or 'I need help.' The *fear* of shame is pervasive. This vulnerability is often seen as a weakness by young men who have what you might describe as 'traditional' masculine values. Most of these young players are in denial about needing help.

Some time ago I worked with a young centre forward who played in the North-West. Heading the ball wasn't his strongest suit, but he was tipped to play in the Premier League one day. However, for some reason he wasn't getting anywhere near the first-team squad. I asked the manager of the club why that was and he gave me a clear and graphic response: 'He can't fucking head the ball. When I was his age, when everyone else had left, I'd be on the training ground with a football tied to a basketball goal. I'd head it, learn to control the header, the speed and direction of the ball. I'd learn to time my jumping or learn how to dominate the other team's centre half. I'd be building up my neck and shoulder muscles. In the end, I was the best header of the ball at my club. This kid – at the end of training – he can't wait to get away to see his girlfriend.'

'And what would happen if he knocked on your door and asked you for help?'

'I'd help him, and so would the coaching staff here. But remember, I've a squad of thirty-five pros here. I can't go round each and every player and check they can perform what should be a basic skill for a professional player.'

So I went back to my young client, expecting him to be thrilled to hear that all he had to do was ask the manager for help with his heading. I instead got, 'Nah, that's not happening. It's just too embarrassing. I'm never going to do that.' The last I heard he'd left the club and was playing non-league football.

Many of the following stories involve an individual facing down their fears and examining what effect they have had on their careers. Young goalkeeper Ben Phillips feared he'd never be as successful as his older brother, who was already with another football academy. Mark Silver, the snooker player, feared another type of loss – his dazzling girlfriend walking out on him. She enjoyed the limelight and celebrity lifestyle, but he wasn't so keen. Rugby international Edwin Thomas feared life alone if his partner left him too.

For some, it's fear of the unknown, as was the case for former athlete Jane Lovell, who was trying to build a career outside a stifling marriage, with all the anxiety involved in transitioning that leaving the sport brings. But for others, their fear is more existential, as we'll see in the case of Tony Oldfield, who looks back over his career first in football, then in sports broadcasting.

We all have fears. I was apprehensive about embarking on training as a psychotherapist after a long career as a sports broadcaster. I had to commit to five years of study and significant financial outlay, with no guarantee that there would be a viable career at the end of it. Overcoming my fears by committing to the course brought its own rewards – and ultimately allowed me to write this book.*

So what can a trained sports psychotherapist do? First, help players afflicted by fears to stop hiding from them; then help them to enjoy the relief that comes from understanding that their fears are commonplace; and finally help them to realize that fears can be accepted without the anxiety of shame.

Psychotherapy can be crucial because, as Roald Dahl knew, recognizing our own strength diminishes the power the monsters have over us.

---

* I even fear that publishing the book will open me to the ridicule of my previous broadcasting colleagues and possibly even my more recent therapist contemporaries. But when we embrace the fear and don't hide from it, we can make better-informed choices.

Mark Silver

Big Boys Don't Cry

It was a couple of weeks before I saw Mark again and I was interested to hear about the state of his relationship with Jasmine – if they were still together, or his insecurities around the relationship had had a damaging impact. He was playing in tournaments both in the UK and abroad, so I took this gap in our sessions as an opportunity to take my work with Mark to my supervisor, Tom.* Supervision is one of the most effective tools in psychotherapy (and is mandatory in our profession), because it gives us peer support and challenges our thinking around issues like ethics, boundaries and different ways of working with tricky clients.

Tom sighed as he mulled over Mark's story to date.

'He's a bit of a lad, isn't he? All that sex in the swimming-pool stuff. To be honest, the phrase "exhibition match" came to mind when you told me of his frolicking in the pool. I saw him all over the newspapers the other week with his beauty

---

* A more experienced psychotherapist, trained to bring a greater depth and variety to my thinking.

queen girlfriend. It's quite interesting, isn't it? The papers seem to love the narrative – what's she doing with him? But has his form dipped since those two got together? If not, it's certainly dipping now.'

He paused and looked down into his big mug of tea and shook his head.

'We've heard so much about how gorgeous Jasmine is, and we've also heard a lot about how close he is to Dad. I'm just wondering where Mum is in all this. If he's insecure with Jasmine, it could follow that he has an insecurity around his mum leaving him. Perhaps at playgroup, that sort of thing. Have you checked this out?'

As usual, Tom provided valuable insights, but it always left me feeling slightly novice-like when he put his finger on something I hadn't checked out yet. I just had to find the right time to explore the topic of Mark's mum with him.

Mark arrived at his next session looking – to be frank – bloody awful. He had dark rings under his eyes and an unhealthy pallor, and I wondered if he was well enough to be here.

He sat down heavily in his chair and croaked, 'Could I have a glass of water?'

While he was sipping his water, I mentioned he looked a bit under the weather and enquired if he was feeling unwell. He told me he was OK, then went on to describe how he'd just had the mother of all disasters the night before. He was playing in the quarter-final of a big snooker tournament and was on course to receive prize money of £25,000 if he reached the semi-final. He and Jasmine had talked about spending this money on a posh wedding. Mark was the overwhelming favourite to reach the last four and was eight frames ahead in the best-of-nineteen-frame match. Needing a simple green pot to take him within one frame of success, he said he lost his concentration, managed to pot the white ball, lost the next eight frames and the match was delicately poised at nine frames all, going into the last one.

'If I lost, all I could think of was telling Jaz that she wouldn't be able to have her wedding, but I was desperate to win and get the money. Well, you can probably guess what happened. Jaz is so disappointed. I think I could deal with her being angry, but her disappointment is killing me. She's trying to be understanding, but I can tell she's ready to leave me because I can't give her what she wants. Every time I ask her why she's with me she tells me it's because she loves me and she wants us to be together, but why would someone so beautiful want to be with a loser like me?'

I could tell Mark's fear of losing Jasmine was overwhelming his common sense and was likely to lead to trouble between them both if he couldn't rein it in. He confirmed my thinking with his next sentence: 'We ended up having a massive row about me not believing she even wanted to get married. She got really upset and said I needed to get my act together if there was any chance of a future for us. She told me not to contact her for a couple of days and that she was going back home to see her parents. She is close to her mum. I can see them sitting over the kitchen table absolutely slaughtering me for messing up the wedding.'

Mark looked desolate, as if she'd already decided to leave him for good. I asked him why he didn't believe Jasmine when she said she loved him. Had she ever given him reason to doubt her feelings?

He looked uncomfortable and, after shifting in his seat, told me that he couldn't say there was anything specific, only a feeling he had, but they had been arguing a lot lately and she'd been getting really angry with him in a way she hadn't before.

Suddenly an open goal had arrived in the therapy. I asked Mark if he thought his neediness and his suspicion about Jasmine's motives for being with him might be driving her away.

He didn't answer straight away and I could see he was finding it difficult to look at me directly. I decided to leave that possibility with him to consider and moved on to another key area we needed to explore.

'Tell me about your mum, Mark. You've not mentioned her so far.'

His face darkened and he lifted up the glass of water, took a deep drink and replaced it heavily. He then went on to explain that he and his mum weren't close, and that when he was eight, she left the family to set up a relationship with somebody else for a couple of years. Mark and his little brother, who was aged six at the time, lived with their dad and things weren't great domestically while Mum was away.

'It was really crap. Dad couldn't cope. Sometimes we'd come home and there was no tea because either he was working or he'd not been shopping for food. I knew what every chippy looked like within a two-mile radius of our house. When Dad wasn't around, I'd go looking for him at the local working men's club and that's when I first picked up a snooker cue. They served chip butties there with brown sauce, and that was often my main meal of the day. After about eighteen months, Mum's new fella ditched her and she begged Dad to take her back, and in the end he did. I think he did so to make sure the family was looked after properly. I never saw Mum and Dad hug or kiss again. It felt like a matter of convenience between them. I used to have nightmares that I'd come back to the house and it was empty and I'd be shouting for my mum, but she wasn't there. In my dream I realized she'd left again and this time she wasn't coming back.'

Mark was breathing heavily, as if he'd run a 200-metre race.

'Blimey, this ain't half getting heavy. You'll have me in tears next.'

'What would be wrong with crying, Mark? When's the last time you cried?'

'Get lost! You're not gonna get me blubbering like a big girl. When Mum left, I remember crying and Dad gave me a real good hiding. That was the last time.'

There was so much in what Mark had just said, and thoughts and ideas were flying round my head like a white ball smashing into a pyramid of red ones in the opening break.

To begin with, Mark was demonstrating the difference in terms of sport psychology between the challenger state (determined to succeed despite the difficulties) and the threat state (frightened that you're going to lose) and there are different physiological responses in our bodies to these two mental approaches. In the challenger state, our heart rate increases and pumps blood and adrenaline to our limbs and brain, ready for a major challenge, usually associated with combat. In the threat state, once again our heart rate increases, but because of our fear and the chemicals we secrete, blood is *not* pumped as effectively to the limbs and brain and we are left in a state of anxiety. The best metaphor to explain this mental state is revving up a car without putting it in gear. It doesn't do the engine much good, so imagine what it does to your body over a long period of time!

Interestingly, Mark was suffering from the threat state in terms of his form and also in his personal life because he felt threatened that Jasmine was about to leave him. This innate belief that a significant caregiver might be about to walk out of his life had some historical basis, because that's exactly what his mother did when Mark was little. The results of his mother's departure were not a positive experience for Mark, so I imagine the thought of Jasmine leaving him brought back similar emotions. These would have included the feeling that he couldn't cope, and the fact that he went hungry when his mum disappeared might explain Mark's tricky relationship with food and alcohol.

Mark's main presenting issue was his loss of form and that meant explaining to him that he was increasingly in the threat rather than the challenger state.

Looking down at his adidas trainers, Mark said, 'I couldn't cope if Jaz left me. I would want to do myself in. I'm just pathetic! Fat baldy bloke with a Miss UK beauty queen? As if.'

He was quickly slipping into despondency. 'I'm pretty sure she's in contact with an old flame who lives close to her mum and dad, and I wouldn't mind betting that she will go and see him and moan about what a useless lardy arse I am. Her mum and dad are gonna be right hacked off, because I know they were already making early plans for the wedding, and God knows what she's gone home telling them.'

Mark reminded me of many clients I had seen who enter a relationship, are over-needy, overcommit, become manipulative in order to try and control the other person, and then get very anxious that their partners are going to leave them.

I saw Mark's eyes get redder and redder and a solitary tear ran down his round cheek.

'Bastard! Look what you've made me do now. I've turned into that big girl my dad told me I'd turn into.'

'I know this is a weird question, Mark, but how old do you feel right now?'

He looked up at me with a mixture of anger, disgust, shame and fear.

'About eight,' he said.

Tony Oldfield

Cold Comfort

I decided to take Tony Oldfield's case to my supervisor and we discussed my work in Tom's ramshackle Victorian terrace house, a few days before Tony's next session. I needed to explain how Tony had low self-esteem after seeing his careers diminish, both as an ex-player and now as a broadcaster, and also financially. I was having mild concerns around his personal safety too. This last issue is normally a compelling enough reason to take a case to a supervisor.

As usual, Tom was on hand with a mug of tea and a warm smile. We went over the details of my work with Tony and he was particularly intrigued by Tony's relationship with Anna, and why he put up with her cruel behaviour towards him.

'We really need to know more about Tony's early life. You say he was married, but he's not doing too well with his relationships, is he? He's fallen out with his son, divorced his ex-wife and he's now on track to really piss off his girlfriend. Added to that, I wonder what the football club are feeling about him throwing a "sickie" the night before a big game. He certainly likes bashing into people, doesn't he?'

Tom wondered where Tony's 'soft place to land' (a place of warmth and comfort where a person can feel safe*) was. This gave me plenty to think over.

At our next session, Tony looked very different. Gone were the jauntiness and the smart, pristine outfit; instead he was unshaven, and his clothes looked as if he'd slept in them. As I registered his appearance, a wave of sadness washed over me. While the skill of a therapist comes from being able to tune in and pick up on a client's emotions, this was simply the normal human reaction to another person in a clear state of emotional distress.

'What's going on, Tony?'

Tony told me that the football club had decided to let him go after complaints in the sponsors' lounge about his behaviour and also his poor timekeeping. There had been a particular incident when he was rude to a young fan who didn't recognize him; apparently the term 'you little shit' was used.

His main issue with what had happened was that the football club was his main source of income and had kept him above the breadline for the last few years. He looked desolate. I recognized that the loss of this work would be a major blow not only to his bank account, but also to his self-esteem, as he would no longer have the recognition as an ex-player. He went on to say that he did have some work coming up – as a co-commentator on a Swedish second-division game for an international audience out of a recording studio near Heathrow. This involved sitting in an airless booth approximately

---

* There are several theories around this topic, but one of the more straightforward is psychologist Abraham Maslow's hierarchy of needs, which states that physiological and safety needs are part of our basic requirements for life.

ten feet square with another commentator and offering his comments about how he thought the match was going.

'It's come to this,' he said, shaking his head with a deep sigh. 'Big-shot Tony Oldfield, who was the darling of the TV world when the Premier League came into existence, is reduced to giving his thoughts on a sodding second-division Swedish league match. Under normal circumstances, if that game was going on in my back garden, I'd draw the curtains!'

At least his sense of humour was still intact!

Tony told me how, years ago, Sky TV had come knocking on his door when the Premier League started. They couldn't get enough of him and once a month he'd sit down with the football show producer, who'd book him for about ten matches at a time. It was good money and Tony admitted that he really enjoyed being recognized in the pubs and bars when he went out drinking. Every football fan wanted to hear his views on their team.

'Nobody wants to know what I think about football any more, or even who I am. It's so hard to get any bookings. I feel if I walked down the street naked nobody would give a toss. I doubt I'd even get arrested.'

The thought of Tony walking down the road naked was not necessarily an image I wanted to dwell on. I decided to change the subject.

'How are things with Anna?'

'Oh, God, they've gone from bad to worse. I went to see her to say that I'd lost my work in the sponsors' lounge, and she went off on one about how she's not surprised they sacked me, who would want *me* hanging around their club – "a has-been that nobody cares about".'

I must admit to cringing inwardly at Anna's cruelty and felt heartened when Tony told me that, once again, he turned and left Anna mid-tirade, walking out of her house and driving away. He told me the anger he'd felt previously wasn't there. He just felt numb and needed to get away from her so he could breathe.

I could see, though, that the impact of her words had hit Tony hard. He was not up to dealing with the emotions they dredged up just at this time and wanted to distance himself from that event. To give him some respite from the emotions he was struggling with, I moved the session away from her behaviour and asked him what he was afraid of.

He sat in silence for a few minutes, then said, 'I'm so scared that I'm going to run out of money. It's what spurred me on when I was a kid and wanted to be a professional footballer. I didn't want to live in a two-up two-down like Mum and Dad.'

I think it's helpful to find out from a client what their real fear is. I could hear his financial concerns – Tony talked a lot about his lack of money – but soon the conversation meandered on to how lonely he would be if he left Anna, and how he missed his son – a twenty-three-year-old footballer with a Scottish club who lived with his mum up near Edinburgh. He told me with some sadness that since they moved to Scotland about ten years ago, he'd not had much contact with his boy. The regular fortnightly visits he used to make up there when they first moved became more like monthly, and then quarterly as Tony's resentment grew at having to do all the travelling given it was his ex-wife's decision to move so far away.

He attempted to keep in contact in between visits via phone, text and email, but over time his son stopped returning his calls, his texts became more and more monosyllabic, and whenever Tony did make the journey, he found he had less and less to say to his son when they were together.

About six months ago, Tony had travelled north specifically to watch a game his boy was playing in, and after the
match he'd tried to speak to his son, but the boy blanked
him. That had really hurt. He had not travelled up there since
and had not managed to make contact over the phone or by
text. It had left him feeling really alone.

Tony then went on to tell me about an incident with Anna
that had happened the previous Wednesday. Unusually for
him, he was feeling really rather ill. He had a high temperature and had run out of paracetamol. He called Anna to ask
her to drop by and bring him some tablets (perhaps hoping
she might make him a cup of tea and give him a little TLC),
but the response he got was as unexpected as it was crushing:
'What has you feeling ill got to do with me?' Tony admitted
to being stunned by her indifference. Anna was sceptical
about how poorly Tony was and took some convincing, but
then reluctantly said she'd see what she could do.

'I fell into a fitful sleep and woke two hours later. There was
no sign of Anna, so I phoned her. She seemed quite angry and
told me to look on the bloody doorstep and stop playing the
invalid. I got out of bed and the room was spinning, but eventually I managed to get downstairs and open the front door.
There, in a small plastic bag, was the smallest packet of tablets
I'd ever seen. She claims to have rung the doorbell but I don't
believe her – it would have woken me up. It would have been
nice for her to just check to see if I was OK, but no.'

'Tony, can you describe your feelings when you saw the
packet of tablets on the ground?' I asked.

He paused, then went on to describe how, when he was
sick as a child, his mother used to get cross with him and
blamed him for inconveniencing her, making her take time
off work to look after him.

'I always felt when I was ill as a kid that somehow I'd done something wrong.'

It occurred to me that there was likely to be a connection between his mother's cruel behaviour towards Tony when he was growing up and his willingness to endure similar behaviour from Anna, in a relationship completely compromised by her lack of care towards him. I asked him about his relationship with his estranged wife, Sandra, and, not too surprisingly, when Tony described the early days of their marriage it seemed that she was not always kind. The marriage lasted fifteen years before Tony decided he couldn't take any more and walked out, yet even so he had paid well over the required child maintenance to Sandra and continued to make regular payments, even though his son was likely to have his own lucrative academy contract. Since their divorce, Sandra had continually asked Tony for more and more money and he was unable, or unwilling, to say no.

I could see the work with Tony was really to help him think about the rules and boundaries of his life so as to be able to say no to people who clearly took advantage of him. This was learned behaviour that went back to when his mum was less than kind to him as a little boy. I'm always struck by how often clients want to repeat relationships: there is a level of comfort about being in a situation that is familiar, no matter how damaging it might be. We will put up with poor behaviour that we're used to, rather than challenge what's going on in the here and now, mainly out of fear of the consequences of making that challenge, but also of being left isolated and alone.

To make matters worse for Tony, his elderly mother had not been well in the last fortnight and had been assessed for needing care in a nursing home, which would have to be funded by selling her house. Tony had been hoping to inherit the house, as he was the only child and had been banking on the proceeds to provide him with a pension in his later years. I could sense his desperation as the plans he had for his life were quickly unravelling.

'To be honest, I'm at a loss what to do right now. I don't have any other relatives to fall back on for help other than my mum, and now she's becoming more and more frail. You know, I've only just started thinking about this, but I'm going to end up like her, aren't I?' he asked, with a sense of shock at the realization, then said, 'Once my mum goes, I'll have no one. My son has no time for me. Look at me now — a sad and bitter ex-player nobody wants to employ, except for commentating on second-division Swedish football. What exactly have I got to look forward to?'

Eddie Stamp

Little Big Man

Following my session with Eddie Stamp, I was expecting a text from Jack Braithwaite, the manager, to bring my time with Eddie to an end. But when none came, I reflected on what my supervisor always said to me, that the volatility of a football club will bring up lots of raw emotion and it was my job to contain it and not be affected by it.

I thought about the two meetings I had had with Eddie and decided that things could go one of two ways. Maybe Jack Braithwaite *had* overreacted and it was just one of those training-ground spats that happen all the time. Or Eddie had a real anger issue that needed resolving with either myself or another therapist. Either way, given Eddie's unwillingness to engage with the therapeutic process, it seemed unlikely that I'd hear from the club again. However, I'd forgotten that issues in therapy are like buses – if you miss one there's bound to be another along shortly. I was about to find out that this situation was no different.

The next Saturday I was watching the results programme on Sky Sports. The TV presenter said there had been an incident in the match involving Eddie Stamp's team and the referee had been forced to resolve a conflict between the coaching staff of both teams on the touchline. They went over to the reporter at the match, who recounted how all hell had broken loose at the interval. There was unedifying footage of pushing and shoving on the pitch, then the reporter ended her report with the words, 'Ah, Eddie Stamp, as combative a coach as he ever was as a player.'

I was settling down to an early supper when my mobile rang. It was Jack Braithwaite, who told me that Eddie was in hot water. Apparently, the pushing and shouting had continued into the dressing-room area at half-time. Eddie had thrown a punch at a coach from the opposing team. He'd been sent to the stands by the referee and a complaint had been made. Jack explained they were waiting to hear the judgement of the Football Association and he would get back to me once he had a clearer idea of what needed to be done.

A few days later I read that Eddie had been charged by the Football Association with improper conduct, banned from being pitchside for the next three games and told he needed to attend anger management therapy. The original charge was assault, but the club appealed and managed to smooth over the ruffled feathers of the other team so were able to avoid police involvement.

The story was all over the local press and I felt pity for whichever poor practitioner ended up having to work with Eddie given the reaction I'd received. Jack had not contacted me again, so I assumed that they'd gone elsewhere for Eddie's therapy and I was off the hook. Frankly, I was relieved, but I thought I'd do a little research about Eddie's past misdemeanours just in case Jack came looking to me for help. What I read made it clear that here was someone with a history of violence. There were reports of serious assaults on opposition players, but also of drunken brawls with teammates and fans throughout his playing days.

Three days after the FA decision, my mobile rang and Eddie Stamp was back in my life. The following week and another two-hour train journey later, I was back at the club's training ground. Jack had asked me if, while I was with them, I had time to see an academy player who'd been finding it hard to settle after moving south from Scotland. I agreed.

I was in the middle of a session with the fifteen-year-old apprentice when there was a knock on the door and it opened before I could say anything. Eddie walked in, looking defiant and ready for a confrontation, saw the academy player sitting there and barked, 'Damien, piss off. I need to speak to Gaz.'

Damien immediately leapt to his feet and was about to dash out of the room. I was almost ready to follow him, but this was a direct challenge to my authority. I needed to stand firm, otherwise I would have no credibility with Eddie, or the rest of the club. I told Damien to sit back down and then spoke to Eddie, telling him that I was in the middle of a session and I'd see him when I'd finished in about twenty minutes' time. He looked as if he was about to explode, but he turned and walked out of the room, slamming the door behind him. I took a deep breath and let it out slowly, before resuming my conversation with the quivering Damien.

I didn't expect Eddie to return, but to my surprise, and mild trepidation, twenty minutes later he did. As he sat down, he put his mobile phone face up on the table. Again.

'Please can you put your mobile phone away, Eddie, and tell me why you're here?'

Once more, his eyes locked on mine and for about fifteen

seconds there was an uneasy stand-off. It was a long fifteen seconds. Then, with an exaggerated deep sigh, he slowly reached out to pick up his phone and very deliberately put it in his tracksuit pocket.

'Gaz, let's get started on the anger management shit. I haven't got all day.'

'Eddie, I'll be honest, I'm surprised you wanted me to do that work with you. I could have put you in touch with plenty of other therapists who would have helped.'

He shook his head.

'I can't be arsed finding someone else. Jack rates you. That's good enough for me. But, to be honest, I think all this psycho-babble is a waste of fucking time.'

'You're entitled to your opinion, but here's the deal. If you work with me you are going to have to cooperate. Nor do I want you ordering other people I'm working with out of the room. This is how I work. Your choice.'

I could see that Eddie wanted to snarl at me, but he managed a tight smile as he reluctantly nodded his acceptance of my terms.

I asked him to explain what had happened at the weekend and caused the incident with the opposition team's coaching staff.

He told me that there had been a bit of an exchange between the two managers over a dangerous tackle on the pitch, then their assistant coach got involved and voices were growing louder. Eddie jumped to his manager's defence and that's when things got out of hand. As he was going over the events in the tunnel, I realized Eddie didn't seem to have any remorse about what had happened – in fact quite the opposite.

'The cheeky gobshite knew he was wrong, but then he

started laughing at me. I just lost it. As far as I'm concerned, he had it coming.'

The vehemence of the words 'laughing at me' left me surprised, and seemed unrelated to the actual on-the-field event, which seemed rather innocuous.

I asked him if he 'lost it' because he was being laughed at.

He looked at me, his eyes narrowed as if measuring what my response might be before he answered, and eventually shrugged and said, 'It's just not something I enjoy.'

I could tell he'd decided against telling me his real reasons, but I pressed him.

'Eddie, there's so much behind that statement. I think to make any progress with managing your anger, we need to explore what's behind it. What has happened to make you react that way?'

He scowled, but when I prompted him he began by telling me how, growing up, he was a scrawny kid and often got beaten up by his two older brothers, and his dad used to regularly give him a good hiding as well. Things only got worse after his father lost his job in a local factory. His father blamed anyone and everyone for being unemployed and spent much of his time drinking in the local pub. Consequently, violence was commonplace in the household, with Eddie as the youngest receiving the lion's share.

He described himself as a youngster as being 'scrawny but hard as nails'. He proudly recounted a story about a childhood family holiday at the seaside when he and his brothers were treated to a game of crazy golf. After continually missing a shot on a hole shaped like a clown, and being subjected to his brothers' spiteful mockery, Eddie proceeded to smash up the clown figure with his putter, much to the amusement of his brothers. He earned himself a good hiding from his father, none too pleased at having to pay for the damage, and it was the last time he went on a family holiday, doomed to stay at home with his grandma instead.

It seemed that the more Eddie reacted with violence to his dad's abusive behaviour, the less violence came Eddie's way, as if Eddie's violence gained his father's approval. This is what psychologists would call behavioural conditioning. Eddie's brothers seemed to delight in taunting and ridiculing him, especially in front of Eddie's friends at school, and when Eddie tried to fight back, they recruited their larger friends to join in the public humiliation. Eddie's school was less than sympathetic as he was a regular in detention for fighting, but while his education suffered, he learned not to be afraid of pain.

As he grew older, violence was still an everyday occurrence at home, and Mum couldn't prevent it, so when he was old enough he went to the school gym to beef up. He described how, when he started developing as a player, the coaching staff used to say he was 'as hard as nails'. It made him feel good, but even then he realized he had a temper which could sometimes be a problem.

'Nobody was going to push me around and laugh at me again. I was a half-decent footballer and by the age of about fourteen, when I was playing, we might have lost the odd game here and there, but if it came to a punch-up, I won every time. If anybody was taking the piss, they knew what was coming.

'When their assistant coach began mouthing off at me, all I could think of was everyone can see he's laughing at me, they're all going to think I'm weak. It felt like I *had* to get him to shut up and stop laughing. I couldn't take the laughing and completely lost it.' He shook his head and said, 'It is what it is, Gaz. You can't fix this.'

Eddie's violent programming from his youth was still alive and well, and Eddie was presenting it as something he had no control over. He needed to understand that there are ways to overwrite this. I could help him do that, but first his fear of being ridiculed was something he had to learn to recognize and manage.

He pulled out his mobile phone and put it on the table, but noticed my glare and returned it to his pocket.

'I hated being that little kid who couldn't defend himself, and ever since then I've never run away from a fight and I never will. I'm a fighter, Gaz, and there's nothing you or anyone else can do to change that.'

Jane Lovell

You Must Be in Seine

Sunlight spilled through my supervisor's window. Our session had reached its natural conclusion slightly earlier than usual.

Tom sighed and said, 'Same time next week?'

I nodded.

'Actually, we've a couple of minutes to go, so tell me how Jane's getting on.'

I shuffled though my clinical notes while Tom continued.

'Psychotherapy, you know, it's all about rupture and repair between client and therapist. But I was thinking about your work with Jane the other day and the thought came into my head that a different type of rupture will come. Maybe a divorce, or possibly a rupture in her relationship with Dad. Your job is to help her make sense of her life after the possible rupture's occurred. But it's going to be painful.'

'For her, her daughter, her husband?' I asked.

'Maybe even for you, as her therapist.'

Tom beamed his avuncular smile and a few minutes later I was outside his house, listening to the cars in low gear labouring up the hill where he lived.

Tom's words stayed with me as Jane's next appointment drew near. I knew I had to take her gently through that painful process (whatever it was going to look like) without guiding her in any particular direction.

At the next session Jane flopped down in the armchair in my clinic and exhaled heavily before saying, 'I feel it's becoming increasingly difficult to just stay on my feet at the moment.'

I pictured Jane finding it difficult to stand without her dad and husband as crutches. So often the imagery or metaphors clients use in therapy might be a clue to a deeper understanding of how they are feeling. 'Put it in the margin,' a supervisor's voice said inside my head, as I scribbled the word 'crutches' down on a pad beside me, to remind me to pick it up later in the session.

Jane was a mixture of elation and fear. She'd decided to speak at the charity event after all and it had gone well. So well in fact that a TV producer who was in the crowd approached her afterwards and asked if she'd consider work as a trackside pundit for the upcoming European Athletics Championships, which were being held at the Stade Charléty in Paris. Someone had dropped out due to illness and the TV company wondered if Jane would consider going. It would mean being away from the family for a week in total. Jane told me that she'd have to miss a modelling assignment in London if she went.

'I really, really want to do this. I feel it will be great PR, and Alan thinks it will give a huge boost to the charity and to the role of the ambassador, if I chose to take it. But it hasn't gone down well at home or with my dad. They think I should turn it down. They think I'll be useless.'

'But what do *you* think?'

Jane's situation was turning into a question of transitioning. What happens when we leave behind an old profession and start a new one? Or, in her case, leave behind her old life and forge a new life and career for herself?

Many sportspeople I've worked with eventually reach this point. What happens when they come to the end of their time as an athlete? Many are desperate to hang on to former glories and be part of the sporting culture. As one footballer once said to me, 'Don't tell the gaffer, but I'd play for nothing next season, so long as I get a contract!'

Jane's feelings of low self-esteem were attacking her fledgling TV career. Fear crept into the space between us. I suspected the transitioning fear was also about her leaving her marriage. The fear of change strangles the dreams of so many of us and we are left with those dreaded words 'if only'.

Many people stay in bad jobs and bad relationships because they fear what's on the other side. They become stuck, with the same thoughts going round and round in their heads for months if not years: 'What if I don't find another job/relationship/friends/place to live?' So we stay in a safe place, or a place we *think* is safe, and in the end we suffer a slow, painful existence that eventually leaves us diminished.

Jane went on to explain that the TV punditry work was what she really wanted to do and that it would be more professionally rewarding for her than being a model.

'I want young women to see me as a former athlete, not some brainless bimbo flogging make-up or breath freshener. My husband says I should stick with the modelling – he thinks it's really cool his wife's on TV advertising stuff, and I've heard him on the phone boasting to his mates how much money those ads bring in.'

Jane told me that there had been yet another row at home and her father had once again got involved, telling her that she should concentrate on the modelling career as she wouldn't be as good as a TV trackside reporter, and the job could just be a one-off.

'Alan is the only one who disagrees and says I should take the TV job. He's told me to follow my dreams. At home it's a bloody nightmare right now!'

Jane's shoulders slumped in defeat and I could see she was finding it difficult to gather her strength. There were so many competing interests in Jane's life at the moment and they all seemed to be fighting for air: Jane the mum, Jane the wife, Jane the daughter, Jane the model, Jane the TV trackside reporter, Jane the charity ambassador. It occurred to me that the trip to Paris might offer an opportunity for Jane to create some space for herself in order to gain some perspective, specifically around her relationship with her husband. It was clearly going to cause trouble at home and I did ask myself whether she could do this job and deal with the consequences.

In my experience, fear of failure when it comes up in therapy is rarely about somebody trying something and it not working out. That could be seen simply as a learning experience. Fear of failure normally presents itself with such words as 'there's no point in trying' or 'what's the point, it's bound to go wrong'. Jane's father was pushing that agenda. His opinion that it would all go wrong was designed to undermine Jane's self-belief in order to control her. There was a strong flavour of the row he'd had with Jane when she was a teenager and he forbade her to attend that teenage party. The fact that she went, had a dreadful time and was humiliated would only have compounded her ambivalent feelings towards ignoring her father's advice again and going to Paris. As adults we often remember much more clearly the emotions of an event rather than the details.

Jane wasn't stupid. She knew she was being manipulated by her husband and her father, but she was still undecided about accepting the TV punditry role. She was fearful it could spell an abrupt end to her marriage, when she wanted to be clear in her mind what she wanted to do with that relationship before its end was forced upon her. And then there was the question of whether it was worth it when there was no promise of future work in TV.

'I never really knew I'd made the right choice about being an athlete rather than a model, and I'm at the same point again,' she said tearfully. 'Dad was insistent that I gave athletics my all. I did, and I was successful, but it never really gave me lasting happiness. What if I make the wrong decision again, whichever way I turn?'

'Well, Jane, we can only deal with choices that are placed in front of us. If the TV work isn't a success you can do something else. But it strikes me you're stuck, between your own choices and the choices of others. Whose hand is on the steering wheel of your life?'

She couldn't answer, but when, after a few minutes, she had regained her composure she said, 'You know what's the real kicker, and I haven't mentioned this yet, but that bastard of a husband of mine is now blaming me for our daughter being bullied at school. Seems some kid in her class has found some old stuff online of my Commonwealth Games events. He's teasing my daughter about having a "fit mum" and now my husband's telling her that I might be going away to do a job in Paris and won't be able to attend her parents' evening. So, to top it all off, I'm a bad mum now. I mean, what the hell am I meant to do with my life?'

Kwasi Adepodji

Stairway to Hell

After Kwasi's brush with the local media, I'd spoken to John Anderson, the manager, and told him Kwasi was fit for the weekend. John immediately picked him to play. Kwasi's mum had arrived from Ghana and was staying in a local hotel, and things were beginning to settle down.

The club's regular centre forward, Simon Cooper, was suspended after picking up too many yellow cards in recent games. If Kwasi was thought a little too soft to be a target man, and easily dominated by opposing centre halves, Simon was the opposite. He'd even been red-carded this season for picking a fight with the opposing team's kit man, whom he described as 'too fucking fat to fit in any team's kit'. In short, Kwasi had some big boots to fill.

I was due to see Kwasi again on the Thursday before the weekend match. Prior to our session, I began to think about the impact of cultural differences in client work. I'm a white, middle-class English therapist, having had a grammar school upbringing in a leafy English suburb. What could I possibly know about Kwasi's life experiences to date? How could I help him?

From what Kwasi had told me about his culture, the Church was very involved with providing the sort of pastoral care that I was engaged in at the football club. He'd admitted that he'd never met a psychotherapist and said that the only psychological support offered at his Belgian club was a name on a small business card pinned to the dressing-room noticeboard.

I thought about how a sportsperson's form and career trajectory might be influenced by living away from the culture they're used to. Kwasi plainly hadn't reached his potential since leaving Ghana, where he was highly thought of. Many elite athletes find it difficult to settle away from their familiar surroundings, especially when they are young, and are often unable to perform at their best with all of their support structures left behind. Fans rarely take this into account and are unforgiving. Kwasi's inappropriate socializing could have been a cry for intimacy that didn't exist elsewhere in his life.

Kwasi told me that back home he had loved to dribble with the ball, and it was this skill that prompted a decent Belgian team to sign him. But European tactics are different and he'd had to adapt his game. Opposition defences in Belgium soon learned that Kwasi was predominantly right-footed. By forcing him to use his left foot, they significantly diminished his effectiveness, and likewise his confidence. This would have been less of an issue had he stayed playing in Ghana. His move to England was both surprising and fortuitous.

Kwasi was still trying to reinvent his game since making the significant step up after moving to Belgium, and while John Anderson had a good reputation for developing young players with talent, Kwasi was struggling to understand what exactly was expected of him. His vulnerability and fear were preventing him from asking for the help he needed.

A few years back I'd worked with a Premier League star who admitted he was terrified of what his incredibly famous football manager thought of him. The manager would come to the edge of the technical area and bark instructions to his players, followed by cutting insults if they did something wrong. The player's form took a dramatic upturn when we worked on him playing *his* game, using his instinct, instead of fearing a grade-one bollocking from one of the most respected football managers in the world. One day the manager called him into his office and said, 'You're playing out of your skin, son. See what happens when you listen to me!'

Kwasi came to our session fresh from the training ground. Perspiration ran in rivulets down his face and he sniffed frequently. He seemed in a brighter mood and was excited to tell me the morning's news.

'The gaffer says I'm definitely playing Saturday. I'm in for Simon. It's been a while since I started, so that's good news, and they're all really happy with me in training.'

I saw his face cloud and prompted him with a 'But?'

'I suppose I'm just a bit nervous of all that racist stuff from the opposition fans.'

'Kwasi, there's nothing you can do to control what those fans think or say.'

Racism in sport is a big problem, though it's getting better, and this was a conversation I'd had with countless sports stars and indeed non-sporting clients too. Racist abuse from fans is unacceptable and the response from officials and the club should be swift and severe. But when it comes to the individual I'm advising about their psychological response, the mantra is simple: 'Control the controllables.' If we can manage to do that, fear often slips away.

Once Kwasi accepted that he had no way of changing what insults the fans might choose to throw at him, he seemed more at ease and we moved on to examine the changes he'd undergone since leaving Ghana to play in Belgium. In the telling of his story, his speech slowed right down.

Such is the kudos for a Ghanaian to work abroad that many will opt for low-paid jobs in another country. Kwasi told me about his friend from back home, Danquah, who worked as a builder in the UAE, and his mother and father were so proud they were boasting about him to all who'd listen. The truth is, he could have earned way more money stacking shelves in the local supermarket in Accra.

'Are your parents proud of you, Kwasi?'

He snorted with hollow laughter. 'That's unlikely now.' I didn't respond, but gave him space to continue while he was in a talkative mood. He told me that because of the support of the local community and the money given to the Church by even the poorest, there's a joke in Ghana that there are no poor pastors in the country. 'It's not true, of course, but compared to many kids growing up we had it good. Money's a big problem between me and my dad. He says I should be sending money back home but I never do.'

'I thought you said your parents don't need the money.'

'They don't, but that's kind of the norm for African players in Europe, and Dad's church always has lots of projects on the go. You know, build a school here, a medical clinic there, and he gives me loads of grief that I don't contribute like the rich footballer he thinks I am. He doesn't even want me to play football!'

The last part was said with such indignation, it was almost comical.

'Is that why you don't send any money home?' I asked.

'Yeah, well, I get to decide what I do with my cash.' The indignation was gone and in its place was sullen defiance.

I could tell his chattiness was beginning to dry up, so I swung the conversation round to how he was faring, checking on his sleep and general well-being.

He mentioned he'd been having difficulty sleeping recently and had asked the club doctor for some sleeping pills. It was tricky to know if he was simply suffering from nerves about being in the first team at the weekend or was struggling with a more deep-seated anxiety.

'Kwasi, I'd like to get to the bottom of what you are nervous about. Let's play a game. It's called "down the stairs".'

Kwasi's eyes narrowed. Distrust was back.

'What's that?'

'I'm going to ask you some questions and we'll try to work out the root of your fear that's keeping you up at nights. That OK?'

Kwasi nodded, but I could see he wasn't sure.

'OK, we're going to start at the top of the stairs and go down, one step at a time. First step, you play badly on Saturday – what happens then?' I began.

'I wouldn't get another chance to play at this club,' he said promptly.

'OK, if you left this club what would happen?'

'I'd be on the next plane back to my Belgian club.'

'Then what?'

'They'd terminate my contract. Send me back home to Ghana.'

'Then what?'

'I'd be back in Accra. My football career would be over.'

'Then what?'

'I'd have to work for the Church or something.'

Kwasi's voice was diminishing in strength.

'Kwasi, just think for a moment. If you went back to the Church, then what?'

By now Kwasi's eyes were looking straight at his laces and he appeared much younger than his years.

'I'd be my dad's bitch.' He looked at me, then sideways as if reeling in shock, then back at me again. 'Shit, man.'

Kwasi had done what so many of us do when placed in anxiety-provoking situations: he'd begun catastrophizing. He had locked on to his primal fear of being back under his father's control. He'd stopped seeing a host of other alternatives, like playing for another club, changing profession, travelling the world – all of which existed between his fear of being sacked by his present club and digging foundations for a school building in a small village in the countryside outside Accra because his dad told him to.

Catastrophic thinking pervades sport. Think how some football clubs sack their manager after a series of poor results. They rarely stop to ask 'Why?' or 'What can we do to support him?' The directors and owners are often hugely influenced by irate supporters who are engaging in their own catastrophic thinking: 'If we don't sack him now, we will go down/won't win the title/are going to have another trophy-less season.' I often wonder what would happen if you gave that beleaguered manager psychological support inside the club. The truth is that most would refuse it. Why? Because they think it looks weak.

Kwasi looked anything but weak in Friday's training and when the manager named the squad to the press later that day, Kwasi's name was on the team sheet. He left his team-mates in the canteen where lunch was being served and asked if he could have a quiet word.

'Can you help me to concentrate tomorrow?' he asked earnestly.

I went through some basic sports psychology techniques with him to help him focus on the pitch and block out any nasty comments from opposition fans. I also told him to get a piece of the white tape that normally keeps his shin pads in place and put some of it around his wrist. On the tape he needed to write a message to remind himself of what matters during the match. I asked him what that message would be.

Kwasi thought for a moment, then told me, 'It'll say, "I'm not going home."'

Saturday's match was not the team's best of the season, but nor was it the worst. Kwasi's side won 1–0 due to a hotly disputed penalty. Kwasi had done OK, but after barely playing any regular first-team football since arriving at the club, the manager realized he was clearly still short of full match fitness, so had decided to substitute him with seventy-five minutes gone.

As Kwasi left the pitch, the home supporters gave him a standing ovation. The away fans, however, were not as appreciative and, as if rehearsed, burst into song, singing to Kwasi:

> 'Score in a brothel,
> You couldn't score in a brothel . . .
> Score in a brothel . . .'

Ouch!

Ben Phillips

Tears for Fears

As expected, the next time I saw Ben his back pain was still the same. In order to understand its severity, I had asked Ben to score the pain out of ten, with ten being the worst pain ever and zero being completely pain-free. He reported a steady seven every day. Nothing he did or ate, his quality of sleep, levels of exercise or emotional state seemed to make any difference. Pain relief also had no effect and even if he was having a brilliant day the pain stayed the same. It was there when he went to sleep at night and there when he woke up, and stayed with him throughout the day. Physical exercise made no difference, except he admitted to being nervous about playing in a competitive football match in case he made a mistake because of the pain. If I asked him to describe the pain, he said, 'Dunno, it just hurts.' Four words that told me absolutely nothing about how he was feeling.

In these circumstances, I often talk to the client about when or how the pain began. Ben told me that he had twisted his back in training about eighteen months previously and that the pain seemed to get worse over the next few weeks.

Mum took him to the local doctor, then to NHS specialists, and he also had some physio treatment, which seemed to improve things a little at first, but just as he appeared to be getting better he was injured again when one of his defenders kneed him in the back as the pair went up to defend a corner kick.

Ben then had more physiotherapy, but this time there was no improvement. He also went for X-rays, which revealed nothing significant, and had MRI scans, which showed there was no tissue damage, leaving the specialists stumped as to the cause of Ben's ongoing pain. In short, everything should have cleared up.

The relationship between stress and pain is well documented – think, for example, of stress headaches. Sometimes, when a person has an injury in a particular area, the body holds a physical and emotional memory of the original injury. This area can then become vulnerable in times of prolonged stress. Could it be that Ben's ongoing back pain was due to psychological distress at not having enough attention from his family?

Since the last specialist had seen Ben, things had gone downhill in terms of the limitations on his activities: he was not allowed to do PE at school (his favourite subject) and training for the local academy was becoming increasingly impossible. All of the above seemed quite normal in these circumstances, but the next bit began to trouble me.

In one of our sessions Ben described how his pain was getting worse in the morning and Mum had to help him get dressed, brush his teeth, prepare his breakfast and carry his rucksack into school every morning. He told me all this in a flat monotone.

I felt the longer this went on, the worse it would get,

because Ben was decompensating (spiralling down) into a much younger version of himself, becoming increasingly dependent on Mum's physical intervention. This, in my experience, is not uncommon in young men who find it hard to break away from their mothers. They will often enjoy the physical comfort of being close to their main caregiver and create circumstances in which more and more care is lavished on them. Thinking about this, elderly people can sometimes do the same, wanting their children to carry out tasks which they are more than capable of carrying out themselves.

I was becoming increasingly uneasy about Ben's situation, so I decided to take the case to my supervisor, Tom, who is an expert in working with young people in schools and said he'd met hundreds of Bens in his time.

'Ben's back issue is actually quite a positive outcome for him, in some respects,' Tom said. 'Think about it. Ben, who is struggling for attention from the family, who are all concerned about Keiron's career, gets this wonderful attention from Mum. She even puts sugar on his cornflakes. Who wouldn't want that? Why would he want it to end? He's hardly ever been the centre of the family's focus historically, while Keiron has been mopping up all the adoration of both his parents because of his promising football career. Every time Keiron scores another goal, Ben gets reminded of the pecking order.

'I'm not hearing any real joy, satisfaction or even interest from Mum or Dad about Ben's goalkeeping career. Does Dad even go and watch Ben play? Also, I'm not sure about Ben's relationship with Keiron. Ben says he looks up to him, but I don't know. Where's the sibling rivalry between the two? Every brother hates his brother at some level. Do you have a brother?'

'Yes.'

'And how do you get on with him?'

I didn't answer.

With a knowing look, Tom continued, 'Ben is trying to forge a career of his own as a goalkeeper and yet the back injury would be a good way of putting that on hold.'

'Putting it on hold? What do you mean?'

'Well, we can all be the best bloody goalkeeper in our football club when we're injured, but it's another thing actually doing it during a big game. I wonder if Ben doesn't have to worry about being the best goalkeeper in his year group at the club because he has the excuse that he has a bad back. Have you ever asked Ben what it would be like to be pain-free? Would that be scary for him? Also, it defines Ben – the great goalkeeper who can't quite make it because of his back injury. It's a useful narrative not only in the family but also in his school.'

Tom had given me plenty to think about, but I couldn't go tearing into Ben with Tom's ideas. It often took a few days for the full weight of Tom's words and thoughts to percolate through, so I could work out how to make the best use of them. I recognized that this was the way Tom might have dealt with the situation, but Ben was *my* client and I had to work out *my* way to deal with it.

There was another issue. Tom's thinking was about an event in the therapy which had already passed and I didn't feel comfortable steering the conversation back unnaturally to that point. If the point was important it would come back around again and I just had to make sure I was ready for it this time. As usual, I would have to sit with these uncertainties and see what came out.

At our next session I discussed with Ben how he felt about his mum looking after him, helping him get dressed in the morning, brushing his teeth and carrying his rucksack into school.

Ben reverted to his minimalist teenage style of speech. 'Yeah, it's OK.' He dipped his head again, so his fringe covered his eyes. I felt as if curtains were being drawn across his face and our conversation.

I decided to take Tom's lead and asked Ben what it would be like to be able to play without pain, and if he could see himself playing professional football. I thought it was an innocuous question, but it produced a significant gear change in our therapeutic relationship. Ben reached for a tissue from the box in front of him. He said nothing.

'Ben, what's going on right now for you?' I asked gently.

I could hear the sobs before I saw the reddening of his face.

'You don't get it, do you?' he said. And before I could answer he went on, 'All I'm known as is Ben the injured goalkeeper. I'm not stupid. This won't last for ever. I'm gonna get chucked out of the academy if I don't get better. They've already given another goalkeeper a trial. Don't get me wrong, they've been brilliant so far, but I'm stuffed if I don't start playing football again soon.'

Silence hung in the room as I wondered if I dare ask the question which was on my lips. I decided to go for it.

'Ben, I know this is a shitty question, but I'm going to ask it anyway. What would it be like if you couldn't play football ever again?'

More sobs.

'I couldn't cope. Football is everything to me. Keiron is top dog in our family because of his goal scoring, and Mum and Dad and even Jenny now love him because he bangs in lots of goals. What am I going to be? Keiron's younger brother who has a bad back?'

Like many young people who define themselves about what they *do* rather than who they *are*, Ben was now in a tricky place. Things had been made much worse by his parents creating this same model for Keiron, whose career was going into overdrive. So the only way Ben felt he could get their attention was to be an outstanding goalkeeper. And now he had the ultimate excuse as to why he couldn't compete with his brother in the 'outstanding' stakes. But while he was getting the longed-for attention, he knew this approach could only be a short-term strategy and was obviously not looking forward to the next chapter.

He looked like a lost little boy as the tears rolled down his smooth cheeks.

James Holmes

Holmes and Away

When I talk with fellow therapists about the sport of cricket, a familiar comment often drifts into the conversation at some stage. It goes something like this: in terms of team sports, cricket is the most psychologically demanding game there is; for individual sports, it's golf.

The psychological battle between batsman and bowler is at the heart of cricket's culture. There's even a term batsmen use when they have just entered the game: playing yourself in – meaning to get used to being bowled at, become familiar with the speed of the ball and sharpen hand–eye coordination. Inevitably, when first arriving at the crease, a batsman might be feeling a few nerves, so quelling these and being able to engage the prefrontal cortex (the computer or rational part of the brain) is key.

If you make a mistake in rugby or football you are not usually ejected from the game. As a batsman you are. I often think about the humiliation a batsman might feel making the long walk back to the pavilion if he is out for a low score. Being compared to a duck (the term when you're dismissed after scoring no runs) is hardly something you're going to be proud of.* Ouch!

The psyche of a bowler is also fascinating. His is a destructive art (breaking or smashing the carefully erected wicket). He uses power, guile and technique to fool the batsman. After weeks of not hearing from James Holmes, I too felt like a batsman facing one of his deliveries. He couldn't bowl or catch me out in our first session, so he'd taken his bat and ball home – quite literally, as I was about to find out.

I hadn't seen James since I'd refused to give him a medical report justifying his return from the Indian tour, and assumed I'd seen the last of him. Four weeks after our abortive session, I'd contacted the Professional Cricketers' Association and told them I thought my work with James had come to an end. So it was with considerable surprise that, one Tuesday afternoon, I received a phone call from an unrecognized number.

'Hello. This is Annabel. I'm James Holmes's partner.'

I immediately hoped nothing untoward had happened to James and then began to wonder why his girlfriend was contacting me.

She told me that things were not going well with them and asked if I had availability for James to restart therapy. When a parent, friend or partner contacts me to ask for therapy for a loved one, I have to ask myself who the therapy is really for.

'James would have phoned you himself,' she said, 'but he was embarrassed. He told me things hadn't gone that well between you, but all he wanted then was his medical report. He got one through the club medical officer, but he's getting

* The term 'duck' derives from the shape of a duck's egg, signifying 0.

worse. These days he doesn't even want me to leave the house to go to work. He checks up on me regularly, thinking something terrible might have happened. My mobile battery died last week and he couldn't get hold of me. He went nuts at me when I came home. He's always on the phone to his mum and dad – maybe half a dozen times a day – checking on them. It was they who suggested I get in touch with you. He's not well, he knows that, and we all had a chat. He agreed to me calling you.'

I quickly weighed things up in my head, asking myself who this was a problem for. If what Annabel was saying was true, James would be moved into action and contact me. If not, and James was perfectly happy with how things were, then maybe she or James's mother and father needed the help.

'Thanks for getting in touch, Annabel. Ask James to text me and I'll arrange an appointment.'

James's text arrived moments after I'd ended the call with Annabel. It was as forceful as his fast bowling: 'WHICH DAY AND WHAT TIME?'

James arrived for his appointment promptly at the agreed time. He immediately took out his phone, said he needed to check in with Annabel, but put it away again and sat with his hands on his lap when he saw my enquiring look.

'James, it's really good to see you again, but it would be helpful for me to understand what brought you back to therapy, and in particular why you came back to see me.'

He looked rather like a naughty boy as I let that question hang in the air between us for a short moment.

'I suppose I'm here because Mum and Dad and Annabel think I'm not 100 per cent, and rather than trying to find another therapist, I thought I'd try again with you.'

I have long since come to realize that sportspeople can

often be lazy when dealing with things on the periphery of their lives, preferring to put all their focus and energies into their sport.

'What per cent do you think you are, James?'

'Dunno, really – 70, 60, 50. I think it's pretty normal to worry about your mum and dad, or your partner. Don't you care about your parents?'

'Of course I do and of course you are right. But this isn't about me, James. Let's work out what's going on for you. How long has this worry about Mum and Dad gone on for?'

James waited a moment, then looked about the clinic space.

'Yeah, a long time, I guess. Always been there. It just gets worse on tour, you know. I can't, well, look after them properly if I'm in some country thousands of miles away.'

'Are your parents in poor health, James?'

'No. Not at all. They're OK for their age.'

I had a feeling I was approaching something that was lurking just below the surface. If I went too quickly James would veer off in another direction. Steady as she goes. This type of work is influenced by *psychodynamic* therapy, which has its roots in psychoanalysis. It rests on the assumption that past events in our lives reveal themselves in the present through our everyday behaviours. Some therapists believe this is the only way to work as *all* our behaviours are based on previous experiences.

I often use a genogram – a picture that displays a client's family relationships – to help me understand who the key people in their lives are. This is the sort of thing you'd see on a genealogy website. I'll draw this during a session and ask questions.

'Have Mum and Dad any previous marriages or divorces?'

James looked surprised at the question and answered in a millisecond, 'Of course not!'

The response felt too guarded, defensive. I had the impression he was hiding something. So far, the narrative of James's early family life was all household harmony, immaculate whites, cucumber sandwiches, village green cricket and sun-drenched lazy Sunday afternoons. It sounded seductively wonderful but also unreal. Real families argue, bicker and get cross with each other, as well as love and cherish each other. There had to be a shadow side, the antithesis of this idealized version of English family summer life. I tried again.

'Did Mum and Dad ever have any serious marital issues?'

James looked straight ahead and then spoke in a low emotion-less tone. 'No, not really. Dad said Mum could have had post-natal depression after having me, but it was never discussed.'

He stopped, as if undecided about how to go on, but even-tually said, 'I wondered, as I was coming here today, whether this would come up, so we better get it out of the way. It's no biggie and I'm not sure it's even relevant, but when I was about seven Mum got pretty ill. She had a burst appendix and was rushed to hospital. She was there for a while, things didn't look good. Me and my sister were sent to live with our grand-parents, Dad's parents, for a few weeks. But as things didn't improve, we ended up having to go to a local school while we were there, which wasn't great.

'The worst thing was that my dad and grandparents wouldn't tell me what was going on with Mum. I knew some-thing was the matter, that whatever was going on was really quite serious, but essentially everyone was lying to me and I knew it. Even my older sister, Debbie, had an idea of what was going on, but the more I said I wanted to see my mum the more the excuses would come, thick and fast.'

I could well imagine that the adults were keeping to the strategy of 'not upsetting the children', but in so doing, by denying the reality of the situation, they managed only to instil a level of distrust within the child they were ultimately trying to protect.

James continued, 'After eight weeks we finally went back home. Mum's parents had moved in to help my dad, who, we later learned, fell to pieces when Mum was very ill. I suppose ever since I've been a bit worried when Mum or Dad fell ill. I felt I needed to be close to them, you know, look after them, not be shipped off far away.'

'Like India?'

His look was one of chagrin mixed with irritation.

'James, it sounds like you were unable to trust other people to be honest with you if something did happen and so felt you had to be there yourself. I am also thinking that your worry about Annabel is connected too as she became more important to you.'

James presented as if he was suffering from a form of PTSD, with part of him stuck in a poignant time warp that froze him at the emotional age of seven. Most of his life was played out as an adult, but once he encountered the feelings of having to leave his loved ones, he was instantly transported back to the fear and anguish he had felt when his mum was so poorly and his father couldn't bring himself to talk about her condition, let alone reassure the young James that everything was going to be OK. And everyone else lied to him. Staying close to home allowed him to feel a modicum of control, to be reassured that if something as urgent and life-threatening happened again to any of his family, he would be able to do something about it this time, because he wasn't a helpless seven-year-old any more.

I suspected that his childhood experience had left him feeling quite uncertain as to the truthfulness of any type of authority figure, and as an adult, when presented with a message he didn't want to hear, his instinct was to shoot the messenger. So in this instance, maybe I was the authority figure he felt he couldn't trust, just like the grandparents who hadn't told him the truth about his mother.

He got up smartly, buttoned his jacket and said, 'I'll be in touch if I need another appointment.'

Edwin Thomas

Under My Thumb

Control is a peculiar thing. It comes up in my work in so many ways, but usually it has to do with the emotion of fear – fear of letting go and what happens when you do. Many men find it hard to admit they are controlling in their relationships with their partners, friends or business colleagues. It often induces feelings of shame and has negative connotations of bullying, but many clients who think they are the sweetest, most caring partners to their wives or husbands are decidedly coercive in their behaviour, texting their partners to 'check they're OK', for example, when the real reason is they're wondering where their partner is and are unable to deal with their own anxiety.

The ultimate fear, born out of insecurity and low self-esteem, is of course that a partner might just up sticks at any time. To avoid that eventuality and make ourselves feel better, we sometimes try to exert power over the person we hold most dear. We want to be sure that our world isn't in danger of imminent collapse and need constant reassurance from them that they aren't about to leave, so we require them to keep reaffirming their feelings towards us.

I once worked with a young man who smothered his new girlfriend with scores of texts and phone calls.

'Why are you doing that?' I asked.

'I need to check she still wants to be with me.'

I looked at him.

'Imagine you're on the beach and you pick up a handful of dry sand and squeeze hard. What happens?'

'The sand runs through your fingers,' he said.

'Now imagine the same handful of sand and you cup your palm. What happens now?'

'The sand stays there.'

'Is your hand open or shut with this girl?'

The next time I saw Edwin he told me that Cerys was living with her mum and dad virtually full-time. He was also unhappy that he hadn't been able to break back into his rugby team. He said he'd had a crisis of confidence following a shoulder injury and was now getting neck pain every time he trained.

'Things are a bit shit to be honest,' he said. 'I went round to the in-laws, and her dad answered the door. Big bugger he is, played prop in his day. He tells me in no uncertain terms to sling my hook and that he and Cerys's mum had found a counsellor for her, and this so-called counsellor was the best person to help their daughter right now. Well, I said my piece about his daughter's place being at home with me. He then gets all polite with me, says he accepts my views and respects the fact I'm married to her.'

'So what happened then?'

'After his polite speech he told me to "piss off" and leave them all in peace. He had no right to say that to me.' There was real fire in his eyes as he remembered his father-in-law's words to him.

Often when a couple are going through a tough patch, I'll ask the client about their 'less than loved one right at this moment' and how they got together. It can be a useful reminder for a husband or wife as to why they first fell in love and then married that person, triggering long-forgotten emotions.

Edwin's response intrigued me. He told me that she'd caught his eye in the stadium of his previous club, as she was involved in the conference and events management side of the operation, and he was very taken with her. He saw her as someone needing a lot of polish but with plenty of potential. Cerys, however, wasn't that interested in him initially, so he made it his business to charm and woo her until she relented and agreed to meet him for a drink.

Things developed from there, with Edwin guiding Cerys on how she should dress for certain occasions she attended with him and encouraging her to become more groomed and (in his eyes) socially adept. Within a year, Cerys had changed. Slimmer and more sharply dressed, she now fitted Edwin's view of how a player's wife and girlfriend (WAG) should look, and she played the role to perfection. A mixture of sultry seductress and domestic goddess, depending on what company she and Edwin were keeping.

Edwin was keen to get Cerys to move in with him, and after Cerys had a huge row with her parents, seemingly about her relationship with Edwin, Edwin encouraged her to make the leap.

He instructed her about what foods they needed to eat to optimize his body for the training and playing regime for a Welsh international fly half. He chose their meals, and even guided her on hair colour and style.

I was cringing on the inside.

They were the pin-up couple of Welsh rugby – the 'Posh

and Becks of the Valleys', as one local newspaper called them, he told me. He thought that maintaining their image was vital to his continued success. Edwin told me that they'd once had a huge row when he'd found a secret stash of chocolate bars on top of the kitchen cabinet when he was looking for batteries for a remote control. From that point on, there were no more chocolate bars (or anything else which might interfere in the achievement of perfection for the couple) allowed in the house and Edwin kept an even closer eye on her shopping habits.

'Those early days were bloody brilliant and we got on like a house on fire. She stopped seeing her scruffy student pals and we spent more and more time together. I told her that she needed to go to the gym if we were going to be at the top of our game. We even got £5,000 for a photo shoot for a Welsh fashion magazine when we got married.'

Life, it seemed, was good then. Cerys was working part-time at a posh hotel and Edwin's rugby ball was sailing over the posts.

'I could chuck the ball blindfolded, left or right, and somehow it always dropped into the hands of one of my teammates.' Talk about conceit.

I asked how long ago the couple had begun experiencing marital difficulties. Edwin looked a little uneasy and explained things had started to get a little tricky after he said they should try for a baby, as it was the obvious next step in the development of their relationship. They'd been trying for a few months when he noticed that Cerys had begun to lose weight and was starting to look rather gaunt. He'd noticed over that period that she never seemed hungry and that, when they were out with friends for a meal, she ordered only a starter, but he had put it down to her wanting to look good for her impending pregnancy, so was quite supportive of her limiting her eating.

'Suddenly, I noticed all her clothes were baggy and –' he lowered his voice – 'I could start to see a bit of a moustache forming. I thought she must be ill, so I insisted we went to the doctor. It was then that she admitted she'd stopped having periods, so the chances of conceiving were zero. The doctor suggested that my Cerys might have an eating disorder.'

I asked him how hearing that from the doctor had made him feel.

'Obviously, I was really cross with Cerys.'

Obviously! I mentally clocked the phrase 'my Cerys' and that the emotion he expressed was not concern for Cerys's well-being but anger that she was messing up his plans.

Edwin looked confused, but, more than that, he was exasperated. 'I just don't get it. She has bloody everything. A fabulous roof over her head, a car, an amazing lifestyle, fame, money, everything . . . She's the envy of most of the other wives. She wants for nothing. Now, just because she can't get pregnant, she develops an eating disorder.'

I asked him why he thought the eating disorder had come about 'just because she can't get pregnant', or if there might be other reasons. Edwin went on to say that their sex life had suffered a complete dysfunction from this point and they hadn't been 'amorous', as he put it, for months.

'How the hell does she expect to get pregnant if she's never in the bloody mood, eh?'

Edwin was ashamed of his wife, the fact that her once feminine form and attractive figure had become the shape of, in his words, a young boy.

'I don't want to sleep with a bleeding skeleton. She's all skin and bone.'

I could see his frustration around his inability to change the situation: his once happy and ordered life was becoming a train wreck and he felt powerless to stop it getting worse. I thought this was the time to challenge Edwin's thinking. I felt I needed to help him examine his perspective on his wife and his core beliefs that she was 'my Cerys' who lived in 'my house'.

'Edwin, just a short while ago you gave a list of all the things Cerys has: a home, a car, money etc. But I didn't hear you mention she has your love.'

Edwin looked at me with a mixture of contempt and impatience, as if I'd not been listening for the last five sessions, and then spoke clearly and slowly as if talking to someone for whom English was not their first language. 'Of course she has my love. Isn't that what she's had for the last six years we've been together? All the help I've given her to improve herself, that was given out of love. The reason I want her back is because I want to look after her and get her well so we can get back on track with starting a family. But her bloody parents keep getting in the way!' He paused, then lifted his head triumphantly. 'Anyway, she'll be back soon, because I've got a plan.'

He said this with great relish, almost rubbing his hands with glee at the thought of what he was going to do. I was expecting to hear about the charm offensive he was planning to launch, the love-bombing and begging and pleading for her to come back.

'I'm going to start taking away some of her privileges, one by one, until she comes back, cancelling her credit card, taking her car back – that sort of thing.'

So, no love-bombing then! I felt I needed to try to get Edwin to understand why Cerys might be suffering with an eating disorder. Maybe then he could apply all that energy and enthusiasm to really helping her.

'Would you like me to look at Cerys's eating disorder, and the part you *both* play in the mess you currently find yourself in?'

'I'm really not sure how this has got anything to do with me,' Edwin said defiantly.

'Well, Edwin, maybe that's just the start of the problem. And I'm afraid eating disorders are rarely about food.'

Madison King

Risk It for a Biscuit

After her emotional outburst at the end of the last session when she discussed her head injury and the possibility of losing her flatmate and oldest friend, Becky, Madison sat down at the start of the next session and immediately produced a box of expensive biscuits.

'These are for you,' she said. 'Maybe I was a bit shouty last time, so these are as an apology.'

I'm always slightly thrown by a client who offers gifts. What do they mean and what are they for? When I was training, my teacher would suggest I return gifts, as they could complicate the work, with someone asking, for example, 'Why is my therapist saying horrid things to me when I bought them a present last week?'

Once I was working with a Premier League player who was particularly impressed by a piece of work a financial adviser had done on his behalf. He told me, 'I asked my adviser what kind of car his missus drives, and he told me it was a beat-up VW, which she liked. I had a new one delivered to his house with a big ribbon on it the next week. He was well chuffed.'

Ethically, I would have to refuse such a gift, but what was he trying to tell me? Maybe it was 'I can buy and sell you and everyone else in my life, so don't go too hard on me' or maybe 'I want everyone to like me and if they don't, no worries, I'll buy them an expensive gift.'

While not quite in the same league as a car, I was also left wondering about the reason for Madison's gift. She was clearly unnerved by the thought that her anger was too great for me and maybe wanted to offset this with something sweet. Sugar for her bile? Was that what was going on? I felt it important that she understood that her anger and fear were both welcome in the sessions.

Fear makes us do all kinds of things, and this session we concentrated on Madison's catastrophic (black and white) thinking. She'd had a tough week. Becky had stayed away from the home she shared with Madison, taking a work assignment up in Leeds for six weeks. In addition, Madison's club was involved in a complicated back and forth with the insurance company, which was questioning Madison's medical history and whether she was properly covered. Then Madison had had a stumble at home during a dizzy spell, and so it went on.

But the biggest trigger for her fears was, surprisingly, the announcement of the Scottish training squad for the forth-coming Women's World Cup in France. Obviously Madison's name wasn't there, as she hadn't played competitive football for four months because of her head injury, which still hadn't been fully resolved.

Under normal circumstances Madison would have been a shoo-in for the squad. She would also have had a strong claim to captain the team. It would have been her first (and almost certainly her last) World Cup. The squad announcement brought into focus the fact that her international career was almost certainly over. Her status as an international player also brought significant financial benefits, like player endorsements, personal appearances and squad bonus money. Players get payments through a bonus system based on national squad selection, match fees for appearing for the national team, more fees for winning and bonuses for advancing through the various rounds of a tournament. While not insignificant, all of these payments can easily be dwarfed by the promotional fees available to senior players for advertising and promotional activities attached to a huge tournament like the World Cup. Madison would be missing out on all of this. In short, her financial health was spiralling down along with her physical and mental health.

'Madison, firstly thank you for your kind gift, but it wasn't necessary. It's OK to get angry here or frightened about the future.'

I took the biscuits, not really knowing what else to do, and put them away in the cupboard – I would deal with my conscience, and the biscuits, later.

'I think I'm going to end up some washed-up drunk footballer without a penny to her name. Becky will end up fabulously rich and married to some successful investment banker with three gorgeous kids and a mansion in the country. I'll be that sad, pathetic ex-friend who's a hanger-on and has no life of her own. Or even worse, I'll end up a wheelchair user and just be a burden to anyone who cares about me. If I ever manage to find a boyfriend I'll be the basketcase girlfriend who's no use for anything.'

Many clients have irrational fears of being attacked or murdered by complete strangers, being killed in a car accident or dying in an aeroplane crash. While not impossible, the chances of any of these actually happening are extremely slim. Yet thousands of people make choices and decisions every day based on their irrational fears. I have friends who refuse to drive on a motorway because they feel the three-lane highways are too dangerous. In fact, motorways are the safest roads we'll ever drive on. Interestingly, their fear doesn't stop many of those same people causing long, slow damage to their own bodies by poor diet, lack of exercise, drinking and smoking.

Things had not improved much the next time we met.

'Things are getting worse,' she said. 'Last night I was alone in the house. Becky's not returned yet and I was going down to the kitchen for a drink of water quite late. Suddenly I'd slipped down three stairs and I grabbed the banister for dear life. I ended up on my arse, hitting every step all the way to the bottom. I sat at the foot of the stairs with my heart racing. First, I laughed, just relieved to be alive and in one piece, then I started crying and feeling sorry for myself. I wanted Becky, I wanted my mum, I wanted anyone to put their arms around me and tell me it was all going to be all right.

'I hobbled back to bed and cried for a couple of hours before I got too tired and fell asleep. First thing in the morning, I phoned the hospital and the special unit I'm under and had another scan this morning. They said they couldn't see any changes but would get a senior consultant to have a look at the scans. They told me to contact them if things got worse.' She shook her head with frustration. 'For crying out loud, I'm still having these episodes even without kicking or heading a ball.'

I felt I needed to help Madison understand the relationship between fear and risk, laying bare the sort of life she was moving towards if she stayed at home for the rest of her life. Even at home there's no guarantee of safety, as her recent fall had shown. Risk is a part of life – for everyone. It's how you deal with it that's important. Do you carefully weigh up the chances of not succeeding or shrug aside the fear of failure when embarking on a new relationship or making a new job application?

Those who are consumed by fear choose a narrow path, one where they fear failure to such a degree that in situations like taking exams they don't revise and then have an excuse for their failure – creating a self-fulfilling prophecy born out of fear. Their weighing process is skewed. By not even trying, they won't have to face the terrifying possibility that they really are not good enough.

I've met hundreds of 'I never quite made it' potential international footballers who never went to that final trial or decided they were injured the night before a big game. Then there were those who froze with fear when their big chance really did come along. Failure is not getting something wrong. That's learning. Fear – and this is true failure – is never even trying or starting a project or carrying on. Olympic ice-skating world champions are just that because they fell on the ice hundreds of times and still got up and tried again.

This is what my profession calls a 'mind trap', where a person is locked into a negative thought process which prevents them from taking any action. Madison had crashed and needed the confidence to risk failing again.

In our next session, Madison's fears were soon rising to the top of her mind again like oil on water. Just about every thought she shared might have had the words 'what if' prefixed. Our fears are all about the future and are like stories. The main characters are usually us, and the story has a beginning, a middle and an end. They usually involve vivid if disturbing images and have a large dollop of suspense (what will happen to me?). Madison's future image was her, alone, in a wheelchair or bedridden.

She looked at me pleadingly. 'So, what am I to do?'

'I'm not here to give advice, but I can help you think through another narrative, another story you might wish to believe. A subtler story, a more positive one. A life that's filled with love and affection and thoughtfulness rather than anger, regret and bitterness. I can't bring back your football career or even fix the physical damage (whatever that is) to your brain. But I can help you to manage your anger and to be more aware of those around you and of how you will fit in with your new world, whatever that looks like.'

'Shit,' Madison blurted out. 'That sounds really scary.'

'It is, Madison.'

She looked pensive for a moment as she digested my words, then said, 'I don't suppose you still have any of those biscuits I brought you. I could do with one!'

Jealousy and Envy

Of Christianity's seven deadly sins, some are worse to endure than others. I'd certainly rather suffer from gluttony or lust than envy, or envy's cousin, jealousy. Of all the so-called 'sins', this must be the most painful.

Envy and jealousy are often mistakenly used interchangeably. But what's the difference between them? Envy involves two people: 'If only X wasn't at the club, I'd be in the team instead' or 'I want the manager's job at the club. I don't want X to have it.' Jealousy involves more than two people and usually the perception of loss as well. A husband might be jealous of a love rival for his wife's affections. It tends to get complicated when jealousy and envy are present in the same scenario, as we'll see in this chapter with Madison King. Untangling the two is tricky.

In sporting terms, envy is stitched into the DNA of most of our teams, as players are constantly scanning which other squad members might take their place. For example, I once worked with a goalkeeper who was the automatic first choice for his Premier League club. In truth the back-up goalkeeper wasn't anywhere near the quality of my client and all was working very well in the goalkeeping department of the club. But then the back-up goalkeeper got injured and the club brought in a cover goalkeeper. The new arrival was a particularly shy character who kept himself to himself. Suddenly my client took an irrational dislike to the new arrival at the club and there was real tension during training. My client's place in the first team wasn't in jeopardy, but each counselling session with him would involve a highly critical deconstruction of his rival's skills or personality. He'd say things like, 'You know, he's just not one of the lads. Keeps himself to himself. Rubbish on crosses. If I get injured the team is fucked because he simply isn't up to it.' At the same time my client's form dipped and he blamed the pressure he was under from the new arrival. Yet the pressure was all self-made.

Many people both inside and outside sport also suffer from unconscious jealousy or envy – that is, they are completely unaware of having such feelings. Unconscious envy is also present in all professional sports clubs, and it can flow the other way too, with successful sportspeople left mystified and hurt by the petty envies of the less successful.

I once worked with the manager of a London club. He was amiable in nature, open-minded and had what psychologists might describe as a 'growth mindset', being open to new ideas and constantly reviewing his practices and methods. However, he'd been appointed ahead of another candidate who was already working with the first team and had been hoping for promotion from assistant manager to manager. What often happens in these circumstances is that the successful external candidate brings his own assistants and backroom staff with him. But in this case my client kept on the assistant manager to see how things would pan out for a few months and have some continuity. Results were poor and before too long the assistant had gone to the board of directors behind the manager's back to tell them that the players no longer respected the boss and if they wanted the club to progress the manager would have to go.

My client came to our sessions depressed and angry. 'I gave that bastard a chance. I could have, should have, chucked him out. He wants my job, that's obvious. Every time I give a bleeding team talk, he raises his eyebrows in front of the other players, and when I say anything to the team, within seconds, he's offering a "yeah, but".'

'Why did you keep him on?' I asked.

What came out was that the manager wanted to be liked by the board, the players, the backroom staff and the fans. When we worked through this realization, he got angry, then sacked his assistant and sold the centre half who'd been siding with the assistant. The fans weren't happy, but my client ignored the criticism. Results picked up and so did his mood. Wanting to be liked was the issue. It left him very susceptible to petty envies and jealousies. And that left him deeply unhappy.

Something my successful clients often come to realize is that finding success is hard enough, but finding someone who is genuinely happy for them is even harder.

Ben Phillips

The Last Cut is the Deepest

My work with Ben continued for another three weeks and in that period I introduced an element of cognitive behavioural therapy (CBT), whereby I asked Ben to continue with the diary of his pain levels, but also identify when the pain was at its worst and what might aggravate or alleviate it, to give both Ben and his mum a greater understanding of pain triggers. He asked his academy physio for some gentle exercises, and with a better diet, better sleep patterns and a bit of mindfulness thrown in, Ben's back pain, while not disappearing entirely, gradually became a bit more manageable.

He was able to start going to PE lessons again, which he really enjoyed and allowed him to have greater socialization with his peer group, boosting his confidence, and though he didn't go over the top in terms of strenuous activity, he was beginning to feel much more positive about his future. His academy club was working hard getting him up to full fitness and he was aiming to play in a big cup tie in three weeks' time.

Most of our therapy sessions explored the relationship Ben had with his brother, Keiron, and the conflicting emotions that he had about him. On the one hand, Ben hero-worshipped Keiron and talked enthusiastically about the day he saw coming when Keiron would be playing Premier League football, maybe even representing his country. It all seemed inevitable. He talked excitedly about the possibility of Keiron and himself playing in the same match on opposing sides and Ben saving one of Keiron's penalties. Ben genuinely enjoyed spending time in Keiron's company and they loved playing computer games together, as the two brothers chatted non-stop about football and teased each other.

But Ben also accepted that Keiron had taken up much of the oxygen in his early family life and that Keiron's footballing career had been centre stage. He knew this wasn't ideal but found it hard to be critical of his parents. Who wouldn't be proud of such a talented, popular young guy like Keiron? Ben was proud to be his brother. In fact, it pleased Ben no end when, inside his own football club, other players and coaches said, 'That's Ben Phillips, Keiron Phillips's brother — you know, at City.' If only Ben could have been as good a player as his brother everything would have fitted together perfectly in his family, but that was never going to be possible. Mum and Dad were now divorced, and Keiron was going places. The only place Ben was going was to a therapist, and, in his eyes, this was a failure.

At times Ben's voice was comically deep, as is common with teenagers, and he mumbled terribly, so I often found it hard to make out what he was saying. I considered this to be a defence mechanism, so people didn't really need to look at him or take notice of him. I thought the same of his long fringe. At times Ben wanted to be completely anonymous and yet paradoxically, through the phantom back pain, it was as if his body was screaming to be heard.

In about our fourth or fifth session, Ben came in looking slightly shocked and drawn. My hunch was that he had picked up another injury, but he was moving quite freely and sat down in the chair in a smooth movement. He asked for a glass of water, which was unusual for him, and sat bolt upright in the chair. I didn't want to rush him, so as usual I asked him how his back was.

The usual teenage response: 'Yeah, it's fine.'

I tried to encourage Ben to go into a few more details and his head dipped again. Here came the curtains.

'Can you tell me what you mean by "fine", Ben? For the last eighteen months it certainly hasn't been fine and even since we have been working together it's still only just beginning to be "OK".'

'Yeah, the pain is gone.'

Usually, such a significant development would be accompanied by quite a lot of happiness or excited chatter, but there was none of that. He sat there sullen-faced and I wondered if there was bad news about his mother or father, or whether there was trouble at school.

'That's great news, Ben. I bet your mum and dad are really pleased that the back pain is gone, right?' I guessed the answer before it came.

'No. They don't know.'

'Really? I find that rather odd.'

But then Ben explained that, out of the blue, Keiron had been cut from his academy. Nobody had seen it coming and the club simply said that they had a better player who had recently had a trial and performed better than Keiron in his position. The club was very sorry and gave Ben's parents a brochure with lots of telephone numbers of support people, and a list of other clubs where he could try out.

'Mum and Dad have gone completely apeshit. Suddenly, from pretending to be his mum, Jenny now doesn't seem to want anything to do with him any more.'

What emerged was that Ben felt guilty about Keiron being cut from his academy. Ben had always dreamed of having the limelight in his family and now it could well be heading his way, although he didn't want it under these circumstances. Keiron was always going to be the professional footballer and have all the glory, but now the script had been ripped up. Ben said he felt guilty about keeping his place in his academy, especially after all the back issues he'd suffered.

'Keiron's never been injured at City's academy and yet he's lost his place. He said his career in football is over. He's not interested at all in finding another club and he's being really pig-headed. I just don't get it. He's such a brilliant player he could easily find another club. I thought about asking my club to have a look at him, but Keiron isn't having it. I can't tell Mum and Dad about my back because all they can think about is Keiron, and making sure he's all right. I tried to mention it to Mum the other night, but she told me to stop moaning and be a bit more "sensitive" about Keiron's situation. I wanted to tell Dad that I might be playing in this big cup tie at the weekend, but it's a waste of time because nobody's listening to me. It's still Keiron this and Keiron that.'

Ben's envy of Keiron was complex. On the one hand he wanted his brother to do well and have a career in football, and yet on the other hand he wanted to have a share of the family limelight. But Keiron's dismissal from his academy had altered the narrative of the family. How would Ben deal with this?

I thought it interesting that no one, apart from me, knew that his back pain had gone. It certainly wasn't outside the realms of possibility that Ben might *never* tell his family he was out of pain because the pain served a useful purpose, and right now all the interest was still swirling around Keiron.

It intrigues me that families create their own narratives. This is the clever brother, this is the dumb one; this one will succeed, this one never will. And so when events overtake that narrative, we are all left trying to make some sense of a senseless situation.

I hoped Ben's family would reconsider the way they viewed his goalkeeping career, but this was wider than that. I wanted them to see him as a young man, not just their son and a goalkeeper. Could I help Ben achieve that? And who was Keiron to them now, after he had been rejected?

'Do you think I should ask Dad to come and see me play in the cup tie? I really would like that, but what happens if he says no?'

Ben's gentle, open face was full of trepidation at the idea of his dad actually cheering him on for a change, but he recognized the very real possibility that Dad might say he was unable to come along. How could Ben feel his parents were behind him when they were wrapped up in their grief over the loss of Keiron's footballing career, which had held such promise? When young footballing careers are cut short in this way, it can be something akin to a bereavement in the whole family, as hopes and dreams of the potential fame and riches the game will bring are ended.

It was obvious that Ben was torn over the disappointment he too felt for his brother and the opportunity he now saw to step into the limelight. It was also clear that he recognized the behaviour of his parents was not going to change any time soon, given they had only ever seen Keiron as the success of the family and would struggle to see Ben in that light.

Keiron's lack of a supportive social structure made it likely that he would struggle to adapt to life without football and this was something I felt it was important to bolster Ben against in case it became his turn to be cut from the academy. Only 1 per cent of academy players actually make it to become a professional footballer playing first-team football; the rest have to deal with the disappointment of failing to make the grade.

I was curious as to whether or not Ben would feel the need to punish his parents by not telling them his back pain had gone, thus relieving them of their anxiety about it. Maybe this was his opportunity to stab them in the back?

Madison King

All Roads Lead to Leeds

Tom stared down into his striped mug of tea, which he rested on his paunch. It was supervision hour again and I'd decided to discuss Madison with him to see if there was anything I was missing. I suppose I had concerns about Madison's well-being and, if I was truly honest, I had a sense of her decompensating – a term therapists use for spiralling down and down further into negative thoughts. When that occurs, the worry is that a client will begin to wonder if their life is even worth living any more. One psychiatrist has called suicide 'death by depression'.

Tom stared into the steam from the mug and, when it had sufficiently fogged up his wire-rimmed glasses, he looked at me.

'Hmm, I'm kind of interested in the roles of Madison and Becky in each other's lives. They're essentially sisters, with all the attendant sibling rivalry that biological sisters might have.'

I looked unsure and he continued, 'Any sibling rivalry is complicated. Even though they may have very different strengths and weaknesses, there is bound to be some envy as well as jealousy at play here. Yet at the same time they love each other. The problem I see in this type of friendship is that they are not family, so it begs the question, "What's the glue that binds them together?"'

I thought for a moment, then said, 'It's quite complicated, Tom, to be honest. They met at boarding school when they were both aged nine, and as only children they bonded immediately. Both were homesick and, from what I understand, Becky was the recipient of some typical boarding-school bullying. Madison was always slightly more physically mature and often came to the aid of Becky, who was teased for being "swotty". Madison had apparently "saved" Becky's childhood and they created a mutual support unit which lasted throughout all the time at boarding school until they went their separate ways at eighteen.

'Becky went off to uni to study finance, while through some contacts at school Madison managed to get a soccer scholarship to a US college. Years later they met up again when Madison returned to the UK to play for a London team and Becky got a job in the City with an investment bank.'

Tom said, 'Ahh, I see. It was all well and good when Madison was a successful footballer and Becky was doing well at work, but now all bets are off. From sisters, this could be – and I stress *could* be – heading towards a codependent relationship in which Becky is the mum looking after Madison the sick child. That will cause a fracture because it's not part of their original "fit", when they teamed up at boarding school and learned to rely on each other. I imagine that's part of the issue here. Due to her accident Madison has unintentionally moved the goalposts, 'scuse the pun.'

Tom had given me much to consider, but he wasn't finished just yet.

'Poor girls. You need to help Madison realize the dynamic at play here. She thinks Becky owes it to her to look after her for a change, and Becky feels she's done enough looking after. It's not healthy. Becky needs to branch out on her own without her sister and so does Madison. Only then can they work out what they want their adult friendship to look like given the different circumstances.'

I thought about my own sibling rivalry. Those siblings who say 'it doesn't exist' always trouble me.

Tom took a large gulp of his cooling tea. 'I see some interesting struggles here. And you say Becky's away for the time being?'

'Yes. Working up in Leeds.'

'Can't say I blame her. She needs to get on with her career. Leeds, though. Bloody hell, what an awful place!'

'We've got a rocky week ahead,' I said. 'The provisional World Cup squad is being announced and Madison won't be included in the international line-up for the first time in four years.'

Tom winced. 'I saw Scotland's opening game is against Brazil. Madison would have started that game, I'm guessing?'

'Probably captained the side too,' I added.

'That's going to be tough. Poor Madison. Sometimes we get just one of those chances in a lifetime.'

When I saw Madison for our next therapy session, she looked tired and drawn. She had dark rings under her eyes which gave her usual tanned skin a greyish hue. Her hair was lank and dirty, and she made little pretence that she was doing well. She told me she hadn't been out of the house for days and Deliveroo were doing a roaring trade from her fast-depleting bank account.

'No one from the squad's been in touch with me, even just to see how I am. It's obvious my name's been completely erased from their consciousness. Oh well, good luck to them.'

Despite her supportive words, there was a 'see if I care' tone to her voice. But I felt there was something deeper and more personal going on. Madison surely knew she wouldn't make the squad, so the announcement with her exclusion was not going to be that much of a revelation. Maybe it was more the realization that Madison's time as an international player was over. She hadn't made this crucial squad selection and, barring a miraculous recovery, wouldn't be going to this World Cup or any future ones.

There was something about the rhetoric that didn't ring true. The session fell into silence. Like a deflating balloon, Madison had exhausted all the hot air and we stared at each other.

'Well?' she said.

'I'm not sure why, but I feel there's something you're not telling me, Madison.'

After a long exhale of breath, she told me I was right. She paused for a few minutes, then she began again.

'Becky's Instagram account is going nuts with all the fun she's having in Leeds. Out every night on the lash with her new mates from the Leeds office. She's palled up with another girl, Leanne Hutchison. I feel like I'm being edged out of the picture.

'Becky came back to the house to pick up some stuff for Leeds and we had a huge row. I accused her of deliberately asking to be moved up north so she could get away from me. How humiliating is that?' There was an increasing note of hysteria in her voice now. 'I lose my health, my career, and now I have to watch as my best friend drops me – the loopy mate.

I mean, who can blame her, to be honest? It's a great chance for her, but she's out there living this exciting big life and I'm sitting here with mine shrivelled like a deflated balloon.'

Madison's mouth opened wide and I thought she was about to shout, but no words came out, just a set of strangled noises, as if some centre forward had put two hands around her neck. Her face reddened and for a moment I wondered if she was choking. Then the tears began and didn't stop for many minutes. Madison had been hit with a double whammy. It's easy to mix up envy and jealousy because sometimes they arrive together, like muggers, to attack.

First, she was feeling envious of Becky, because her oldest pal was embarking on a new phase in a successful career with fun times aplenty. As I've already mentioned, envy usually involves just two people, with one wishing to have elements of the other's personality, good looks, intellect, emotional intelligence, wealth, professional success etc.

Then there was jealousy. This usually involves a third person when we are worried we're going to 'lose' somebody or something to that third person. Madison had already decided that the budding friendship between Becky and Leanne was a threat to her own friendship with Becky. The irony was that her jealousy brought the likelihood of a fracture closer rather than helping to heal the relationship between them.

While Madison had already made this leap in her jealous delusion, I thought it highly unlikely that Becky would replace Madison with Leanne so easily. The roots of their relationship went deep and I didn't see Becky wanting to force the issue right now unless Madison made her choose between their friendship and her career.

At our next session Madison's mood hadn't improved, and when I asked her, 'How's your week been, Madison?' she replied with obvious irritation, 'Do you know, you're the only person who calls me Madison, other than my parents when they're cross with me!'

I asked her if she thought I was cross with her, but with a monosyllabic 'No', she'd never sounded more like a sulky teenager.

'What does everyone else call you?'

She replied sullenly, 'Maddy.'

'What would you like me to call you?'

I was met with a dismissive, 'It's up to you.'

The session wasn't going well. In these situations I've found it best to be clear with a client that I don't feel they are engaged enough in the therapeutic process for anything positive to happen, and I question the point in continuing. It seemed to do the trick here and she snapped out of her teenage mode.

'I'm really pissed off. Becky says she has a chance to stay in Leeds to work on a project with Leanne.' Madison said her name with exaggerated sarcasm. 'All I hear about is Leanne this and bloody Leanne that. I wouldn't be at all surprised if I got my marching orders from the flat and Leanne was tucked up in there before I'd even packed!'

Like so many clients struggling with anxiety, Madison had engaged in catastrophic thinking. As far as she was concerned, the only options here were for her either to get chucked out on the street and watch Leanne move in, or to get better and go back to playing football. She couldn't see how selfish and whiney she sounded, but I felt now was not the time to tell her – she needed to be stronger to deal with some harsh truths.

Madison shook her head. 'I mean, I know it's a long shot, but maybe I can get myself fit again.'

Her symptoms were getting worse and medically there wasn't even a plan in place to start phasing in a return to her playing football. I felt it was unhelpful to collude with her, so I told her that we both knew how unlikely this was and we would be far better focusing our time on the things we could change.

Over the rest of the session we examined the subtle changes now becoming easy to identify in her personality, probably due to neurological changes following the head trauma. She said she had noticed that she was now quicker to get angry, and I helped her to recognize two distinct personalities attached to each temper state that we labelled 'Madison' (less tolerant) and 'Maddy' (more tolerant). Having a label is sometimes helpful for a client, enabling them to identify what mood they are in. Once we had that understanding we could work on isolating the 'triggers' that took her from one persona to the other.

I suggested some exercises for her to do to recognize what 'state' she was experiencing at any given moment, and whether she was 'Madison' or 'Maddy', with the main aim being to get back to tolerant 'Maddy'.

'Am I ever going to get better?' she asked as she got up to leave.

'Depends what you mean by better, Maddy. But I think you can be happier.'

Eddie Stamp

Second-class Stamp

Many coaches and managers in professional elite sport suffer from unconscious envy. That is, many don't realize it. But that envy isn't straightforward. Some of it is physical, in that younger players are fitter and able to do what coaches and managers could only do ten years previously, if at all. But there's another sort of envy too, because the financial rewards for a modern player outstrip anything that their coaches or managers were earning decades before, and there's sometimes a huge difference in the wages of first-team coaches and the players they are working with. There are not many industries where the management's wages are dwarfed by the people they are managing.

For example, a few years back an international goalkeeper went to his manager and asked for the following day off to go to a modelling shoot with a well-known international fashion house.

'Miss training and I'll fine you twenty grand,' said the manager.

'That's fine,' said the keeper. 'The fashion shoot is earning me five times that. See you Friday!'

Eddie Stamp had not arranged any more anger management sessions and if I texted him he would reply with a cursory 'Too busy'. But when a letter arrived at his house from the FA, asking him to confirm how many sessions he'd had, with only one under his belt he decided he had no choice but to ask me to come north again. I suspect he saw our sessions as a necessary evil he would have to tolerate in order to finish his course.

When we did eventually meet, I was hopeful that the letter from the FA would mean he was prepared to engage more fully with the process. I decided to begin gently by discussing the early part of his life and I asked him what his football career had been like at the start. He told me he'd been rejected because of his small size by club after club and had got deeply frustrated.

'I found it hard to take. Lads with virtually no skill at all were getting contracts and yet, because of my size, nobody wanted to even take a look at me, even though I could run rings round the bigger lads. I went to one trial and the academy coach there took one look at me and told me I was too small and to not even bother getting changed. Never even got chance to put my boots on.'

He went on to describe the growing anger he felt at one rejection after another, so he turned to weight training at the local gym. When he eventually got an opportunity at an academy that decided to take a chance on him, he knew he had to give them something special.

'When I went into a fifty-fifty tackle there was only one winner and I got the reputation of being a hard little bastard. Not like the pros of today. A puff of wind and they fall over.'

Back in the day managers liked the 'hard man' reputation he'd carved out for himself, because they knew he'd run all day and never be afraid when it came to the physical part of the game. He'd had a decent career – played in the Premier League and had a good run in the Championship – but his last club tarnished things for him when he was coming to the end of his playing career. Eddie told me how the manager had called him into his office, and he was expecting to be told it was all over, because he'd had a season disrupted by knee injuries. Instead, the manager had sat Eddie down and offered him an unbelievable one-year contract extension, but at the end of his offer said, 'It'll cost you.'

Essentially, the deal was £25,000 a week, but the manager wanted a quarter of Eddie's wages, otherwise he wouldn't sign him. Eddie knew he wouldn't be playing many more matches, and the manager wasn't bothered if he played or not. Eddie spent most of that season injured or on holiday with his wife, and every month he had to give the manager a quarter of what he was earning. Eddie soon found out that he wasn't the only one with that arrangement at the club. It seemed this was quite commonplace within the industry around twenty-five years ago.

Eddie saw out the remainder of his contract and completed his coaching exams, and soon afterwards he got a telephone call from the manager of the club he now works at, Jack Braithwaite. 'He told me there was a position here for his assistant and asked if I would be interested in coming to the club. He said it was a sleeping giant!

'Ha! I told him to fuck off, said the club was more like a sleeping pygmy! We both laughed and I signed the deal the next day to come here. I had played for this mob for about two seasons a few years previously, so it felt like coming home. I know everybody here, from the tea lady to the laundry assistant. But the players are soft. Jack said he could see that when he came here, and he wanted me to harden them up. We ain't going to get out of this division playing tippy-tappy football. We don't have those players. We ain't Man City. Not yet,' he smirked.

Eddie then told me about some dark times in his career when he was injured and used to numb his pain both physically and emotionally with alcohol.

'There were periods of my career that I simply don't remember. I was pissed or hungover most of the time. The club I was at had some drinkers, but I wasn't going to be out-drunk by them. I've cleaned up my act a lot since then, but my anger just got worse. I don't think the drink helped. When I see these young lads making no effort at all and picking up £40 and £50K a week, I'm furious and I just want to smash into them and make them realize how lucky they are.'

'Eddie, there's a massive difference between anger and aggression and we have to work out which is which. Aggression can help you win football matches when it's measured and planned, but violence and anger are your undoing.'

I could see he was beginning to get angry again, but I wasn't finished.

'I have to say, I think the issues go deeper than this.'

He snarled at me, 'What do you mean by that?'

'I believe the anger is a symptom, just like a runny nose is a symptom of a cold, and from what I've seen I think the anger is a result of your envy of the younger players. Players who have more skill than you did, are better paid than you are and whose careers are blossoming, while your playing career is over. I don't think you can hack it. That's why you can't control yourself when you play in those practice games and end up kicking the shit out of the lads. You can't control it and you're going to have to.'

I could see Eddie was just about ready to launch at me, but I had to continue. 'Your envy and anger are fused together and we need to work out how to pull them apart. And if you're not careful, you could end up being envious of your own son, who could potentially have the career you didn't.'

Something within that last comment managed to hit home and caused Eddie to take a breath.

'How does your wife cope with your anger, Eddie?'

I saw his lip curl in disgust as he seemed to feel on much safer ground with this aspect.

'She doesn't. I blow up like a volcano and she runs up to the bathroom and hides and locks the door. We've had some real ding-dongs down the years. Some time ago she said she couldn't go on any more and that her nerves weren't good. I sent her to the doctor and she's been on these pills ever since. She's much better now.'

He seemed oblivious to the obvious.

'Do you think she will need those pills if you get on top of your anger issues? What about your son? Do you think his behaviour at school is anything to do with how angry you get at home?' I asked.

He looked at me with a mixture of slight confusion and irritation.

'I can be a real bastard to live with, I know that – but, Gaz, it is what it is,' Eddie said, then was quiet for a short while. The irritation seemed to be fading, leaving confusion in its place.

I took advantage of his calm to ask, 'Do you miss being a player?'

'Course I do. Who doesn't?'

'I'm not talking about everybody else, I'm talking about you, because I think the hurt you feel about not being able to play is driving the anger.'

'I can't help it – I just lose it. It's who I am. I didn't need you to tell me this.'

'But you do need me to tell you why it's happening, and unless you address it, it's not going to go away.'

Eddie rubbed his shaven head, as if trying to rub away some of his thoughts, and reached for his phone. With that, he got up and went to the door, but then he paused with his hand on the door handle, his head bowed, and just stood there – no words, head leaning against the door with his hand still on the door handle.

He turned a few moments later and his eyes were red. He said just one word: 'Bastard.'

Jane Lovell

Taking the Mic

I had a text from Jane during the week to say that she had decided to take the job in Paris and, being away, would have to cancel her next session. She rebooked for after the championships. I was moving house that week so didn't get much opportunity to watch Jane making her TV debut and the media coverage of the week-long event. However, towards the end of the championships, I was sitting on a train to London and the man opposite me was reading the sports section of a national newspaper. In the newsprint facing me was the headline 'GB team slammed by ex-athletics coach' and underneath was a smaller headline: 'TV pundit Jane Lovell's dad says GB coaches are out of touch'.

I looked away, deciding not to read any more. I didn't want to reach any conclusions about what was going on in Paris before Jane came back to therapy. Words like 'sabotage' sprang to mind and I quickly tried to dampen down my anger at Jane's father. I had to remember that I had no idea what was really going on, and in my experience of working with athletes caught up in a media story, truth and the reported facts were rarely bedfellows. As one editor used to say to me during my journalist days, 'Never let the facts get in the way of a good story.'

Jane was slightly early for her first session after Paris. She didn't really smile at me as she came into the clinic and barely kept eye contact either as I invited her to sit down. I guessed I wouldn't have to say very much before she got into her stride and I was correct. She never asked me if I knew what had happened in Paris, when her father was quoted in the national sports press, she just launched into a tirade from the start. The gun had sounded.

'My father is an utter bastard,' she began. She was almost spitting out her words. 'Do you know what that selfish arse went and did while I was away? He only gave an interview to the local paper. They phoned him up to do a feature on how he felt about his daughter appearing on national television, and he gave them the sort of scoop they wouldn't have had in twenty years. He slags off Team GB, the coaches, the back-up staff, the physios, everyone. Oh, and he's not finished yet. Says I could have wiped the floor with any of the current squad, and – listen to this – had I not had my head turned by modelling, I'd have made it as an Olympic champion!

'He was talking utter shite! I didn't make it because he pushed me to a point where I injured myself and could never run as fast again.'

The article in the local paper had been picked up by the national press and was soon the hot topic of discussion over croissants and café au lait in Team GB's athletics accommodation. One less-than-impressed sprint coach cornered Jane just as she was about to go on air and apparently there was a rather frank, one-way conversation. Jane, clearly upset, did her 'piece to camera' reporting on the 200-metre heats and, in a slip of the tongue (which she didn't realize or correct) referred to the winning athlete as Canadian rather than from the USA.

'After my producer told me, I just went to my hotel room and bawled my eyes out. What a stupid mistake. In front of millions of people. There wasn't even a Canadian in the heat!'

'It happens, Jane.'

'Not to me! I phoned my idiot of a father up and we had one of our worst fights ever. He said the fact that I'd made a fool of myself on air proved he was right, and that I should never have agreed to work there, and what was I doing leaving my husband and kid for a week? Well, that was it. I let him have it. I'd never spoken to him like that, but boy did he have it coming. I told him he sabotaged my career as an athlete by pushing my body beyond its limits and now he's probably screwed up my TV career. He knew what he was doing by giving that sodding interview. Once again, it's Jane Lovell the failed TV reporter, the failed athlete, the failed mother and daughter. I just can't keep doing this!'

In my opinion Jane had reached her FIP (Fuck It Point). It's when we stop worrying about the consequences of saying something that's been left unsaid for years. Most FIPs involve no planning or reasoning – it's more like a balloon that inflates inside us and carries on inflating until we can contain it no longer. Most of us reach a FIP with our parents eventually. My supervisor, Tom, reckons that most successful child–parent relationships are built after the FIP, because that's when both parties have a degree of honesty and authenticity that might have been lacking before.

Rather than agree with Jane and fuel her rant, I decided to

see if she could dig a bit deeper into her relationship with her father, so I said, 'Tell me about your dad, Jane. I don't think I know very much about him.'

Jimmy Turner was a decent 400-metre sprinter in his day. He'd been a county champion in the 1960s, but couldn't quite make the step up to national level. A teacher by profession, he taught geography and PE at a southern grammar school and had been put in charge of the school's athletics team. When Jane showed some promise as a sprinter in her all-girls school, Dad, who was never really close to his daughter, suddenly took over her athletics development and they began training together at weekends. As Jane's confidence grew, so did Jimmy's pride in her. She sailed through the county trials and was soon knocking on the door of the junior national teams. Training was at Crystal Palace, but it was quite a journey from the family home and Jimmy would train with Jane at a local non-league football stadium.

'I know Dad was an aspiring sprinter himself, but the training brought us together. I just wanted to be a daddy's girl and please him, so I did what he said, and certainly early on it brought success. He taught me about being prepared at the gun at the start of the race. When I was a teenager, I had a five-metre start from the off. I really felt he knew his stuff. But then my mum told me that a local sports photographer had taken a picture of me running and it somehow got into the hands of a modelling agency. Next thing I knew I was being offered modelling work. Dad was furious. Mum and Dad argued a lot then. She said that Dad was putting far too much pressure on me. Dad said I could be an Olympic champion. I did the odd photo shoot in my late teens, but it caused such a rumpus at home I packed it in.'

Jane's career was in full flow at the start of the century. She missed out on the Athens games due to injury but was expected to get back to form in time for Beijing in 2008. Her dad played down the significance of the ankle injury that kept her away from Athens, but planned her rehab training programme badly and, after repeated recurrences of her ankle injury, she broke down in the spring of 2008, her weakened ankle finally unable to withstand the demands of elite heptathlon disciplines. She never competed professionally again.

'As my career died, so did his. He'd made quite a few enemies in Team GB and they wouldn't have anything to do with him after I quit. Several of the top coaches told me I needed to ditch my dad and find a better coach, but how could I do that? It'd have broken him. It was pathetic. My modelling career was beginning to take off, and I also got an offer to work for a European Sports Channel based in Holland. It didn't really work out though – they told me I was difficult. One day I travelled out to their studios to talk about Olympic competing in a sports TV chat show. When I arrived after a bloody awful journey, they told me the programme schedule had changed and they wanted me to commentate off tube [sitting in a small studio with a TV monitor and pretending you're in the stadium] on the shot put and discus. I refused and that was the end of my TV career. Dad told me it served me right and my modelling made me look like a "tart".'

At each turn in her career or personal life, Dad seemed ready to pounce on Jane's decisions when they went wrong, like a cat waiting for a mouse. At no point was he ever positive about her choices.

While jealousy and envy are complex, the person on the receiving end of these emotions may find them hurtful and confusing. Jane was trying to please her father by achieving success, but in so doing somehow displeased him, possibly because she was no longer following his agenda and was now out of his sphere of control. As her coach, he enjoyed the indirect attention her success brought, and was often quoted in the national and local press. Through her he had finally become somebody. With her retirement as a result of injury, he was reduced to being a nobody.

We can often blame ourselves for other people's jealousy and envy of us, and at worst alter our behaviour to fit in with their perceived dislike of our success. Many parents have unconscious envy of their children, seeing their youth and prospects eclipse their own. One client's father would regularly remind his son how well he was doing when he was the son's age. It left my client baffled and angry, with feelings that he'd never live up to his father's success. They are still estranged to this day.

'Jane, what does it feel like when you're broadcasting?'

'When I'm holding the mic it feels like I get to say what I want to say, without anyone else interfering.'

Her eyes were bright with the sense of freedom she was reliving.

'Imagine that you're holding the mic right now, what would you like to say to your dad?'

I could see her struggling to form the words she had been longing to say for years but had suppressed out of a sense of loyalty and love, neither of which she felt was adequately returned.

I prompted her. 'Can you ever forgive him for how he's behaved?'

'Forgive him? Right now, I want to shove that microphone down his throat. Sideways!'

Tony Oldfield

Poison Envy

I had thought a lot about Tony Oldfield since our last session together, imagining him commentating on a Swedish second-division game and the feelings of worthlessness this had brought up in him. He was a nice enough guy – the sort you might enjoy spending an hour or two in a pub with – but there was a reek of disappointment about him and I would have found it hard to be a friend of his in more normal circumstances. His behaviour was just too inconsistent to be comfortable around, and his inability to say no catapulted him into very difficult areas with his personal relationships. To quote a friend of mine, 'He's the type of bloke to change lanes without indicating.'

But I did have some sympathy for him. It must have been tough that his playing career came to an end just before the Premier League began, when money from satellite broadcasting brought riches to the players in the top division of English football. Had he managed to carry on playing for, say, another three years, I doubt whether he would have been in this financial pickle. Then again, maybe his desire to fund a lifestyle that was beyond his means meant he would have burned through his money quite quickly anyway.

I admired his tenacity in coming back to therapy, even though many of our sessions were quite bleak. I knew I had to help him understand what money represented to him and how often he used it to try to buy friendships and relationships. This was true not only of Tony but of course of many other people who use their wealth to try to find kindness, love and happiness. Who was I to criticize Tony when the world and his brother were doing exactly the same?

But with Tony there were obviously issues around self-esteem and his propensity to latch on to cruel women – issues that, I suspected, were a throwback to his relationship with his mum, who had treated him badly when he was growing up. Tony had already told me that his parents had split up when he was little. His father was a distant figure and his mum had found it difficult to cope, taking out her frustrations on Tony. Now he sought women who weren't always kind to him.

Obviously, I couldn't be sure that Anna was as cruel as Tony had made out. All clients bring versions of their loved ones into the therapy space and I try to keep an open mind as to whether their depictions are accurate. Very occasionally, I will invite a parent or partner into a single session with a client if there is a particular knotty problem to resolve. A so-called 'tyrannical' partner or loved one often turns out to have a very different persona from the one that has been portrayed by the client.

In our next session, Tony looked as low as I'd ever seen him as he slumped down in the chair. He had the air of a man who'd lost a £20 note only to find a fiver. When clients behave like this, I believe they are actively signalling to the therapist to ask 'What's the matter?', so I duly obliged.

'What a week, what a crazy week. I have just been cheated out of a job that would have been perfect for me.'

He banged his fist on the arm of the chair as he spoke the word 'perfect', then went on to explain that he'd been contacted by a big TV production company that was putting together a series about football players from the 1980s. They had asked Tony to audition for the presenter's role. He went for a screen test, which they said went well, so Tony thought it was only a matter of time before he got the job, as the other people in the running had never played at his level.

The job was worth £10,000, Tony told me, and he had kept ringing the producer to find out whether they'd made a decision and when filming was due to start. The producer had answered his first call, but after that he didn't pick up. A few weeks later Tony heard that a well-known ex-footballer, who was now a TV personality and football pundit, had got the gig.

'For Christ's sake, he's on every bleeding TV commercial these days and must be making hundreds of thousands of pounds a year. It wouldn't have hurt them to give me the gig. And that producer, what a real git! Didn't even have the bottle to ring me up and tell me. I had to find out on Twitter, on frigging Twitter!'

Tony's bitterness about the football industry was laid bare. He couldn't wait to pour out story after story about the avarice of managers and players, when all he wanted was a small 'wedge' of £10K. He had gone into victim mode, as if the football industry was somehow conspiring against him. Even the ex-player who had got the job ahead of him was somehow also in on this conspiracy to make sure Tony didn't earn any money.

This is sometimes called a 'childlike state', where we become helpless in the face of the world's ups and downs.

Tony was refusing to take responsibility for what was going on in his life and somehow it was everybody else's fault except his own.

I asked Tony why the £10,000 was so important to him.

'I wanted to treat Anna, buy her some nice jewellery, and send some money up to Sandra in Scotland,' he said, as if I should have known the answer.

I then asked him to imagine he didn't have to spend this money on Anna or send any to his ex-wife. What would he do with it, then? He looked completely nonplussed.

'You see, I do get it, Tony. But much of your financial pressure comes from wanting to keep everybody happy. I'm just wondering what would make *you* really happy. I suppose what concerns me is where do *you* find comfort and love?'

He had no answer. And here was my dilemma. Should I collude with him, like everybody else in his life had always done, and tell him that it was OK to feel bad about missing out on the wealth the game had denied him? Or should I be kind and tell him what somebody should have told him years ago? I felt that beating around the bush at this stage would be futile.

'Anna doesn't seem to be very kind to you, like the incident with the paracetamol, and I simply don't understand why you want to continually try to please her, or Sandra for that matter. I think you've been doing this for many, many years, as you probably did with your mum, constantly running back to these people and trying to please them.' I told him that I thought it was something he was doing with the football industry too. The question was, how many times did he want to be rejected? How long was it going to be before he decided enough was enough?

As I was talking, I could see him slowly shrinking even further into the chair, as if to try and hide from my words.

But what would be the point of not telling him what was plain for everyone else to see, even though he couldn't.

'I know you don't want to hear this, Tony, but football doesn't need you any more, and the acid inside you which burns with envy about what should have been and could have been is only damaging you, and damaging all your relationships.'

He just sat there staring at me, obviously shocked and unable to speak for a few moments, and I could see the shame on his face as my words sank in. He eventually took a deep breath.

'Blimey, you don't sit on the fence, do you?'

He lapsed back into silence for a few moments, looking down at the carpet, and then he looked back up at me again. I felt a mixture of panic and fear rise in me that maybe I had gone too far, that I'd irreversibly breached the Tony Oldfield protective outer shell, and now there was no way for the inner Tony to defend himself against the realities of life suddenly streaming through.

'Did you have to be such an utter bastard?' he said calmly, looking me straight in the eye.

Mark Silver

Jung Hearts

Once again it was a few weeks before I saw Mark Silver for another session. There was always some snooker tournament or other going on, and he often cancelled a session with me at the eleventh hour, making some excuse about how 'useless he was' and saying he found it difficult running his diary effectively with Jasmine still staying with her mum and dad, as that was something she usually did for him. She hadn't returned yet.

I reviewed my notes of the last session with Mark and concluded that Jasmine was very much a stereotype that Mark went for. Most of us will have a 'type' we're attracted to. This theory comes from the work of psychologist Carl Jung. All of us, from early adolescence, fixate on what our ideal boyfriend/girlfriend might look like. Some of these fantasies are absorbed through our early exposure to children's fairy tales – think of the princes and princesses of books and films. In Western cultures, many a teenage girl will have the 'chase me' fantasy, where the boy has to ask the girl out and there is an expectation that they both play certain roles in the courtship. Theory suggests that this is how we make sense of the world and how we connect to other human beings.

I suspect Jasmine was Mark's manifestation of his ideal woman, and he'd fallen in love with a concept or image rather than with a real person. Many men and women fall into this trap and then, after their relationship develops, they realize they're with a complete stranger who bears no resemblance to the person they thought they'd met at the start. In layman's terms, this could be described as the trophy wife/girlfriend phenomenon: men going for what they *want* not what they *need*.

This can be a difficult concept to understand when we are whipped up into a frenzy of positive feelings after meeting some gorgeous person we want to believe is 'perfect'. How do we get an objective view of the relationship when all we can see is an idealized version of the other person? This is particularly true of teenagers, who are desperate to seek the approval of others and often enter relationships based on a whole set of jumbled ideas about what is cool and what is not.

I remember my first early crushes as a teenager and feeling ten feet tall after receiving a pretty girl's attention. A love letter (if you remember love letters rather than texts or WhatsApp messages) would send me soaring, believing that I was Romeo incarnate. Once that brief connection was lost and the object of my love turned her attention to somebody else, I felt utterly crushed. This is not love, but rather a reflection of ourselves in someone else's mirror. As mature adults, it's often more helpful to understand who we are, and why we should value ourselves, instead of seeking that value in another person.

Mark felt valued by Jasmine's love. But when he couldn't

feel that, he went into a cycle of despair which then involved jealousy, as he became convinced that she had already re-directed her love elsewhere.

Having expected Mark to cancel yet another session, I was surprised when he turned up on time. He was all apologies, making excuses about the difficulty of travelling while he was playing tournaments and saying he hadn't 'been himself' while Jasmine was staying with her mum and dad.

'It's getting harder rather than easier her being away. I've not been able to concentrate at all in the tournaments I've been playing in and, to be honest, I've been drinking a bit more. I just want to start playing better snooker again and forget about Jasmine for the time being. It's doing my nut in trying to forget about her, though. That's why I've come to see you, to help me concentrate.'

Once again we went through the theory of the 'challenger state' (determined to succeed despite the difficulties) versus the 'threat state' (frightened that you're going to lose) and this time I could see it was making much more sense to him because he realized how it could be used in his next snooker match.

I asked Mark how he was getting on at home and how he was managing on his own. He told me for the first time about his younger brother, Jim (who sounded a bit like a pirate, both in name and in behaviour), who had moved in while Jasmine was away to 'keep an eye on the place'. Fortunately, Jim was available as he was between jobs at the moment, so was really keen to 'help out' when Mark mentioned that he was on his own.

Mark described Jim as the more attractive of the two brothers. Taller and physically stronger, he used to play semi-professional rugby and was a bit of a hit with the ladies. Mark told me that, having spent so much time in working men's clubs as a child when he was looking for his father, he then found refuge there playing snooker and pool after losing out to his more dashing younger brother with many of his early crushes. But in the intervening years, Mark had overtaken Jim in terms of career success, and he admitted that he was desperate to hold on to Jasmine as a symbol of that success.

'Problem is, Jasmine has agreed to come back at the weekend and I know Jim will be all over her like a rash. It's the worst of all worlds, mate. Jim is a really good cook and has looked after me and the house while Jasmine's been away, and I've been really enjoying his company. But I can't help feeling that as soon as Jasmine comes back it's all going to kick off between them.'

I got the feeling that this was more about Mark's insecurity around Jasmine than the likelihood his brother was going to make a move on her.

Mark sighed, looking really glum as he told me, 'After Mum came back home and her and Dad got back together, I had a bit of success round the snooker halls and started dating this girl called Hayley. I was only about eighteen years old and I thought Hayley was just perfect. I made the mistake of inviting her round for Sunday lunch one week. Mum, Dad and Jim were there. Mum is pretending we're all posh. Dad's pissing himself laughing and teasing Mum, asking her why we had the best cutlery out etc. Jim was about sixteen at this stage and he and Hayley just hit it off from the get-go. The next week she dropped a note through the door to say she didn't want to go out with me any more because she had a date with Jim that night. I was livid. I had it out with Jim and he laughed at me, saying it wasn't his fault she preferred him over me. He was a spotty sixteen-year-old! I tell you what, it really crushed my confidence. It took me ages to ask out another girl and I *never* brought one back to our house.'

Mark was lost. Did he 'bring' Jasmine home and run the risk of Jim hitting on her, or did he chuck his brother out of his house, despite his culinary skills and the real affection he had for his roguish younger sibling?

Therapeutically, this was interesting. Mark's brother represented a mother figure – part of his family who looked after him by feeding him – yet he was also the rival sibling. Jasmine also fulfilled the same 'motherly' role. This illustrated Mark's hunger to find someone to look after him, and his underdeveloped ability to nurture himself. Even two people (in addition to his real mother) might not have been enough. Could Mark feel loved or cared for by either of them in this situation?

I wasn't sure whether Mark's anxieties about Jim were real or imagined – Jim was a child when he 'stole' Mark's date, after all – but I did feel that if Mark and Jasmine were to sort out their problems, they needed an empty space in which to do so and Jim would be a distraction. The sorts of repairs their relationship needed would require time and space, and the last thing Jasmine would want, I felt, was another love interest, real or imagined. It's hard not to give advice in these situations and I tried to examine with Mark what he felt he should do.

'I don't know. I feel like I need my brother around but really want him to piss off when Jasmine comes back. We have to sort things out by ourselves.'

'Can't you tell him that?'

'It's not that easy. He doesn't really have anywhere to go.

I felt a sense of responsibility for him when I was growing up and I still feel that for him now.'

'Who do you trust more, Jasmine or Jim?'

Mark sighed. 'Now that, my friend, is a really good question.'

Love

Ahhhh, *l'amour.* Everyone thinks they know what love is, but philosophers, scientists and psychologists across the ages have often disagreed about it. The ancient Greeks identified no fewer than eight different types of love: self-love, the love of a parent for a child, platonic love for a friend, obsessive (and often destructive) love, the enduring love of an elderly couple, the flirtatious and playful love of early infatuation, the unconditional love that is often associated with religion and not forgetting the romantic love sung about in songs. Anthropologically, it is argued love is necessary for the continuation of our species, but the psychologist Abraham Maslow suggested that love was more of a basic need to belong or to be loved.

This section recognizes that love can be a driver for many human behaviours, not only in relationships but also in sport. Love is manifested strongly in sport – think of the love of fans for their team, as can be heard on the terraces in supporters' chants. But that love must withstand painful, humiliating defeats and disappointments. For an individual, the pain that comes from the loss of a desired object, person or even career (imagined or real) can be catastrophic. For instance, I once counselled the chairman of a football club who said he couldn't bear to watch the games, because he became 'a toxic presence' when the team was losing, so he hid away in his office instead.

In psychological terms, sportspeople are usually young and, when at their physical peak, their relative youth means they are still in the process of separating from their parents or caregivers. For some young football players, living away from home for the first time builds a longing for a mentor, which can be transferred to the coaching staff within the club, and it's noticeable that a football coach or manager will sometimes refer to a player as 'son'.

In her 2003 book *Why Love Matters*, psychotherapist Sue Gerhardt explains that the earliest relationships in childhood shape the development of a baby's brain and can have an influence on future neural development. Without the experience in infancy and childhood of being nurtured, cared for and loved, certain neurological pathways are not developed, resulting in difficulty forming and maintaining healthy relationships as an adult.

The search for love can lead young elite athletes into compulsive or addictive behaviours. In my work I often find that problems around food, drink and sex are associated with a lack of love (real or perceived) in a client's early life, as we'll see in this section in relation to Eddie Stamp and Kwasi Adepodji. This is particularly relevant in a team sport, where the needs of an individual are balanced against the needs of the team. The team I support, for example, Leeds United, have adopted the slogan 'Side Above Self Every Time'. The same is equally true in other sports, like cricket. However, this isn't always easy, as James Holmes found out when he couldn't put the needs of his cricket team above his own desire to be back home in the safety of his family.

In the drive to be the best that they can be, a young athlete sometimes finds it difficult to distinguish between personal performance and what's right for the team – and of course, these are often in conflict. I once worked with a talented young footballer, Dan, who'd come from a troubled background. He used his success at football to feel better about himself. However, he was highly self-critical in every match he played and each misplaced pass would deeply affect him. If he wasn't voted 'Man of the Match' he'd be upset and obsess why another player had got the award.

Dan hadn't scored for several matches and made it clear to me it was getting him down. He'd had several assists (creating successful goal-scoring chances for other players) but somehow he couldn't find the target. I had a sense that he was trying too hard and that it was affecting his game.

In the next game, with the score 0–0, Dan received the ball and charged down the wing into the opposition's penalty area. After a clumsy tackle by their full back the referee awarded a penalty. Dan was not the team's regular penalty taker, but he jumped to his feet and picked up the ball as if to take the penalty immediately. The other players in his team realized to their horror that he was about to take the spot kick and dashed over to prevent him. What ensued was a tug-of-war, with the regular penalty taker trying to snatch the ball away from the younger player. This lasted for several seconds as the crowd laughed at the pantomime being played out in front of them. Eventually the team's captain shoved Dan out of the way, snatched the ball and gave it to the team's regular penalty taker, who duly scored.

When I caught up with Dan afterwards, I asked him what was going on.

'I was desperate to score. I wasn't thinking. I've never taken a penalty in my life, but I'd won it so I thought I should take it too.'

Sports clients who value and look after themselves both physically and mentally, often have successful careers. They have clear boundaries and good self-esteem. They don't put themselves down and don't usually need external validation from coaches, fans, social media or the press to know if they are doing OK. But these are the sports clients I rarely see.

Sport seems to attract many people who are seeking something that has been missing in their lives and which is made up for by the adoration of the roaring crowd or receiving a medal. This section is concerned with the basic human desire to belong and be loved. I often smile when I see a player kissing the club badge on his shirt after scoring – and believe me, we all need a badge to kiss.

Tony Oldfield

Had Enough Bad Love

Tony Oldfield didn't turn up for his next session – in fact he cancelled just in time to avoid paying my fee, sending me a brief text saying that he couldn't make it and would rebook when he was ready. There was nothing to suggest when or even if he'd book another session with me, which left me pondering whether I was likely to see him again.

I suspected that Tony felt challenged by my words in our last session, when I had made it clear that the football and broadcast industries didn't owe him a living, and the only way he would ever be able to have a real relationship was to deal with this fact head on. He was doing what therapists call 'acting out', which is a therapeutic term used to describe the unconscious motivations for the behaviour of clients who are struggling to understand their emotions. Their actions may be impulsive and self-destructive, as if to demonstrate – to 'act out' – the conflicted, painful feelings distressing them, taking the chaos inside and almost putting it on a stage in a weird kind of hope someone will understand when they see it.

I debated whether I should have said what I said in the last session, but came to the conclusion that there was nothing to be gained from shielding Tony from my therapeutic understanding of his situation. My hope was that he would return so we could continue the work, with him hopefully finding his own way forward towards a more fulfilled life. Maybe he was thrown by my lack of retaliation, expecting perhaps an aggressive response to his calling me an 'utter bastard', but that was part of the training of a therapist – the ability not to be triggered by the client but to contain a situation instead of inflaming it.

Maybe I had been just as cruel as Tony's mum or his current girlfriend, Anna, and was playing out the same scenario that everybody seemed to do when coming into contact with him, including the football club – which had likewise decided they'd had enough of him. But why had Tony elicited these responses? I suspected it was to do with his inability to be kind to himself. Essentially, Tony didn't value himself, so why should anyone else?

As individuals we often get pushed around by others, and Tony had to learn what was good for his soul and what wasn't. I don't think this had ever occurred to him and he was left in dark shadowlands, always trying to please someone – mother, football coach, TV producer, wife and now girlfriend. I wondered if I could be added at the end of this long list. So when Tony called a few days later to book his next session, I admit to feeling relieved.

Tony looked more presentable when he came in and I thought I'd tackle his absence the week before at the beginning of the session. He squirmed in his chair, telling me how busy he'd been, with seemingly every television station in the world trying to get hold of him. More second-division

Swedish football, commercials, football clubs galore, they all wanted him.

It all sounded positive, but the evasive way in which he couldn't meet my gaze indicated that his version of events may not have been entirely accurate. When I dug a little deeper, asking which clubs and television stations had been in contact, he floundered and then just slumped in the chair in silence, giving up, all semblance of trying to present a positive front gone.

'What's really going on, Tony?' I enquired gently.

Again he came up with a series of childlike lies as he tried to present his situation as being if not quite so positive still less than dire. When I didn't respond, he looked directly at me and snapped, 'Do we have to do this?'

When I didn't respond I could feel his anger towards me, not least because I was now forcing him to confront the emotions he had spent a lifetime trying to hide from.

'OK, I was pissed off with you. There! Really pissed off after our last session and I didn't want to come any more. I just wanted out.'

I was encouraged that Tony had come back. Clients sometimes end therapy suddenly to gain power in a powerless situation. Of course, the relationship between a therapist and a client is unequal, but sudden departures often trouble me. Not knowing what has happened to a client, I wonder about their welfare. Sometimes there's no explanation and my texts and emails are ignored. Nowadays there's a term for it, 'ghosting', and depending on the length of the relationship, ghosting can be almost like experiencing a sudden bereavement.

A previous supervisor once told me, 'Remember, the worse you feel, the better the client will feel. You see, they have projected much of their negative emotions on to you, leaving them feeling unburdened and much lighter.' I think the worst examples of this are young athletes who come to me in a terrible emotional condition but leave after one or two sessions. In therapeutic circles, we call this a 'flight into health', or, to put it more bluntly, 'I'm feeling better now so fuck off!' But who are they kidding?

I explained it was fine for Tony to feel angry with me and I asked why he felt it difficult to express that anger. Tony explained that he often got angry with people but instead of challenging them, he simply slipped out of the back door, mainly because he didn't feel he could control his anger and he'd say something he might regret, causing more upset than he could handle. He was sorely tempted to do that in our relationship but decided to come over and give me one last chance.

I asked him why he was willing to give me another chance and he thought for a moment, then a slight smile passed his lips and he said, 'I was intrigued by you. I called you a bastard and you didn't flinch, and I don't feel like I have to justify myself to you – quite novel for me.'

I asked if he had felt he needed to justify himself during his marriage.

'Constantly!'

For the first time Tony talked of his marriage breakdown, which was caused by a short-lived affair with a young TV production assistant at a satellite channel. Tony recognized that he was wrong to have begun a relationship with another woman, but defended his actions by stating his wife, Sandra, was never loving and warm towards him. He recalled that frequently, whenever he returned after working away for a week or so on a football tournament, her habit was to thrust his son at him and say it was his turn to do the childcare, while she went to stay with her parents for a break. He often felt she resented his work, especially when it took him away, and that she could never forgive him for leaving her on her own to look after their son.

The affair proved to be the last straw for his wife, who said she had dedicated her life to following Tony around the country and bringing up their son, and this was how he repaid her loyalty. Tony was distraught at the thought of being on his own and desperately apologized about his fling (she only knew about the one, but in fact there were many). He felt they could have worked things out, maintaining that fifteen years of marriage was worth trying to save, but his wife didn't share his view.

'She was just so unreasonable, pushing me out of the house and saying the marriage was over. I had nowhere to go and ended up having to stay with my mum, and believe me, that was no barrel of laughs. I'd gone from the frying pan into the fire, balls first. Mum was furious with me for messing up my marriage and called me all the names under the sun. All the ridicule that I remember as a kid came rushing back – that I was a good-for-nothing, that I was stupid, that I was selfish, that I was led by my dick . . . I couldn't take it for very long and I moved out into a small flat. You know, when I think about those few weeks with Mum, it reminds me of being with Anna now. All I wanted was somebody to love me and care about me. That's not a lot to ask, is it?'

'Loving and caring about someone is being honest with them, Tony. And you were not prepared to be honest with your wife. That's why she probably decided enough was enough. Don't you think that's reasonable?'

He looked distinctly uncomfortable, but dismissed it as 'water under the bridge'. But affairs don't happen on their own and in Tony's case I felt it was another case of 'acting out' rather than addressing the issues of the marriage head on. Any confrontation was painful for Tony, but he was making some progress. At least he had come back to therapy after our sharp words in the previous session. He could have easily gone and found another therapist.

The cliché that the greatest gift any of us can have is to love and be loved sprang to mind, and yet this gift seemed to have eluded Tony Oldfield all his life. According to him, his wife hadn't loved him – that's why he was unfaithful – nor did football, nor did Anna.

I'd never heard Tony speak so intently before when he said, 'I have got to end it with Anna. I really have. I don't think I can carry on being with her and be honest with myself. I feel empty. But how can I break it off with her? She'll go potty. But so what?'

I didn't have to contribute, as Tony was having a full-blown conversation with himself, the emotional and rational parts of his brain fighting for control.

'Everybody goes nuts with me – that's hardly new. Maybe I'd be better off on my own. It's not gonna be easy, but I'd rather be without all that hassle. That would bloody well show her.'

Tony's voice had risen and his face had gone quite red by this stage, and I asked him what he was feeling. His emphatic response suggested that the therapy was going in the right direction.

'I'll tell you one thing. I'm thinking I don't deserve this shit any more.'

Richard Davies

Hole in the Soul

'Coffee and Cream, Coffee and bleeding Cream, every sodding day. I'm fed up with those words. I've even stopped going to Starbucks!'

Richard Davies, probably the country's most gifted jump jockey of his generation, sat with his head in his hands in my counselling space looking tormented. He was earning good money and you couldn't pick up the racing section of a national newspaper without reading his name or seeing his grinning face beaming back at you. He was the very image of success. I wondered what the readers would have made of my client right now as he spoke in a childlike whine.

'My dad keeps going on about this bloody horse, Coffee and Cream, that he wants me to ride next April at Aintree. He says he's got good contacts with another trainer who's looking for a jockey. Dad says we'll break the family duck at Aintree. Every sodding day, it's "You'd like the horse, he's a 'stayer', what do you think?" It's doing my head in. To be honest, I'm not sure I could get down to the weight they'd want anyway. Frankly, I don't even know if I want to do the National next year.'

Many jockeys struggle with maintaining their weight, as they must reach a target weight – the weight of both horse and jockey combined – with every horse they ride, and they might race three or four horses a day at any course. If that's not difficult enough, each horse's weight can fluctuate between races, depending on the current handicap of the horse.

The handicap is the weight applied to try and slow the horse down, which is meant to make the race fairer so that in theory all the horses finish the race together. The horse will wear lead weights in the saddle and the handicap weight will increase if the horse has done well in its previous races.

The target weight for a horse is usually released just five days before a race, so jockeys have only that time to lose any excess pounds to make sure they're within the weight limits for each of those horses. It is not unusual to have to lose anything up to ten pounds, with the typical approaches to reducing weight being forced vomiting, extended saunas and starvation. Often, Richard would casually tell me about feeling so light-headed from lack of food he could barely drive, existing on sweets and sugary drinks on race days to get him through.

'What's your diet like at the moment, Richard?'

He shot me a pained look mixed with shame.

'Terrible. I have a sweet tooth. You should see the glove compartment of my car. It looks like a bloody sweet shop. Chocolate, wine gums, Liquorice Allsorts – those are my favourites.'

Consuming large amounts of sugar is thought to be beneficial just before a game and most sports club dressing rooms have a large stash of sweets for players. It's not uncommon for some players to use legal stimulants, such as caffeine-laced products or a nicotine-based product called

Snus, which is a form of snuff originating from Sweden. It is sold in what looks like tiny tea bags and a player will put a bag under his top lip. It's supposed to give a nicotine buzz at the time of competition. Research has shown it has little or no benefit, but it's highly addictive, just like sugar, and many players I work with are using ten to fifteen bags a day – even when they're not playing.

'I just can't seem to get off the sweets. It's now got so bad I have this fear of driving somewhere and finding that the glove compartment's empty. I never fill up with petrol and buy just fuel. Sometimes I've already eaten my first chocolate bar on the way back to the car after paying for the fuel. Keira goes mad if she finds empty sweet wrappers in the car door compartments. She thinks I'm ruining any chance I might have of long-term success, even though I've ridden more winners this season than any other jockey out there.' He said the last comment with a tinge of bitterness.

Eating disorders are notoriously difficult to work with. They are rarely about food and often involve a client using their food intake as one of the few things they can control in their lives. Often working with issues around food, sex and money (cynics would claim you can never have enough of all three!), I believe that a client is 'filling up' on one of these as a substitute for lack of love or attention.

As Richard spoke about his sweet tooth my mind wandered to consider his key relationships. So far, he'd discussed the critical father, desperate for Richard to have an Aintree winner, but he'd mentioned relatively little about his mother or his girlfriend, who herself came from a racing family. She too was desperate for Richard to succeed.

'Richard, tell me about the women in your life.'

'Where do you want me to start? We had a right to-do at

Newbury last week. Mum and Dad came with Keira to watch me ride. As luck would have it, I was riding on the favourite in the last race of the day. I came in three or four lengths clear and as I dismounted Mum and Dad were there in the winners' enclosure. Mum enjoys racing days because she gets to socialize with the other wives, but that day it was obvious that she'd had a few too many Pinot Grigios, and with the path being a bit uneven, the next thing we know she's stumbled and was down on all fours. Well, my old man goes all red-faced and then lets rip at Mum, calling her a "drunk" and a "disgrace", and then storms off.

'Me and Keira bundled Mum, who was all apologies and tears by this point, into my car and took her home, where we sat her down with some coffee to help her sober up and checked she was OK. Thankfully, she had got away with only a slight scape to one knee.'

Richard then went on to describe one of those seminal conversations you sometimes have with a parent when all the parent–child dynamics melt away and what's left is two vulnerable people being honest with each other. I remember mine with my own father a few days before he died. Richard's mum thought this was the moment to be honest with her son about her unhappiness in the marriage, and how she'd found herself regularly drinking greater and greater amounts of wine to dull her unhappiness. Like Richard, she'd been a promising fine art student when she'd met Richard's father, but had been seduced by the racing world and his place in it. After years of watching her husband never quite seem to achieve his full potential, and growing tired of supporting him, Richard's mother decided she'd like to re-ignite her painting career, but whenever she discussed it with him, she was met with ridicule. She was saddened to see

Richard lose his interest in art, and hoped he didn't end up regretting his move into racing in the same way she had.

'I asked my mum why she'd never told me this until now. She said she loved my dad, but felt that if she went against his wishes, the marriage would likely be over.'

It's all about love. Richard's mother stayed in an unhappy marriage because she couldn't bear not to be loved, so she behaved in a certain way to maintain the relationship, dulling the pain with drink. For his part, Richard ate sweets and chocolate to offset the pain that he too was living a life that, while successful, was empty and not bringing him happiness. They both had a hole in their soul.

Two days later I was in supervision with Tom and the work with Richard took up most of our time together. Tom looked at me over his spectacles as he scribbled notes on his A4 pad.

'What's going on with the girlfriend? How does she feel about his painting?' he said without looking up.

'Keira's complaining that Richard isn't taking his riding career seriously and wants him to forget about his hobby of painting.'

I waited for a moment before sharing with Tom what had transpired towards the end of my last session with Richard. Tom slurped his mug of tea and thought for a moment.

'Hmm', he eventually said. 'Just like his dad wanted his mum to give it up, I wonder if Dad is dealing with his own demons about smothering both his wife's and his son's fledgling art careers. Of course, Dad's defence to this could be that the end – as in Richard's successful racing career – justified the means.'

I took a moment to absorb this.

Then Tom asked, 'What are Richard's paintings about?'

'Always horses.'

Richard had brought a couple of his paintings in a few sessions back. A client's artistic life can be illuminating as to what might be going on for them internally. The imagination is a wonderful window to the unconscious and if I'm stuck with a sports client and appear to be getting nowhere, I'll sometimes ask them what their favourite films, books, art or pastimes are.

I once asked a rugby player to bring in an illustration of an artwork he'd like to discuss. He arrived with a postcard of Marcel Duchamp's *Fountain*, a porcelain men's urinal. It took forty minutes of the session for the prop forward to realize that he'd always believed the world was 'pissing on him'.

Richard's paintings of his horses were never peaceful. The faces, always in close-up, were angry, or in pain, or disturbed – frightened by unseen events. I had asked Richard in one session what he thought of the images. Nothing. Then I realized my mistake and asked him what he *felt* about the pictures.

'Angry. Just so fucking angry.'

'Like the horses, Richard?'

'No, they're scared.'

'Are you scared?'

Richard explained that he realized he was confused about his emotional life and knew deep down that he wasn't being true to himself by continuing to ride, however successful he'd become. The paintings of the scared horses were a message. Maybe that's why Keira didn't like them.

Richard had been about to leave the session, when he paused and turned to me. 'This isn't about Aintree, is it?' he asked.

My supervision session with Tom was coming to an end, just like the daylight outside, when Tom blindsided me.

'Do you think the girlfriend is afraid of the violent paintings and fears for Richard's sanity, and possibly even her own safety? Maybe she's not so much afraid of the fact he is painting, more of *what* he's painting.'

As usual, Tom's thinking provided a dimension to my work I hadn't fully considered. In a similar vein, Richard's father must have had his own concerns about his son's mental health when he saw the paintings.

Tom asked me if I had any concerns for Richard's state of mind or the welfare of his girlfriend.

'It's a fair question, but my feeling is no. I think the paintings are Richard's safety valve and they are trying to tell those around him something very important.'

Tom nodded in agreement, adding, 'Your job is to help him move from implicit communication to explicit.'

Tom put his pad down and sighed.

'He's an angry boy on an angry horse. He needs to find a sense of loving himself. All the sweets and chocolate in the world can't take away the bitter taste in his mouth.'

Eddie Stamp

Had Too Much to Think

I was never sure Eddie Stamp would turn up for any of our sessions because he always seemed reluctant to commit to a time and date. Each time I boarded the train north I wondered whether it was going to be a wasted journey. Unusually, however, Eddie had requested another session out of the blue, and after juggling a few appointments in my diary, and using the meeting as an opportunity to catch up with an old friend who lived nearby the night before, I went to see him.

He had asked to see me before training at 8.30 a.m. I sat alone in the training-ground clinic space, and after fifteen minutes of waiting, I presumed Eddie wasn't coming. I reflected on our last session and remembered the emotional outburst when I'd suggested Eddie's envy of the younger players might be driving his anger, and how he could end up being envious of his own son.

And then Eddie came in, looking terrible. He was bleary-eyed, as if he hadn't slept, and looked shaken. He apologized and said he'd been feeling unwell for the last twenty-four hours, so I asked him if he was well enough to start the session or even be at the training ground, because if he was still ill, it was possible he could pass any illness on to the other players. I got a strong whiff of shame from Eddie, followed by a stronger whiff of alcohol. Eddie said he'd had to come because the FA had been checking up on him to make sure he had been attending our sessions.

The odour of alcohol and stale sweat hit my nostrils as he sat down in the chair opposite me, and I noticed Eddie's hands were shaking slightly when he placed his mobile phone on the table. Face down this time. Ethically and professionally, I cannot treat people who are under the influence of drugs or alcohol and I let Eddie know this. He denied he'd been drinking and started to get angry when he saw I didn't believe him.

Silence hung in the room. I said nothing in the face of his angry stare, waiting for Eddie to start talking again.

'OK, OK, I was on the piss last night, all right? I may have had a few more than usual but I'm perfectly fine now. To be honest, I was quite nervous about today's session, so thought I'd have a drink to relax last night – I might have had more than I needed just to relax. I could have done without the hassle this morning, though. I've just been pulled over by a copper. He said I was speeding, but I don't think I was. Anyway, luckily he was a massive fan of this club and told me to get here safely and get some breakfast inside me.'

He was rubbing his forehead with his hand. I wasn't sure if he was trying to smooth his thinking or soothe his aching head.

I stayed silent until he looked at me and said, with an air of faint desperation in his voice, 'Shit. I know I've had a lucky escape. That's why my hands are shaking.'

There was silence again.

Eddie had put me in a very difficult position. Should I tell anyone at the club about a potential drinking problem which could impact on his professional duties, or was this a one-off indiscretion I was meant to overlook? He certainly didn't look in a position to take a training session, and I could insist that he report in sick and go home as soon as possible after he'd sobered up from the previous night. What really wound me up was that Eddie was suggesting that it was my fault that he'd been drinking the night before because he was nervous about our session today, worried he would have another emotional breakdown like the last time.

Once again, I didn't know what to do. Should I stop the session because Eddie had been drinking in the last twelve hours or carry on? I quickly made a decision. I thought that Eddie, because of what had just happened to him, might be more truthful and honest with me, hoping I'd keep quiet about it. I decided to press on.

'Eddie, are you finding the sessions with me hard?'

He burped loudly. 'Let's put it this way, I wouldn't have drunk last night if I hadn't had to come and see you this morning. Things seem to be getting worse since you and I started talking to each other.'

I asked him in what way they were getting worse.

'Now, when I get angry, I'm frightened about what I'm going to say and do. Previously, I didn't even think about it, but since our last session, I've not been able to sleep properly and I keep worrying that if I get too angry I might not be able to control it.'

He looked a bit lost, and I felt a wave of sympathy for him, as he was having to deal with completely alien emotions that he had no idea how to manage.

'That's really positive progress, Eddie. Have you been really angry since our last session?'

He looked at me with deep suspicion. 'I don't know what you've done to me, but I hope you know what you're doing and I'm not some sort of guinea pig.'

Ignoring his outburst, I explained to Eddie what psycho-therapy is all about – that by talking about issues that are troubling us, it opens up deep and sometimes painful mem-ories that have formed our behaviours over the years. The point is to try and identify why we behave the way we do, because then, by understanding why we do something, we can change it. Basically, it's not magic but, just like lancing a boil, it can be quite painful before ultimately making us better.

I asked him about his drinking, how often and how much? I told him that he needed to be honest with himself, not me. He admitted to worrying levels of alcohol consumption, but for him, he said, they were relatively low, and he kept his drinking to the weekends after matches usually.

I talked to him about what alcohol does to the brain and in particular how the limbic (emotional) part of the brain gets even stronger when fuelled by alcohol. I also described the dopamine hit he got every time he drank alcohol and discussed his self-care, how he looked after himself and who looked after him. He was transformed from the grizzled, hardened scrapper to a lost little boy.

'Blimey, Gaz, I've no idea. Never really thought about it. I don't think anyone has ever really looked after me. I look after loads of people – my elderly dad, my missus, my son, who plays havoc at school – everybody. I do my best. My mum and dad were not gushy, huggy people. I'm not one for talking about my feelings and such. Just like when I was a lad, if my lad goes over the top, he knows what's coming and it ain't pretty.'

His phone bleeped a notification and, lost in thought, he

picked it up and put it in his pocket. I felt a small thrill of accomplishment that he had put his phone away without being asked, but I couldn't revel in the success, knowing that we were at a major point in Eddie's therapeutic journey.

'Do you love your son, Eddie?'

He looked uncomfortable before replying, 'What sort of question's that? Of course, I love him. Fuck off! I pay for all his computer games. I go to watch him play for his academy. I give him a clip round his ear when he's misbehaved.'

I thought of an old pop song by the band Squeeze: 'Is That Love?'

What Eddie had effectively disclosed was that he found it very hard to be a benevolent parent, using a kindly voice, a gentle touch. It struck me that Eddie simply ignored his son, paid for stuff or chastised him. Eddie was only repeating what had happened to him earlier in his life, when there was a clear lack of benevolent love, and now he didn't know how to deal with his own emotions, or the emotions of his wife or son.

I asked Eddie if he thought that his boy was repeating his own actions and behaviours as a boy – communicating his anger by playing up at school, being aggressive or venting his emotions through violence. I asked if he thought it likely that his lad would end up just like him, maybe covering up his anger with alcohol.

Out came the mobile phone, as if Eddie needed to distract himself by playing with something in his hands. I could see he was really struggling with the strength of his emotions, and I asked him if he could tell me what he was feeling just then. He continued to turn his phone round and round in his hand in silence for a few minutes, not able to look at me, then he managed to get out one word: 'No.' I could see him blinking furiously, so gave him time to compose himself before asking him to tell me about his son.

There was no mistaking the pride and affection he felt for the boy as he talked about how he was such a good footballer, really good at school, much cleverer than Eddie ever was, and he wasn't going to let anyone push him around.

I then asked Eddie if he could see any similarities between his son's behaviour and his. Eddie's shoulders began to shake and they wouldn't stop. It's sometimes difficult to watch a grown man cry and, boy, did Eddie cry. Huge sobs with his head bowed.

He kept uttering the same phrase over and over again: 'He can't be me. He can't be me. He can't be me.'

Eddie carried on crying for a little longer. Years of anger and frustration spilled out of him – years of fights and alcohol and bruising tackles. It began with a trickle and ended up like a waterfall.

Bizarrely, the sobs suddenly stopped and he found a few seconds of utter calm. Long enough to say, 'Lock the door. I can't have anybody seeing me like this.'

Kwasi Adepodji

Growing Pains

A football club dressing room is an emotionally volatile place after a game. Often the manager will come in, say a few brief words and leave it there. The better coaches and managers I've worked with recognize that they themselves are too emotionally involved straight after a game to engage in a post-mortem with their players. In the past ten years, with greater video technology and statistical information at their fingertips, many managers will retreat to their office or find a quiet spot to review footage of a particular incident or goal or miss before talking to the players.

The general atmosphere after the match in which Kwasi played when he'd replaced the regular centre forward who was serving a ban was positive. There was an overall feeling that the team could have done better, but given the conditions (blustery and playing into the wind in the second half) and against a spirited opposition, three points wasn't a bad return for the afternoon's work. Apart from Kwasi being jeered as he left the pitch, it had been a pretty good day overall, and even the crowd numbers were slightly up on normal, meaning more revenue for the club.

As I entered the dressing room I could barely see Kwasi. Many of the players were on their feet, chatting or taking advantage of the portable buffet of pasta and chilli con carne that had arrived as they began the process of 'carbing up' after their exertions. Amid the steam wafting through from the shower room, soiled kit and players chatting excitedly or on their mobile phones, there was Kwasi sitting in the corner. He was still in full kit and was sitting, knees apart and head bowed, staring at the green AstroTurf floor, which was marked out like a football pitch. I saw a couple of players approach him, but he said nothing and didn't even acknowledge their presence.

In these circumstances it's difficult to know what to do for the best, as his emotional temperature was difficult to read – he could have been trying to hold on to a volcanic temper or spiralling down into a pit of despair. Say something to him and risk being the lightning rod for any anger and frustration he might be harbouring, or ignore him and pick it up another time, but face accusations of neglect. There was no point saying 'Well done' to him. Other players had done that and got nowhere.

What was clear was he was not at all present as he sat there cloaked in his own thoughts, and the good wishes and positivity were completely passing him by. I decided to take the plunge and moved over to him. I felt it was important to meet him eye to eye to make sure he couldn't ignore my overture.

I crouched down on my knees and said, 'Kwasi, do you want to talk?'

I wasn't sure he'd heard me at first, but then he shook his head, keeping his gaze locked on the floor in front of him.

'OK, we can pick this up on Tuesday after training, or feel free to phone me tonight if you fancy a chat. You've got my number?'

He nodded.

It is unusual for players to contact me at the weekend, but Kwasi did ring the next evening.

'I hope you don't mind me calling. I've been unable to sleep since the match yesterday. The doc gave me some sleepers but I'm not feeling great,' he said, sounding hesitant, as if unsure why he'd phoned.

'What's going on, Kwasi?'

I try to keep things as open as possible with clients who are in the midst of an emotional tsunami.

'I haven't told anyone this but . . .' His voice dropped to almost a whisper. 'During the match, when our keeper got injured, their centre half came over to me and said that I was a fucking disgrace to the sport. Told me I'm the easiest opponent he's ever played against, I'm not fit and that he was even thinking of not bothering to mark me as it was almost beneath him. He said that as well as "fucking hookers" I was fucking my entire team, because he thought I wasn't even trying. Then he walked away, turned towards me and spat on the ground.'

Kwasi's sense of who he was had taken a good kicking. As his therapist I was powerless to stop such verbal assaults, but my job from now on was to help him be more resilient to them. Then, for the first time, Kwasi started talking about the incident that had brought him this notoriety. He said he was excited to see his friends from Accra, he got a bit giddy, a bit show-offy, and suddenly his friends were with a group of women in a hotel room and things got out of hand.

I suspected that the sexual experiences he had had were, as well as an opportunity to swagger with his friends, an attempt to create some form of intimacy, as he'd seemed unable to find real emotional closeness up to this point. Many people seek out a sexual experience right at the start of a relationship thinking it will bring them the intimacy they crave. It rarely does.

Kwasi talked about how much he enjoyed the freedom of living away from home, able to do exactly what he pleased away from the gaze of his family. He talked about the pressures placed on him to find a 'suitable' woman and settle down in a conventional relationship. When I pushed him about what 'suitable' meant he said ideally Ghanaian or, if not, definitely African at least.

Kwasi said he enjoyed the freedom to date and have liaisons with women of all races, but he feared falling in love with a woman Mum and Dad wouldn't approve of. In short, he wasn't ready to deal with the fallout an 'improper' relationship would generate from his parents. This meant he was condemned to short-term inconsequential relationships that had no future. If they did have some promise, Kwasi said he felt like he'd have to end them.

A few ideas were percolating in my head around this young man and how best to help him. Meanwhile, I had to be mindful of the needs of the team. Simon Cooper, the regular centre forward, had two games left of his three-game ban and Kwasi was the only real alternative in that position. I needed to help Kwasi short term so he would be able to perform on the pitch as well. This is one of the hardest things to deal with in a club. As one manager said to me, 'I don't give a shit about the psychological well-being of the players. If we lose the next six games, I'm gone, and so are you!'

Kwasi's desire for intimacy in his private life was being undermined by short-term flings that left him feeling worse about himself. He was either rejected by women wanting a more substantial relationship or he deliberately sabotaged a healthy relationship for fear of getting too closely involved.

His was a common problem for young men newly unleashed on the world with the wherewithal to buy themselves any pleasure they chose. They all think they want to put it about, trading on the fame that being a footballer brings without having to put in any effort. But when the hangover and excitement have faded, it just leaves them feeling miserable and insecure, not to mention vulnerable to all manner of accusations that could have calamitous consequences.

It was also clear that Kwasi had not yet fully disengaged from his family life back in Ghana and was still under the control, either consciously or unconsciously, of his parents. He was stuck in the dilemma most young people face, wanting to maintain the protection and warmth of their families, while still having the excitement of moving into the big wide world without having to deal with parental judgement.

The goal of therapy is for the client to have a healthy regard for themselves, and that means liking yourself *without* the need for a romantic relationship. Right now, Kwasi needed to be a happier individual, which would allow him to play better, rather than go for the short-term sugar rush of a one-night stand that ultimately left him feeling empty.

The football club was inevitably less than wholly sympathetic in the way it viewed the situation. Eric, the assistant coach, listened to my psychological insights and nodded briefly before leaning in towards me and saying, 'I don't care if he shags half the city, as long as he scores on Saturday.'

In an ideal world, helping a client to gently pull away from

the orbit of their parents and forge a fulfilling life for him-
or herself would take months. But in a football club you don't
have months; sometimes you have only weeks or even days.
I had to get Kwasi mentally ready to face yet another possibly
brutish centre half at the weekend.

James Holmes

Sisters and Smiles

I wasn't sure if I was going to see James again, given that he'd ended the last session telling me he'd be in touch if he needed more therapy. I discussed James's case with Tom, telling him about James's revelations about his mother's emotional distress around the time of his birth and her serious illness when he was seven.

Tom steered me towards considering James's attachment style, as there were two major incidents in his early life that could well have contributed to his adult behaviour. There's a theory about how our personalities develop and it goes something like this. All babies have some primary caregiver (usually a mother) and the quality of the developing attachment between the two of them from birth can go a long way to determining how the child makes, creates and maintains relationships for the rest of their life.

Psychoanalyst John Bowlby was the originator of attachment theory and it was his belief that most of us fall into one of three different 'attachment styles'. With the securely attached child, Mum and baby develop a dependable relationship where the baby thrives in the knowledge that Mum will look after their needs. Such children then grow up, experience the world as a safe place and can adapt to new situations. They tend to take new experiences in their stride, are not thrown by unfamiliar circumstances and are likely to be popular.

With anxious or resistant attachment, Mum finds it hard to really connect with the baby and is emotionally removed in spite of meeting the child's basic needs. This could be for a variety of reasons, such as illness, bereavement, an unplanned pregnancy, sibling rivalry, relationship issues, financial concerns or, in James's case, post-natal depression. Such children grow up afraid of the world and new situations and try to control their surroundings. They might be aggressive if they can't get what they want, becoming involved in fights in the playground at school. Learning to love or even like themselves is quite challenging.

Babies and children who have an avoidant attachment style want closeness with their caregivers, but they can quickly learn to stop seeking closeness or expressing emotion when parents or caregivers are emotionally unavailable. If children become aware that they'll be rejected by the parent or caregiver if they express themselves, they adapt. Such children appear emotionally distant or 'closed off' and find it hard to maintain intimacy or friendships. They might be quite alone at playtime at school, with few if any close friends.

James struck me as someone who had an anxious attachment style and his inability to control his surroundings, as, for example, when on tour, gave me the strongest clue. In later life, the anxiously attached child will often try hard to control others and their environment, because only then can they control their own feelings and emotions.

The fact that James's mum had nearly died was bound to

have had some effect on the mother–child relationship, and as he'd mentioned at some stage 'I'm quite like Mum,' I was guessing there was some anxiety present in Mrs Holmes too. My theory of course could be wrong, but it certainly passed the 'duck test': *If it looks like a duck, swims like a duck and quacks like a duck, then it probably is a duck.*

It was now October and the cricket season was all done and dusted. The radio sports bulletins, which were usually littered with county cricket championship scores, were now refocused on football gossip and groin strains and early managerial changes. I hadn't heard from James for several weeks and, as with many a client who disappears suddenly, I began to believe that he'd gained the strength to not need a therapist and so must be feeling good about something in his life.

Autumn is usually when I see cricketers, because they have a bit more spare time in the off-season, but it was still a surprise when one afternoon a brief text arrived from James: 'CAN YOU SEE ME THIS WEEK?' All capital letters, no explanation. I doubt he could have conveyed his wishes in fewer characters.

I was mildly annoyed by the lack of social niceties. And with it an arrogant assumption that my clinic was quiet enough to accommodate him at a few days' notice. Brushing aside my irritation, I tried to work out what James was conveying, apart from the obvious, and thought his use of capitals might mean 'This is important.'

I texted back that I had had a cancellation in a few days' time and could see him then. When he came, he made no reference to the fact that we hadn't seen each other in several weeks and jumped straight in, saying that he'd been sleeping poorly recently. He also told me that things weren't going smoothly with Annabel, and again it was her suggestion that he came back to therapy.

I spotted the subtext 'I don't want to be here, but my mum/dad/partner said I'd better come' and wondered if it was James's way of not being able to admit he needed help. This attitude often pushes the client into a childlike role, essentially claiming that he or she has no power to challenge another person's wishes.

'James, we should be straight with each other from the get-go. I can't treat a client who is only here because another person has told them they have to be. If you wish to engage in therapy with me, that's great and I'll try to help you, but I think it's about time we stopped dancing around the subject.'

It was a bold statement but I felt I needed to reassert my professional boundaries about how I worked.

'OK, both Annabel and I agreed it was a smart move to come and see you again. We've not been getting on at all well since the season ended, and what's made it worse is that I haven't heard from any of the lads since the end-of-season drinks. Not many of them spoke to me in the pub and I left feeling a bit flat. When I mentioned it to Annabel, she said she wasn't surprised, since I'd been acting all stand-offish and a bit superior.'

'Is she right, James?'

'Well, I've never been the life and soul of the party. Some people might think I'm a bit serious. That's all.'

'How are you feeling about it now? It must be six weeks since you saw your teammates.'

His face creased in pain, as if he'd had to field a stinging catch from a teammate. 'I feel . . . I dunno, it feels like I'm invisible. Like no one can see me, no one cares. As if I'm out of sight, out of mind.'

'Like when you were seven and your parents sent you off to your grandparents when Mum was ill?'

James sat bolt upright in his chair. 'Bloody hell, do we have to keep going back to that?' He took a few deep breaths and let them out slowly. 'I've thought about it quite a bit since we saw each other last. Look, I'm sorry if I reacted badly during that conversation. I think you hit quite a raw nerve.'

'I'm sorry too, James. My intention was never to damage you, but it's a scar that I think needs to heal properly.'

James said that since we met last he'd been to see his mum. He'd never had the chance to talk to her about her burst appendix and the illness that had almost cost her her life.

'It was like a great unmentionable after she recovered,' he said. 'Family life gradually got back to normal and it was kind of decided that everybody had probably overreacted – all a bit of a silly misunderstanding really. You know, Mum was never going to *actually* die, so what was all the fuss about?'

'Do you think it changed you, James?'

'Oh, hard to say. I was just a young lad. I remember after-wards being teased at school for being too serious. The other kids started calling me "Smiler" because I never smiled. Even to this day my teammates use that nickname. I've never been a throw-my-head-back-and-laugh kind of guy. I'm quite like my mum in that respect.'

'Tell me about your mum.'

'She's really kind and we're very close.' There was a soft, dreamy look to his expression.

'Do you remember her smiling and laughing as a child? You talk about your childhood being a happy one – was Mum the source of that fun?'

The question seemed to confuse James, so I asked him if

he understood what I meant. Absently, he said he understood clearly, but was trying to think back to his youth.

'You know, I can't remember her laughing much at all. In fact "fun" isn't a word I'd use to describe Mum at all.'

The contemplative frown told me that James had never really considered this before. He then started revealing more about his mum, describing how when she was pregnant with him, her teenage younger sister died in a car accident, and although she'd never talked about it before, James had a strong feeling it had affected her deeply. His mum had only really started talking to him about it in the last few weeks, telling James that when he was born, all she could think about was that her sister would never get to meet him. He said the way she talked about her sister revealed a profound sadness.

'So, you were born into a house of mourning, James.'

'I guess so. Never really thought about it. What difference would that make?'

And so James and I headed off down the path of psycho-education, with me explaining to him the rudiments of attachment theory and how his mother, so recently bereaved just before childbirth, probably didn't have the usual smiles and giggles for him that most babies would typically experience.

It seems likely that in those very early months of his life, his mother was often preoccupied and even distant. Perhaps his anxious style could be partly attributed to this. Preoccupied, anxious or depressed mothers may make their babies experience them as unreachable or even absent.

In the next few weeks James and I tried to deepen our understanding of his attachment style, why and how it had formed and how it affected his relationship with Annabel, explaining why he would suddenly become angry with her if he didn't get his way or didn't know where she was.

Gradually, James began to loosen his vice-like grip on those around him and a few weeks later 'Smiler' actually laughed in one of our sessions!

Edwin Thomas

It's Eating Away at Me

'Falling' in love – how interesting that we use the verb 'fall' when describing what is essentially a lack of control over our emotions. In my experience, clients who have cushioned the fall and are successful at finding loving relationships have first learned to value themselves and not be afraid of showing their own vulnerability. To really be in love means opening yourself up to the possibility of rejection, hurt and ridicule, but for many the reward is worth it.

However, we often confuse love with lust: we use the promise of love for others to gratify our desires and withhold love to control those for whom we claim to care deeply. The latter felt a very good fit for Edwin Thomas, whose control of his wife, Cerys, had resulted in her moving back home with her parents and needing therapy to deal with an eating disorder. But how did he end up like this? He'd had an ordinary childhood, ordinary parents, ordinary schooling with ordinary exam results, but then things got extraordinary when he picked up a rugby ball.

My supervisor, Tom, says teenage boys often have what he

terms a 'fear of ordinariness' and, working in schools, I've found this to be largely true. Adolescent girls tend to want to fit in, are desperate to be seen to conform and not stick out, whereas boys tend to enjoy having a clear identity in a group, be it bully, comedian or good at sports. Edwin told me his nickname was 'Tricky' Thomas because of his ability to throw a feint during a rugby match and suddenly change direction.

He told me this with great pride. But his love of being the best at rugby in his school and then junior club had created what psychologists might describe as 'maladaptive behaviour' – that is, everything that advanced his rugby career was relished and anything that took away from his career was disposed of quickly. Which of these camps was Cerys now in? She'd certainly helped him build up the celebrity-couple notion, but was he ever going to be able to put her needs – and more pressingly, her basic need of good health – above his career, which, from once being stellar, had begun to slip back towards the ordinary. I suspected Edwin was hurting.

In Edwin's next session he was particularly animated when telling me about a recent incident. He'd been out drinking with a couple of teammates when one of them pulled him aside and said, 'Listen, bud, I'd rather you heard it from me, but there's rumour going around that your missus has moved back in with her parents. Gerry's [the club's full back] mum lives on their street, and you know she's a bit of a gossip, and she says she sees your Cerys around the town most days.'

Edwin told me his mood darkened immediately on hearing this. He spun his teammate a story about Cerys's mum not being very well and said that Cerys had gone to look after her while her dad was out at work.

'Cerys is bloody well mine and I've got to put a stop to this nonsense, don't you think?'

I said nothing. At some point, most of my clients ask for my advice – which I always refuse to offer. Basically, if I do give them advice and it turns out to be good advice, there's a risk I turn them into a child who can't think for themselves, but if it turns out to be the wrong advice they'll think I'm an idiot.

'Cerys and I need to get back on track. What's she doing with her bloody parents? We need to be together so we can, you know, start thinking about having a family.'

I noted the 'we need' – did Cerys share that need?

'Well, she can stay there for a bit longer yet,' Edwin then said.

I noticed the gear change and Edwin also changed position in his seat, before continuing, 'To be honest, I've felt a bit less pressure in the past few weeks. My training's gone a bit better and I'm in with half a chance of starting at the weekend in a Welsh cup game.'

I asked him more about Cerys and he explained that she was getting treatment for her 'so-called' eating disorder and that they'd had a few more 'civil' conversations of late. He said she seemed to be feeling the benefit of her own counselling sessions and while living with her parents she'd put on a few pounds. 'It's obviously her mum's cooking that's fattening her up,' he said with an element of derision.

As he stood up to leave the session Edwin announced, 'You'll see, she'll be back to full fitness in no time and at home with me. Don't forget to send us the bill, mate.'

It was as if he felt the situation had been resolved and he needed to reinforce the employer–employee relationship between us. And with that, he was out of the door.

*

A week later, I went to see my supervisor. Tom answered the door in his usual flannel shirt and a heavy-knit V-neck pullover. He always greeted me with a warm smile as if I was the only person in the world he wanted to see at that moment.

'You're early for supervision! Fancy a cuppa?'

After discussing another rugby player who had a gambling addiction, he asked about Edwin and Cerys. I admitted I was struggling with the work. On the one hand I wanted Edwin to recover his form as soon as possible and, according to Edwin, the best chance of that happening was if Cerys returned. However, his improving form seemed to suggest differently, so was her presence relevant to his rugby performance? Also, I couldn't help feeling that if Cerys was going to live a fulfilling life, she'd be better off away from Edwin.

Tom looked over the top of his glasses and said, 'Look, psychotherapy is about change. This is about *both* Edwin and Cerys making real changes to their lives to make the relationship tenable. From what you say, Cerys is doing the changing, but Edwin doesn't want to or even see the need to. He can't put Cerys's needs above his, because frankly he's never done that in any relationship he's ever had. Rugby has always come first.'

While he was undoubtedly right, for once I didn't find Tom's comments that helpful. Clients can suddenly get better with a change of circumstances. When their frame of reference changes, so does the way they view their situation. As I was soon to discover, for Edwin it was a change of circumstances that altered this story.

When I saw him a few weeks later, Edwin was dressed slightly more formally in a shirt and tie with a sports jacket, and as he sat down, I had the impression that a business meeting was about to take place rather than a therapy session.

'I've got some news to tell you,' he said. 'I've been offered a player-coach role up north on a three-year deal and I think I'm gonna take it. Fresh start and all that. And they've offered Cerys a job too in their marketing department. Double win. I've told Cerys and she's keen to go too, but she's been arguing with her parents, who don't want her to. It's top money for both of us, gives us security, and they've also thrown in a place for us to live in a posh new canal-side development. Cerys took some bloody persuading, but last night she said "yes". There's loads of terms and conditions from Cerys about me easing up on the control stuff, but to be honest, I'd agree to running down the rugby pitch naked right now if it got us up north together!'

Edwin had been to see Cerys, taking her flowers and chocolates (hardly the ideal gift for a woman with an eating disorder!), but despite this lack of sensitivity, his charm offensive had apparently paid off.

'You can tell she's put a bit of weight on – she looks a million dollars now.'

I asked Edwin whether he could go north without Cerys, or if she was part of the package that he needed for his new role. It seemed that her presence wasn't necessary, but Edwin had been adamant that he wouldn't go without her so had negotiated the deal with her very much in mind.

'Do you think Cerys is well enough to go with you at this point?'

I was trying to drill down to find out if Edwin was really able to think about what Cerys needed *before* what he needed. I pointed out that her recovery had come while she'd been living with Mum and Dad and seeing a counsellor. All three people were going to be pulled away from Cerys's life with the move north.

'Look, bud . . .' His words couldn't have been delivered in a more patronizing way. 'I get your concern, like, but I am the best person to look after my sodding wife. Just sorted her out with the deal of the century at one of the best rugby union clubs in the north of England. Whatever she wants she can have. That's the deal if I'm gonna keep my end of the bargain with her.'

I asked him more about the new accommodation.

'We're going to live in one of those places where they've done up some old canal warehouses. Bars, restaurants and all the works within a short rugby pass of my front door. It's gonna be a-mazing. I can coach or I can play. Depending on the tactics of the team, I can . . .'

I let him carry on about how wonderful life would be for them both when they moved, then asked, 'Is there somewhere for Cerys's parents to stay if they want to visit?'

Edwin pointed to the side of his head and tapped a couple of times. He had a self-satisfied smile on his face.

'Yeah, mate. She wants a flat large enough for her parents to stay over and I've told her if that's what she wants, that's what she can have.'

At last we were getting somewhere.

'That's what I've told *her*. What I've told the club, though, is that we only want a one-bedroomed place initially, but with membership to the local gym thrown in as part of the package. I'll break the news when we get up there and tell Cerys the guest bedroom just wasn't possible on the club budget. I can do without her parents stirring things for us like they do here.'

I had a vision of him taking a simple conversion and the crowd clutching their heads in frustration as the ball sailed wide of the posts.

Madison King

French Connection

Tom had talked to me before about therapy being to do with rupture and repair, and although there was pressure on the friendship between Madison and Becky, nothing had pushed them apart – yet. But all that was to change one Monday afternoon when Becky returned unexpectedly from Leeds to the house she had shared with Madison. I say 'unexpected', but Madison must have known that her friend would return at some stage, at the very least to pick up some more clothes. When she did, Madison had been drinking G&Ts all afternoon, so Becky arrived to find the house and Madison in a dreadful state. I suspected this was *exactly* how Madison wished to be found.

'I was completely shitfaced,' admitted Madison in our next session, 'but I'd just got to the stage where I didn't care any more. We had a storm-force-eleven row and I said some stupid things. I told her I was going to return to football again, and if I ended up a cabbage, well, so be it. I cannot stand living in this shadow of being frightened to do this or that. I'd rather risk permanent brain damage and get on with my career.'

She reminded me of a small sulky child threatening to run away from home after being rebuked by a parent and thinking 'Then you'll be sorry!' We all have a duty of self-care and what Madison was doing was thumbing her nose at that. She was threatening her own life and pulling anyone close to her down into the vortex with her. As I saw it, the two women were fighting for survival, and a therapeutic treatment plan for Madison suddenly opened in my mind.

She continued, 'Becky called me all the names under the sun. She said I was being a selfish cow and she couldn't recognize who I was any more. I told her to run off back to Leeds. I was so pissed, to be honest, I couldn't make out what was going on, but suddenly Becky had packed a suitcase and was gone.'

'Maddy, let's go back to the start of the friendship with Becky. When you were both at school, what made it special?'

Madison looked at me quizzically, then said, 'I dunno.'

'It's important for you to understand what it means when someone cares about you. Becky is incredibly compromised right now, torn between her career in Leeds and London, and caring about someone who is in full self-destruct mode. The point I'm getting at, Maddy, is this bond between you isn't measurable. It's slow and gradual, with thousands of tiny acts of kindness that maybe you're hardly aware of. Like noticing when she's not feeling great, the odd compliment, the girls' nights out, sharing intimate chats about your boyfriends, the cup of tea or meal you make for each other, a hug when one of you is down – loads of things where you put someone else before you. You going back to playing football isn't putting Becky or anyone else before you. It could well be locking someone – Becky, your mum and dad or a future boyfriend – into a life of looking after you, or coping with the financial pressure of finding you a carer because you are no longer able to look after yourself, or watching you deteriorate in front of their eyes and not being able to do anything about it. How can you genuinely love anyone if you cannot truly love yourself, Maddy? Returning to playing football again is a form of self-abuse, but in fact you're visiting that abuse on others. Is that really love?'

Madison was silent.

'Look at it this way. After your accident, Becky took advantage of an opportunity that had suddenly opened up – a chance to grow, expand, take on new dimensions. Do you think that is a coincidence? Maybe while she has been involved in keeping an eye on you it has consumed her emotional bandwidth. Now she has a chance to mix properly with her workmates and find a true role for herself in the world. Not just as your friend. If you really care for Becky, you're going to have to support her being the best possible version of herself. And that might be difficult for you, Maddy, while you are in a spiral of despair about the loss of your own career.'

She looked truly shocked now, but I had to keep going.

'Let's suppose you never see her again, do you think any future person in your life is going to buy into this version of the world you have planned?'

I had an image of a personal ad on a dating site: *Bitter former professional female footballer with anger issues seeks compliant chap who might have an interest in being their carer for the next forty years. Must be conversant with dealing with depression, anxiety and some abuse of alcohol.*

Madison let my words sink in for a few moments. I could see her fighting with herself not to get angry, while at the same time trying hard to process the information. I hoped she was reviewing her relationship not only with Becky but also with herself. Had Madison always been selfish, or had she been able to put another person's needs before hers? She twisted her head one way and then the other, as if there were two sets of scales in her head trying to balance each other out.

After a while she began again. 'So what you're saying is that I might be holding Becky back?'

'What I'm saying, Maddy, is what's done is done. It's more about now. Do you have the capacity to support Becky or anyone right now? And what does the friendship with Becky mean to you if all you can concentrate on is how this new friend of hers might replace you? It feels more like a play-ground spat than you really thinking about what's best for yourself and her.'

Madison was quiet for a short while, then she quickly stood and said, 'You really don't understand what's going on for me. I can't lose Becky. I've lost everything else. She has been the one constant in my life. Everything else is going down the fucking plughole.'

'Madison, I do understand, but your behaviour is pushing Becky away, so you're going to end up losing Becky unless you begin to be kinder to yourself.'

Her eyes reddened. 'I can't deal with this. I need to go.' And with that, she left.

Had I pushed Madison too far? Here was another rupture, but this time between client and therapist, and I was feeling thrown by the way she had suddenly left the session. But maybe I had allowed her to see her predicament clearly. Only time would tell. As often happens in these circum-stances, I struggle not to feel like a bad therapist, but thankfully, Madison called me forty-eight hours later and made a new appointment.

When I next saw her, she told me that she didn't want to

lose Becky because she was scared of what life might be like on her own. As she put it, 'I'm 400 miles away from my parents and family. I have no partner and no future. The only person I've been close to since the age of nine is pulling away from me and would rather be in some godforsaken northern city.'

Towards the end of the session, Madison asked me, 'Where the bloody hell do I start? That's why I got so upset last week. I've just no idea what to do.'

'Well, if you want to demonstrate that you can be thoughtful about Becky, you're going to have to demonstrate you can look after yourself.'

The bereavement process was moving gently towards acceptance. It would take a while, but in our next sessions Madison slowly began to realize that her career was over and her thrashing around in self-pity was pointless. Instead we created a timetable of how she would usefully spend her days at home, thinking about a career change and cutting right back on her drinking. We agreed that she wouldn't drink for a seven-day period (between our sessions) and we renewed this each week. I have learned that clients find it easier to agree to a short period of giving something up which is renewed weekly rather than commit to months and years of abstinence.

Without Becky around sparking a domestic row, Madison's moods began to even themselves out. She could recognize her anger ebbing and flowing, learned to do breathing exercises and even enrolled on a local yoga course.

One week she bounded into the session with an energy I'd never seen before.

Breathlessly the words tumbled out of her mouth: 'I'm going to the World Cup, the World Cup. In France.'

I had visions of her somehow planning a return to playing football, with all the risks that would entail for her. I feared we were going backwards.

'I don't understand, Maddy.'

'Scottish TV have asked me. Me, on the box!'

Last Sessions and Impressions

A supervisor once said to me that in therapy you should always have an ending in mind during each and every session, to help set a direction. Just as you wouldn't turn up at a railway station without an idea of where you're going, the same is true in my work. The client may meander here and there to all sorts of interesting backwaters, but the two fundamental questions I am always asking myself are 'Where are we going?' and 'How far are we on the journey?'

When it comes to sport, the endings I have experienced fall somewhere on a scale between those who after one or two sessions claim to be 'cured' and no longer need help and those who see me as a permanent part of their lives, so never get to an ending. The majority fall somewhere in the middle.

Then there are the tricky ones. One footballer I worked with made initial progress, but then suffered an injury and all his psychological demons returned. The intense pressure and stress of being injured often mean the client reverts to the same defence mechanisms that brought them to therapy in the first place – back to square one!

Then there are the sports clients who 'ghost' you. They don't turn up for their session at the allotted time and then fail to respond to a text or voice message. These clients concern me the most, as I'm left with anxiety about their well-being. Maybe that's the point. They want someone to be worried about them, because they don't have the emotional software to worry or care about themselves. Despite my training, I can sometimes get cross about being 'ghosted' and wonder why they can't even be bothered to phone or send a text. But as Tom sometimes needs to remind me, 'Just remember, this isn't about you!'

The best endings are planned between therapist and client, when it is jointly agreed that the therapy is drawing to a conclusion and the number of remaining sessions can be planned. Research has shown that clients' (and therapists') memories and experience of therapy are often coloured by how it ends.

To take an example, think of a romantic relationship that has ended. If that person simply walked out without a goodbye or cheated on you, that would affect how you see the whole relationship. Now compare that to the more grown-up ending of 'We need to talk about this relationship because it's not working. I wonder if we can rescue a friendship out of it.' If that was done in a kind, genuine and authentic way, which would work better for you and how would you view that relationship now?

Unfortunately, in sports psychotherapy many of the endings are unplanned. Players may leave a club or get injured, and maybe you don't see them for weeks, or ever again. In this section we'll see our ten athletes reaching the end of their therapeutic journeys, from the most carefully planned to the downright surreal, and with varying degrees of 'success'. The end of a therapeutic relationship is like any other ending. It can be painful, funny or sad. The best I can aim for is to make it kind, hoping that the client has felt the benefit of therapy and has learned to understand themselves better.

Tony Oldfield

The DNA of DNA

Waiting in my therapy room for Tony to arrive, I noticed the hands on the clock ticking past the appointment time of 3 p.m. He was never usually late, and indeed was usually a few minutes early, so I wondered if there was an issue with traffic that was causing him to run late. I checked my mobile phone. No messages.

Whenever clients are running late, it leaves me with a bit of a conundrum. What should I do? If I chase them it looks as if I'm desperate. If I ignore the situation it could look as if I don't care. I usually wait fifteen minutes before I send as neutral a text as possible. So that's what I did, texting Tony: 'Hope all's OK. We had a session booked today for 3 p.m. Let me know if there's a problem.' Ten minutes later and still no response from Tony. Nada.

This was quite out of character for him. The previous week, he'd been generally upbeat and positive. He said that he was getting closer to finally resolving things with Anna and that he'd had positive feedback about a part-time job he'd applied for as a visiting lecturer on a sports journalism course at a local university. It sounded like he thought the job was his.

I looked back at my session notes. The previous week he had been initially quite self-critical, having spent a considerable amount of money on yet another silent evening out with Anna at an expensive restaurant. 'I was sat there, thinking to myself, "What am I doing here with her?"' He told me all he could think about was the bill for the meal, and how he was choking on his food preparing to spend around £120 that he could ill afford on an evening that he hadn't even enjoyed.

I asked him why he continued to book evenings out with Anna, when he knew he couldn't afford it, or why at the very least he didn't ask her to contribute to the cost. He looked shocked at the idea of asking Anna to contribute, saying, 'You can't take a lady out and ask her to put her hand in her pocket. It's demeaning to both of us!'

I couldn't work out if he was falling back on old-fashioned values out of a genuine sense of chivalry or because it was a convenient excuse to avoid having a confrontation with Anna over whose turn it was to pay.

'Tony, imagine the fire alarm is ringing in that restaurant, what would you do?'

'I'd get out of course. What sort of question is that?'

'Think about your relationship with Anna. Think about the packet of paracetamol. Think about the pearl necklace. Now tell me, is the alarm ringing in this relationship?'

He did not answer, but instead talked about the possibility of ending things with Anna. 'Of course, I'd like to be with someone who at least seems to like me, but then I'm not sure there's anyone out there who would, and what if there isn't and I'm left on my own with absolutely no one to talk to or go out with? I'm not sure it's worth that risk.'

Sometimes my sessions with Tony reminded me of watching someone play tennis on their own up against a wall, returning every serve and shot, just as he answered his own comments and questions. Maybe he was well on the way to becoming his own therapist!

I have many male clients who are caught up in this sort of confusion. Staying isn't safe, leaving is too scary. They end up with a 'rabbit in the headlights syndrome', when the limbic area of the brain, which regulates the emotional side of behaviour, enters a 'fight, flight or freeze' mode. Tony was clearly in deep freeze.

My job is to bring the thinking or logical part of my clients' brain back online, so it is able to work in tandem with the emotional part. Some theorists believe that therapists loan clients their own logical thinking skills to help them make sense of the emotional turmoil that's going on in their own heads. Right now, though, I was trying to make sense of Tony's DNA (did not attend). By this time he was forty minutes late and was clearly a 'no show'. I felt a mixture of crossness and sadness. Cross that Tony had felt it was OK to walk out on our relationship without a word and sad that he clearly felt unable to tell me why. I certainly felt a sense of failure.

As usual I took my work to Tom. Sitting with his customary mug of tea, he took a sip as I explained I was being 'ghosted' by Tony. I expected some theoretical deconstruction of how I'd maybe missed something obvious or gone down a rabbit hole with Tony psychotherapeutically. Instead, Tom was silent for about a minute, deep in thought, and then he began.

'Clients do sometimes drop us like that. It doesn't feel

good and usually isn't warranted, but I'm afraid if you're going to worry about every client who does this to you, you'll end up needing more therapy than you're dishing out.'

Tom's words bit deep.

'Anyway,' he continued, 'you've got to get over your God complex.'

'Sorry?'

'All therapists think they can fix everyone. Tony's kicked you in the nuts and maybe that's a timely reminder that you simply can't fix everyone. Your job is to take Tony (or any other client) as far as you can. And you've done that. Maybe he'll find another therapist one day, maybe he won't, or maybe he'll latch on to another cruel woman, or marry the one he's with. You've done your job. It's the end of this chapter.'

I never saw Tony Oldfield again. But months later I was at a Championship football game in the Midlands and ran into Brian Stephens, who ran the sports journalism course at the university where I suspected Tony was now working. Brian was there with a group of students cutting their teeth on football reporting and mangling every cliché imaginable. Brian and I had once worked in the same newsroom back in the early part of our respective careers. He'd gone into teaching, while I'd followed a psychotherapy path.

Brian was laughing. 'Maybe I'm turning into an old fart, but I've got kids up there,' he said, pointing towards the press box, 'who are still writing "and the ball was in the back of the net". I've told them, "Where would you expect the bloody ball to be if it's a sodding goal?"'

We both laughed, but I wanted to kill off the ghost of Tony Oldfield.

'Brian, you know that job you advertised at your uni,

looking for an ex-player who'd help your students practise post-match interviews. Did you manage to fill the position?'

'No,' he said, 'no one applied. Odd, isn't it? Do you know anyone who might be interested?'

I shook my head. 'No, I don't.'

Richard Davies

'Easely' Does It

Richard had come for his sixth and final session with me paid for by the Riders Union. His issues – anger depicted in his paintings of distressed horses combined with confusion about whether he actually wanted to be a jockey or not, and having a sweet tooth – did not meet their requirement for more funded therapy. Addiction to recreational drugs would have justified further sessions, but to them addiction to Mars bars didn't.

The session was tricky to organize as our dates seemed to clash and it had been moved a number of times – something new in our work together. He didn't mention why his diary was so cluttered all of a sudden, so I waited until our final meeting to tackle it.

Richard arrived in my clinic looking in good health, possibly even slightly younger and certainly more carefree than I remembered from our last meeting. The pallor and darkness under his eyes had vanished and there was a glow to his complexion I hadn't noticed before. I wondered if he'd come straight to the session from 'riding out' (exercising the stables horses), but there were no jodhpurs or any of the sports clothing I was used to seeing him in.

'How's it going, Richard? You're looking well.'

'I'm dangerously well, thank you,' he said, beaming.

'That's excellent news. It's been a few weeks since we last met. I'm just wondering why it's taken us this long to schedule our last meeting.'

'Ah, I thought you'd ask me that. I have some rather big news.'

'Oh, what's that, Richard?'

'I've enrolled in the local art college to do a drawing and painting course. Part-time, one day a week. Keira and Dad aren't too impressed but I don't care. Funnily, my racing form has improved since I began the course three weeks ago. I'm loving it.'

He was in an exceptionally good mood, so I smiled and asked what he was drawing in his art class, bearing in mind that it might be tricky to get his horses into the classroom.

'Sadly, the tutors have asked me not to paint horses for the first few weeks. It's mainly still life – you know bloody fruit or flowers – at the moment, but I'm having a great time. I should have done it years ago. Mum's dead impressed too and wants to see every piece of art I bring home from college. She even mentioned she might come along to a class or two herself. Dad is all "this is a complete waste of time and money", but I've told him it's my time and money, not his.'

I was genuinely impressed with Richard's attitude and was allowing myself to indulge in a little smugness. It's often said that therapy can give clients permission to do the thing they should have done a long time ago. In my work this had cropped up several times. One client said they needed my permission to leave a toxic relationship, another to give up drinking, another to end a career in a sport where he simply wasn't enjoying playing any more. Sometimes clients come to therapy to verify their own thinking, and having another opinion that supports your own can often provide the impetus to take a leap.

The other thing that struck me about Richard's decision was that it demonstrated that he had found his own 'greyscale' between giving up being a jockey on the one hand and painting on the other. It wasn't a case of either/or; he had managed to find resolution in a place of both.

Intriguingly Richard had said little about his relationship with Keira. Throughout our sessions she had often sided with Richard's dad and been dismissive about his desire to pursue a career in art. It's a shame they felt that way, as research into sporting success suggests that if an athlete pursues another sport or outside interest as a hobby it often results in greater success in the primary field of sporting excellence. It's thought that the secondary interest stimulates an area of the brain that enhances rather than detracts from the main sporting focus.

I asked Richard what she felt about his going to college.

'Actually, she's really coming round to the idea. She wasn't that thrilled at first, but since I've been going to college I'm doing better in my races, and also I'm in a much better mood most of the time. She said just the other day that things were certainly less tense around the house.'

'That sounds really positive, Richard,' I told him.

Our final session was ending and both Richard and I expressed in a mildly self-satisfied way that we were happy with what we'd achieved in our time together. An old supervisor once said that in six sessions you can have a good look around the harbour without setting sail to sea. Our time together had a flavour of both. Richard had come with a fear he would never get around Aintree in the Grand National and had ended up at art school. To quote many a football manager, 'That's a result.'

Right at the end I asked if he'd go to Liverpool the following year for the Grand National.

'Yes, I probably will.'

'Really?' I said, a bit puzzled.

'Yes, my tutor suggested drawing a famous building for our end-of-year project.'

'Ah, I see. The iconic grandstand?' I suggested.

'Close,' he said, and winked at me.

Eddie Stamp

A Fond Farewell

My local Costa coffee shop had a drive-through section manned by two slack-jawed teenagers, with two further youthful baristas serving walk-in customers, though both of them seemed determined not to make eye contact with anyone they encountered. After being given my caffè latte, I took a seat at an easy-to-spot table and settled down to wait.

Eddie had asked me to meet him for a 'chat' as he crossed the country for a 'business meeting' and the Costa was on his route. By this stage Eddie's anger management course had been completed and I thought I'd heard the last from him and his football club.

He'd actually asked whether we could have a one-off therapy session among the early-morning caffeine addicts, but I declined and suggested a later time, saying that first thing in the morning the space would be too public for a therapy session. He said he couldn't make it any later as he had to go somewhere, and a visit to my clinic at home was out of the question as he didn't want to have to make a detour, given his time constraints. Frankly, I was a bit confused as to why he had really contacted me.

Eddie had always pushed the boundaries of our therapeutic relationship and this was another example. However long a therapy session lasts, whether it's five or fifty minutes, it needs the client's and the therapist's full attention – a lesson I learned early on in my career when I allowed sessions to go ahead in what were less than ideal circumstances. I've had to end sessions early because I felt the client was too distracted. One tried to convince me he was perfectly happy to have a Zoom video session from a betting shop.

Fifteen minutes later, Eddie turned up, unshaven, wearing a club tracksuit. He said he wanted an 'off the record' chat with me. His attire was hardly the stuff of anonymous meetings and I noticed that other customers had spotted Eddie.

'Sorry, mate,' he gushed as he rushed up to the table where I was sitting. 'The traffic's shite. You've already got yourself a coffee! I was hoping to get here before you so I could get the drinks in.'

I was not in the mood for his seemingly fake contrition and said, 'That might have worked if you were here twenty minutes ago, Eddie.'

He grimaced and raised his hands, palms towards me. 'Bang to rights, Gaz. Let me get myself a coffee and I'll tell you what all this is about.'

Eddie joined the back of a queue of customers, all of whom seemed to want complicated pastry and coffee combinations, but eventually he came back and sat down opposite me. He was now twenty-five minutes late for our meeting. I wasn't doing too well at not feeling impatient with him. I gestured for him to begin.

'Gaz, mate, I need your advice.'

My heart sank. I'd been over the 'I don't give advice' part before with Eddie on a number of occasions. Obviously he hadn't taken much notice and I wondered how much else of what we'd discussed over our sessions, if anything, he had taken in. Eddie went on to tell me that he'd been offered the manager's job at a League Two club and he was on his way to meet the club chairman after this coffee with me. It meant more travelling from his home, but the money and career prospects were better, and he'd have a small budget to buy new players.

'What d'ya think, mate?'

He looked at me expectantly. I noticed the constant use of 'mate'. Eddie's spiky relationship with me could hardly be termed 'matey', so it was rather surprising to now be promoted to this new status.

'It's not my place to give advice, Eddie, especially as I don't understand the running of a football club as well as you would.' I paused and sipped my cooling coffee. 'I would like to ask a couple of questions, though. First, what does your wife think about the move?'

I might well have asked him about the state of the Latvian economy. He looked genuinely stumped by my question. He said nothing.

'Because if you are serious about putting into practice some of the personal changes we've discussed, Eddie, this should be a joint decision. You go off to your new club and she's going to have to shoulder a greater proportion of looking after your lad. If you are going to be a manager and give this job what it deserves, with all those long nights looking at new players, planning training schedules, meetings with players, fans, directors, club staff etc., your wife has certainly got to be on board. Otherwise you're asking for trouble.'

Eddie jumped in now, saying, 'Things have been much better at home since our chats. Things are a lot calmer. And I hear what you say, mate. But I didn't ask you here to tell you I'd been offered a new job.'

'Then why did you ask me to come?'

'The new club wanted to know about our work together. You know, the anger stuff. They were impressed that I'd approached you and was doing all that talking stuff. They brought it up in the job interview. Look, I know I'm being a cheeky bastard here, but they said they might get in touch with you. You know, check I'm "psychologically" fit enough to do the job.'

As Eddie emphasized the word 'psychologically' with air quotes, the mystery of my swift elevation to 'mate' status had just become clear.

'Look, Eddie, I can, with your permission, tell your new club we've worked together as therapist and client, but I won't be able to divulge any details of our work together. It's part of my working practice, I'm afraid.'

I could see he realized he hadn't quite got what he wanted and his anger was rising. He stared at me unblinking and I half expected any moment he'd upend the table and send our coffee mugs flying. When he looked away to check his watch, I decided to push my luck.

'How are you coping with the drinking, Eddie? That concerns me.'

He blinked at me, then his serious face cracked into a cheeky grin. 'Are you asking whether I want another coffee?'

Six days after our meeting and it was Eddie's last game. Press speculation had been rife that a move was imminent. Once again, I found myself watching the Sky Sports coverage of the afternoon's football on the TV. After the final whistles around the country, the presenter announced that Eddie Stamp was changing clubs and had been promoted to the role of manager at a League Two side. I felt a sense of completion in the work. Eddie's new club hadn't been in contact with me to enquire about the psychological work he and I had done together. I'd dodged a bullet.

And that's where the story might have ended, but later that evening, while I was browsing on Twitter, I noticed Eddie Stamp was trending. One of the players had uploaded a video taken in the dressing room following Eddie's last game as assistant manager. I hit the small grey arrow. Players and coaches were congratulating each other after their 2–0 win that afternoon. The camera wobbled slightly before straightening up on Jack's image.

Jack cleared his throat before addressing everyone. 'Lads, lads, you might have seen something in the press and I can now reveal that this was Eddie's last game with us. I just want to thank him for his hard work and loyalty throughout his time with the club and hope that he is successful in his new job. I'm sure the FA haven't seen the last of him, though –' there were jeers and laughter at this point – 'and I pity any poor player who doesn't give him 100 per cent effort.'

More laughter broke out at the end of Jack's speech. I wondered if Eddie was going to say anything, but he didn't seem to be interested. By now he was dressed in 'civvies' – hoodie, jeans and trainers – and was looking impatiently around the room as if he couldn't wait to get out. He was scowling. I could imagine that he felt deeply uncomfortable with the emotional 'gushiness' of the situation. He was closing down.

The team captain moved towards Eddie and extended his

hand, holding a shirt signed by all the players and coaching staff for Eddie to take from him. 'Good luck, Stampy. I'll give you a call.'

Eddie took the shirt briefly before tossing it carelessly on a nearby bench. 'Most of you aren't fit to wear this shirt.' He shook his head. 'I'm out. I fucking hate this place.'

And with that he pulled his holdall over his shoulder and left the room to stunned silence. Eddie Stamp had given the club the only farewell he knew how to.

Mark Silver

Well Known and Alone

Mark sat comfortably in my consulting room. He looked as relaxed as I'd ever seen him and there was a mischievous smile around his lips as he spoke. He seemed to have gained more confidence in recent weeks and was very different from the desolate man who had informed me of the ending of his relationship with Jasmine some months earlier. After some rather unhappy weeks where he seemed dependent on both his brother and our sessions to keep him going, he was now at a stage where he wanted to try and stand on his own two feet.

'So, this is our last session,' he said.

'It is. How do you feel about our work together?'

'I feel great. The question is how I explain my improvement to the other snooker players on the circuit. I can hardly go round telling them my form has improved after seeing a psychotherapist. It's embarrassing. I just tell them I've been working with a performance doctor. They're all dead impressed.'

'How are you managing without Jasmine?'

His face clouded. It had been four months since their

relationship had fallen apart and after several attempts at 'gluing things back together', it had finally disintegrated. Nonetheless, Mark's form had steadily improved. Mark's brother, Jim, had tried to help, moving out and staying with various friends, and had just recently secured a live-in handyman job at a country estate some thirty miles away, but all it had achieved was to leave Mark living alone.

'I'd be telling porkies if I said I didn't miss having her and Jim around, but I have to tell you this – I found out last week. Remember all those times a photographer would just turn up out of the blue to snap us at some swanky club? Well, it turns out it wasn't all in my head, she really had set the whole thing up. Can you believe it? I always had my suspicions, but while I was out with a mate we met up with his mate who works as a freelance snapper [photographer] and the cheeky sod asked me where his next pay cheque was coming from.'

I admitted to being a bit confused.

'Yeah, me too, until he told me she was getting a £100 kickback every time she was snapped with me if the photos were published by a bloody paper! There was me spending eighty quid on our meal out and she'd be making £100 tipping off the snappers.'

I decided to play a straight bat.

'So how are you finding being alone, Mark?'

'Oh, I get a bit lonely at times, but the break from Jaz has given me a chance to breathe. I admit I got a bit narked when I found out she'd started seeing a TV presenter a few weeks after we broke up, but hey, good luck to her.'

'I'm really asking about you, Mark.'

'Well, the most amazing part of it really is my form has returned. I'm certainly drinking less and, as you can see, my new diet is working wonders.' With that he patted his still considerable, but undeniably reduced girth. 'Will have to run around in the shower to get wet soon!' he said, and winked at me.

'I'm really glad the new regime is working. Why do you think your form has improved? Clearly something's going right in your game.'

Mark thought for a moment.

'It's a bit of a mixture of things really. Learning that stuff about me always being in the threat state – you know, always looking over my shoulder and fearing the fella behind me – that's made a big difference. Every time I started a match, I'd think of myself as the challenger and how my opponent is more likely than not to win. Now I think, "Sod him, I'll show him." It gets me into the right frame of mind. Frame – did you see what I did there?' Mark was laughing at his own jokes now.

'You've done well, Mark. The results speak for themselves.'

'You'd have been proud of me last week. I was playing at Ally Pally [Alexandra Palace] when I got hit on by a promotion girl working for the event organizer. I politely declined, had a quiet beer with a few mates in the bar afterwards and was in my pit by 11.30 p.m.'

'Impressive, Mark.'

Hours and hours of therapy work had been undertaken and now it felt to me as if Mark was ready to launch himself into the world alone, not dependent on anyone else's acceptance. I often think that clients such as Mark come to therapy emotionally like children and the therapist's job is to take them through adolescence into adulthood. The actual age of the client is immaterial.

'We've come to the end of the session, Mark. It's time to say goodbye.'

Mark looked reluctant to leave but reached out a hand to shake mine.

'Just one thing,' he said. 'If I need you again one day, will it be OK to contact you?'

'My pleasure, Mark. Any time.'

Jane Lovell

Passing the Baton

I saw Jane for about another six months after her TV work in Paris. In that time, despite her slip of the tongue, she'd been offered more TV work. As a result of her increased visibility in the media, she was picking up more modelling work too, and along with her expanding role as an ambassador for Alan's charity, things couldn't have been more positive for her professionally. But for every action there's an equal and opposite reaction, and as things improved in Jane's working life, domestically they were getting worse.

My sessions with Jane were to help her not take to heart the criticism that was raining down on her from both her father and her husband, with every minor household mishap laid at her door. Through our work together, she learned to tell her father that some decisions were hers and not his, and to back off a bit. But at the same time, she also used his experience to talk through her business opportunities, rather than, to use his expression, 'chasing every five quid like an excited puppy'.

Their relationship began to change from critical parent

(Dad) and naughty avoidant child (Jane) to two adults sharing their love of athletics. To Jane this was like a breath of fresh air. Working with clients, I've found that when we create clear boundaries for ourselves and for others about how we want to be treated, and maintain those boundaries, our sense of self-worth often improves. With Dad no longer able to meddle in her life and with Jane issuing polite but firm reminders when he tried to do so, things between them improved.

Towards the end of our time together, Jane told me she'd been thinking about our sessions. 'Things are so much better. I'm really getting on well with Mum and Dad, and the ambassador role with the charity has opened so many doors. I'm meeting someone from the royal family next week at some gala in London. That sort of thing would have completely thrown me a few months ago. Now it's "Great! Bring it on."'

I asked her how things were at home and her face fell.

'They've gone from bad to worse. My husband and I sleep in separate bedrooms and, other than both looking after our daughter's needs, there's virtually no relationship. He's even given up criticizing me and is spending more and more time away with his mates. He accuses me of having an affair with Alan, and he says things like, "What's good for the goose is good for the gander" and "You'll see, I'll find someone."'

She looked at me with resignation and I asked her if she thought he was looking for another relationship.

'To be honest, I'm almost hoping he does find someone else. At least that would put an end to this constant state of feeling like I'm always in the wrong.'

She looked flat and defeated, but with a deep breath seemed to rally her strength as she continued, 'He often calls me a "stroppy cow" when I answer him back, but I see it more as standing up for myself and not allowing him to browbeat me. It's something I've had to learn to do. Anyway, we were having yet another argument last week when, out of the blue, he suggests couples counselling. At first, I thought he was bluffing, but he mentioned it a few times. What do you think?'

What I thought first was, 'Bloody hell, where's that come from?', then I realized that I actually knew very little about Jane's husband. As with all of my clients, I had only the 'version' they brought into the sessions. This seemed to be another example – it's common in my work – of suddenly having to revise an idea of a third party you've got from the client. Maybe he wasn't as completely unfeeling and insensitive as she had previously implied, and his idea of couples counselling suggested a depth to his thinking that Jane hadn't previously alluded to.

I agreed with Jane's husband. However, one form of therapy should not be mixed and matched with another – it's confusing for clients and the therapists involved wouldn't know which approach was working. I explained that if she decided to pursue couples counselling, we'd have to stop our sessions and she looked downbeat.

'I'll miss our talks,' she said.

'I know, Jane, but you've learned and changed a lot since we began therapy. Couples therapy would have been hard before we did our work, because you may have been beaten down by your husband and agreed to things that might not have worked for you. You're stronger now and can stand up for yourself, and this is an area of your life that needs resolving one way or another. I'm here at the end of your couples counselling if you want to come back. But it's time to sort that bit of your life out.'

Although there had been a massive improvement in Jane's relationship with her dad, and in her ability to be assertive in all her relationships, my job was not to finish the work with Jane but to know and understand what I could and couldn't do to help her. And with that I handed the baton on to another therapist.

Ben Phillips

Keeper of the Faith

I hadn't seen Ben for a couple of weeks when he came back for our next session. The thing I noticed about him immediately was his haircut. Gone was the fringe that covered his eyes (at one stage I'd wondered how he could play in goal without actually seeing the ball!) and, while it wasn't a dramatic haircut, he no longer had to blow his hair out of his eyes to see anything.

As he walked in, there was a more positive bounce in his step and he was wearing an academy club tracksuit for the first time. Did this mean that Ben had truly decided he belonged to the club now that his back pain had subsided? He had a big beaming smile on his face and was keen to start talking.

'I need to tell you about the game at the weekend,' he said.

'Did you win?' I asked, wondering what was bubbling inside him.

'No, we drew and there's a replay in a couple of weeks' time. But that's not it. I want to tell you what happened in the game. We were losing 1–0 with eighty-seven minutes gone.

Their goal was a "worldlie" and to be honest I never got a sniff of the shot. Their number eight biffed it so hard that by the time I'd moved the ball had hit the net. Those ones don't bother me. There was nothing I could do about it.'

I was impressed by Ben's maturity. He had taken on the persona of a professional player being interviewed on national TV.

'Go on . . .'

'Then we got a late corner. I wasn't sure whether or not to go upfield with just a few minutes remaining to see if I could help the team score a goal. I was waiting in my penalty area, when the coach, Toby, tells me to go up. I've never done that before and all I could think of was Keiron and how he used to score loads of goals from corners. Well, Zach, our winger, floats it over and I can see it's heading straight for me. I didn't have to move left or right. It landed straight on my head. I got good contact on the ball, but it's not going in – just wide, you know. But Arthur is there, our centre forward. He can't believe his luck. Unmarked, two yards out, and the goalie nowhere to be seen. He belts the ball over the line, it's 1–1! And then the oddest thing happened. The whole team ran over to mob me.'

'What did Mum and Dad say when they saw you had an assist for the equalizer?'

Ben kept smiling and his response was not what I expected.

'Oh, they weren't there. I didn't tell them, and they didn't ask, and you know what, it was absolutely fine.'

'Sounds like you don't need them to be there.'

'Yeah, well, I can get on all right without them and Keiron. I mean, I don't have to be Ben Phillips, Keiron's little brother, any more, do I?'

'No, you don't, Ben.'

Ben grinned cheekily at me.

Seeing a client, especially one so young and full of potential, transformed in this way is what makes my job worthwhile. The fact that I had believed Ben was experiencing back pain but recognized that it was caused by emotional distress allowed the healing process to begin. His perceived lack of parental attention was replaced by his own feelings of worthiness, so as his pain diminished his emotional distress subsided.

'Mum and Dad still don't know that the back pain's gone. You're not going to tell my mum, are you?'

'No, Ben. It's not my place to tell your truth, but telling the truth is usually a good idea.'

He let out a sigh of relief.

'And you know what? I've asked Toby if I can try out at centre forward for the replay. He told me I was a pain in the arse. Better than being a pain in the back, eh?'

Kwasi Adepodji

Made in Belgium

At precisely thirty seconds after midday Kwasi entered the Zoom call I had arranged. As his image came into view, I was momentarily distracted by the bright purple tracksuit and the unfamiliar badge of the Belgian club he was now back with. He was smiling and had taken his place on an orange sofa in a brightly lit attic space. Even though he was now living in another country, the place screamed 'bachelor pad' and Kwasi looked more relaxed than I had ever seen him face to face. The change of location seemed to be suiting him.

It was a shame this was to be our last counselling session, but his Belgian club had asked Kwasi if they could take over his pastoral care and requested he cut ties with the club he'd been playing for in the UK, where I had worked with him.

'Hey, Kwasi, how's it going?'

'I'm settling in quite nicely, man. Only been a couple of weeks, you know, but really feels like I've never been away. Same shops, same bars, but the club feels a bit different. There's a new assistant manager here and he's working quite hard with me.' Kwasi suddenly snorted. 'You know, I've just discovered my left foot isn't only for walking on! I'm pinging footballs around with my left foot like never before!'

'Sounds like you've no regrets about moving back to your Belgian club, Kwasi.'

'It was all made sweet for me and I even got a small pay rise and these digs. What do you think?'

I smiled at his childlike pleasure in his new surroundings. Kwasi's relatively sudden move had come about as the Belgian club were short of a striker. The next transfer window was weeks away and Kwasi's improved form had caught the attention of their manager. Once Kwasi's UK club had their regular striker back from suspension, the two managers were able to do a speedy deal and Kwasi was on the next plane to Brussels.

'It looks great, Kwasi. Do you live there alone?'

'Ha, ha – no. That's the best thing. The club's signed another Ghanaian player and we're sharing this place.' He was openly grinning now. 'It feels good to know there's someone else from back home here. It's not quite so lonely, you know? We get on great and he's a good player too.'

He looked away for a moment and his mood became more subdued, then he said, 'He knows about what happened in England and says he's gonna make sure I stay on the straight and narrow here!' The grin was back.

Clients often show improvement in therapy because their personal circumstances change. Sometimes it can be a new job or more money, or they begin a new relationship. I believe these 'new things' don't just come about through random accident. It is more likely that the client has moved psychologically to a place where good things can happen to them.

'And what about your mum and dad, Kwasi, do they still want you back home?'

'Ah, things seem to have settled down quite a bit after I returned to Belgium. I scored a goal – just a tap-in really – in my first game back. It made all the papers at home. Suddenly everyone is high-fiving my dad on his brilliant footballer son, so things are a bit better. Since I returned here, I've played three games – started two and came on as a sub in the other. The local newspapers are beginning to say I might get called up to play for Belgium!' Kwasi paused. 'I just wanted to say thank you, man. You've helped me question a lot, and that includes asking the coaches here when I don't under-stand stuff what they're telling me.'

I breathed a sigh of relief.

'I've also really had a good think about what Mum and Dad have said, and about wanting to play football profes-sionally and what it means to me. I've thought how stupid I was doing what I did in the UK at that party. I've had some tough phone calls with them, where we talked about grow-ing up and making my own mistakes and choices.'

'Deep down, I'm sure your parents are very proud of you, Kwasi.'

'Oh, I think they are, but they're struggling to accept a grown-up.'

I smiled. Kwasi had managed to put his finger on the cause of many a parent–young adult conflict. He wouldn't be the last young man struggling with these feelings.

Kwasi turned away from the camera as someone (I am guessing his roommate) entered the room and urged him to hurry up or they'd be late.

'Sorry, man. I've got to go – have a party to get to.'

'Really? What kind of party, Kwasi?'

He laughed, quickly understanding my concern. It was a laugh that I'd not heard from him before.

'Nothing sketchy. Just a birthday party for one of the lads. Thanks for everything.'

And with that he was gone.

Madison King

California Dreamin'

I tried hard not to watch Madison King on TV in her role as a pundit at the Women's World Cup. As I've mentioned in relation to other clients, I fear it could prejudice my therapeutic work to see them doing their everyday jobs.

The aim of therapy is to bring a client's issues to a safe space and any ideas I might have had about Madison's TV performance were best kept well out of the way when she returned. I had mistakenly assumed, though, as she was Scottish, that she would just be used for Scotland's matches, but when I tuned in to watch the favourites, the USA, play in a group match, there was Madison as a pundit. I hit the 'off' button on my remote control.

Madison's players' union had authorized eighteen sessions for our work together. Normally the number isn't so generous, with most players offered between six and ten sessions. But the union saw this as a special case because of the severity of the injury. Her final session was planned for after the tournament in France, but her return date kept moving.

Scotland had gone out at the group stage, but the television company asked her to stay on for the knockout stages of the competition. Madison wasn't expecting this, made a joke in a text to me about running out of clothes and said she'd see me the week after the semi-finals (her last broadcast game).

As I hadn't seen her for a month, I was on the lookout for any obvious changes: facial expression, clothing, demeanour, how she entered the room. My overall impression was that Madison looked confident. She seemed softer, less brittle and maybe less angry than when I had seen her before. I also noticed that she was wearing blue earrings – the first time I had seen her wear earrings in any of our sessions. Sometimes a client will accelerate their improvement in therapy knowing that the final session is coming up, and I had a sense that something had changed. I hoped I would discover what in the next fifty minutes.

Madison was more chatty than usual. She wanted to tell me in detail about her time in Le Havre, where most of her games had taken place. Therapy is about listening hard, listening for the clues buried in the streams of information she was pouring out: the hotel, the terrible plastic food at the football venues, the less than ideal stadium close to the city's docks.

While hearing about her experiences was very interesting, if I wasn't careful our time together would be little more than a verbal picture postcard of the last four weeks of her life. She'd enjoyed the tournament. Met some interesting people. Her symptoms were largely unaltered. She hadn't mentioned Becky once. Those four pieces of information had taken nearly half an hour to reveal. What wasn't she saying?

'Maddy, we've got about twenty-five minutes to go of our last session and I'm just checking that you want to use it to tell me about your time in France. It's great to hear about it all, it really is, but is that why you've come today?'

A look of 'I've been rumbled' came over her face.

'No,' she said. 'There's something I want to ask you. Guess I've been putting it off.'

'What would you like to ask me?'

'I had an unusual offer while I was away. I just don't know what to do.' She shook her head.

I had a horrible feeling that she'd been offered the chance to resume her playing career, with all the dangers that would entail. One more serious blow to her head could permanently disable her. And yet my role as a therapist isn't to offer advice.

'Tell me about your offer, Maddy.'

She explained that while she was away she'd spent quite a lot of time with the USA squad and had befriended a specialist in sports medicine based at Stanford University, California. Madison's new friend, Carly, was on secondment to the national team for the duration of the championships. Apparently, Stanford were involved in some new research involving women who had received traumatic head injuries while playing sport. The women's soccer team at Stanford also had an opening for a new assistant coach. After a flurry of emails and phone calls while Madison was in France, they'd offered her a six-month paid fellowship to be part of their head injury research programme and to coach their women's soccer team at the same time.

'So, what are you unsure of, Maddy?'

If I'd received that offer, I'd be in sunny California already!

'Should I go, of course?' she said.

'I can't answer that, Maddy, it's your choice, but I can ask you what might be stopping you going. I think that's a better way of looking at this.'

She fell silent for a moment, then said, 'I don't know . . . Falling ill, failing, being shit at what I do. Them seeing what a screw-up I am. What if I fail – crash and burn?'

'And what if you don't? What if you fly?'

I let that sink in for a moment, and I saw the competitive look of a sportswoman flash across her face.

'And Becky? How are things going there?'

A slow, sad smile came across Madison's face.

'We've both got some living to do. She'll be just fine.'

Edwin Thomas

Write a Wrong

After his move to coach and play for a rugby union team in the North and his all-too-quick reconciliation with his wife, Cerys, I didn't hear from Edwin Thomas for many months.

I'd occasionally see articles about his club in the rugby sections of the national press, and he seemed to be building rather a negative reputation in his new surroundings. I had the strong impression things were not going too well for him. Headlines like 'THOMAS IN ROW WITH LOCK FORWARD' or 'THOMAS HAS DUST-UP WITH REF AFTER ANOTHER NARROW DEFEAT' seemed to come week after week, and his team was close to bottom of the Premiership table.

I felt sorry for Edwin on some level, because he seemed to be moving backwards in his career. I also wondered how Cerys was coping and whether their marriage was surviving Edwin's controlling tendencies. If Cerys was able to overlook his manipulative personality, then the coaches, officials, players and staff at his new club appeared much less forgiving.

Almost six months to the day since I'd last seen Edwin, he

phoned me out of the blue. I couldn't take the call initially and agreed via text to have a brief chat with him later that day. When we did, his tone suggested we spoke to each other regularly.

'Look, bud,' he began, 'I've got myself into a spot of bother up in this shithole. I need a bit of help, like.'

And there in that one sentence was my issue with Edwin. Entitled, prejudiced and arrogant. My soul shivered. Instead I said, 'Go on . . .'

'Well, I've got involved in a bit of a mess here. I've been having some argy-bargy with a few of the senior players about bonuses, and it all ends up with a row in the dressing room. Anyway, a couple of punches were thrown and I had to get separated from a few of the lads. Nothing too serious, but to cut a long story short, the club seem to think these incidents are happening too frequently. They insisted I see a local psychiatrist, and apparently I now have some sort of "personality disorder". Well, I told him he was talking out of his arse, and that I could provide a letter that proves he's talking utter bollocks.'

'Where are you going to get this letter from, Edwin?'

Edwin chuckled. 'You of course, me old mate. You're the top banana in this field.'

I'm rarely stunned into silence, but here was one occasion when words escaped me. I did manage to ask, 'And what does Cerys think about all this?'

'What does that have to do with anything?'

His words gave proof, if any were needed, of the lack of impact of our work together.

'Well, she's your wife. What was her reaction when you told her what the psychiatrist had said?'

Silence. I tried another tack.

'Have you discussed this with Cerys?'

After a long pause, Edwin admitted he hadn't.

I pushed forward. 'Don't you think Cerys should know what has happened and what the psychiatrist said?'

I felt it was really important that Cerys should be aware that others recognized there was an issue with Edwin.

'Ha, why would I want to tell her anything? Besides, she moved out a month or so back.'

He said these last words so dispassionately, it was as if he was talking about throwing away a pair of old rugby boots.

'Can you tell me how that came about?' I asked him.

'Well, not much to tell really. She was unhappy here and blamed me and moved back to Wales with Mum and Dad. It's that simple. Couldn't cope with the pressure, could she?'

'What pressure, Edwin? What couldn't Cerys cope with?'

'Being a proper wife.'

He was obviously not in a reflective mood, and I was struck by a sense of sadness for Cerys, who had been hoodwinked into moving away from all her support networks and then, when she looked for love and support from the one person who should have been able to provide both in abundance, she found precious little of either.

I didn't know what to say to Edwin that wasn't unprofessional, unkind or unethical. What I felt like saying was, 'You got yourself into this unholy mess, so I suggest you get yourself out of it.' Instead, I said I'd phone him back in a few days.

My supervisor was uncompromising in his assessment of Edwin's reappearance in my life. As usual Tom didn't mince his words.

'Little turd. Who the hell does he think he is? I've got one or two contacts up there in the rugby world as it happens.

Apparently, the club would bankrupt themselves if they sacked Edwin and he knows that. That's probably why he's acting all "Billy Big Balls". Do you think the psychiatrist is right?'

'Come on, Tom, psychiatrists are the highly paid kings of the psychological profession. Do you know the joke about the difference between a psychiatrist and a psychotherapist?'

'No.'

'About 200 quid an hour!'

Tom laughed. 'Very good.'

'The truth is, Tom, I fear the psychiatrist is right. All the signs are there: impulsive behaviour, unstable relationships, difficulty controlling his anger, manipulative, blames others. It certainly passes the "duck test".'

Tom smiled again. 'And that would explain the lack of progress you've managed to make with him. Obviously, you can't write this letter he's after. You and I don't diagnose, we treat, but only those who want to be treated, who want to change.' He took a long slurp of his tea before saying, 'But he's not going to like it when you tell him. I'm just glad I won't be there when you do.'

Tom winked at me.

The next day I phoned Edwin. He sounded relieved to hear from me.

'Ah, bud,' he said. 'All OK with that letter you're going to send me to show my psych up here?'

'I'm sorry, Edwin. I can't do that. As a psychotherapist I don't diagnose things like personality disorders. That's something psychiatrists do. But I can refer you on to a psychiatrist colleague you could have a chat with.'

'What bloody good are you, then?'

And with that, the call and my relationship with Edwin 'Tricky' Thomas were over. Psychotherapy isn't for everyone. He might not have liked the interference of the psychiatrist, but it sounded like, one way or another, Edwin was about to get the help he needed.

James Holmes

Can I Bring the Missus?

Treating children for attachment disorders can be tricky at the best of times, but things become much harder once these thoughts and beliefs form deep patterns in a person's psyche over the course of their lifetime. It can be managed as an adult, but my preferred option is psychological education and, for those with an anxious attachment style, continually reinforcing the message that the individual can cope on their own. These were the issues affecting James, who was transferring his anxiety about his parents on to his new main caregiver, his partner, Annabel.

The cricketers' union had agreed to extend the number of sessions allocated to James, but I'd started to worry that, given his attachment style, if James formed an attachment to me therapeutically it could impact adversely on him when our work eventually came to an end. I thought this fear of getting too close might explain some of his reluctance to being open and engaged in our initial sessions.

My work with James in the cricket off-season (October to February) was making real progress, but our work would soon be coming to end, with just a couple of sessions left to go.

Reviewing my work with him, the majority of it had centred around his ability (or lack of it) to be honest with those who were stakeholders in his life. By being more honest with Annabel on his 'off-days', things began to improve for them as a couple. I encouraged him to tell her when he was feeling vulnerable and needy, and gradually it became a good-natured joke for them – one they could both deal with.

Clients often find it hard to be totally honest with loved ones because they're afraid of the response. They end up telling what I refer to as 'little boy lies' because in essence they're frightened Mummy or Daddy will be cross with them and there is a pathological fear of having to deal with that crossness.

With the new season just around the corner, I helped James be more open with his county team about his ongoing issues and they made it clear they would support him as best they could.

One afternoon in late January, James turned up for his penultimate session with a distinct frown. 'Smiler' definitely wasn't smiling.

'What's the matter, James?'

'The club has announced that we're going on a pre-season warm-weather camp. There's a whisper it's Morocco or possibly a couple of other far-flung places. I want to go, I really do, but I'm bricking it. What if I have another major turn like last year and make a dick of myself?'

'You're a different person from when we first met, James, and after the work we've done, and the fact that you understand why you feel the way you do, I think things will be different for you.'

James wasn't convinced, so I tried again.

'Look, this is now something you have control over. Why not ask the club if you can talk to them about the choice of location? That will make you feel part of the process rather than on the receiving end of it.'

James looked thoughtful, but said no more than, 'We'll see.'

A week later, 'Smiler' was back for his last session, this time looking much more buoyant.

'So, James, are you going away on the warm-weather pre-season tour?'

'You betcha! All set for a week on Saturday. I spoke to the club as we discussed and I have a mate who has a mate who got us in at the Desert Spring Resort in Spain. I can do Spain. The food will be European style and I can cope with it all. It's only going to be for five days. It'll be a breeze. I may even take my golf clubs with me.'

I was purring inside. I'd got James to take control of the situation and there had been a positive outcome. He could feel secure leaving all his loved ones behind and, while away, he could concentrate on his cricket. Who knows, maybe one day he'd win his place back in the England squad.

Just as he left, we had that 'doorknob therapy' moment, when a client who felt unable to tell you something during the session drops a bomb in the room and disappears.

'Thanks for everything,' he said. 'Without you I wouldn't be going on the pre-season tour. Did I mention that the club have allowed Annabel to come with me?'

Final Thoughts . . .

This book gives an insight into my work as a sports psycho-therapist, showing what's really going on for those in the spotlight within sport, and how I attempt to help my clients. As we've seen, the outcomes are more positive in some instances than others – for goalkeeper Ben Phillips as opposed to rugby player Edwin Thomas, for example – but I would never claim that psychotherapy is a magic wand. Success is sometimes about luck, but there's another key ingredient: vulnerability.

As a species, we humans are unique in how slowly our brains develop, making us vulnerable and reliant on caregivers for much longer than other animals. To give just one of a seem-ingly endless list of animals as an example, foals are up on their feet independently within thirty minutes of being born and are able to feed themselves by the age of six months (they can live for about thirty years). A young human, by compari-son, would not be considered self-sufficient until at the earliest thirteen, an age that is recognized in some cultures as mark-ing the transition into adulthood. Despite (hopefully) living into our eighties, we spend much longer in childhood than other animals, which means we're vulnerable for much longer.

Is that a weakness? No. What sets humans apart from other species is how much we are able to thrive as a team – a team of vulnerable individuals forming a successful whole. The ability of an individual adult to be vulnerable, to admit that they need help or that they don't know what they're doing, is a STRENGTH. It can be scary, but having overcome the fear to make that admission, we can harness the thinking, assistance and support of others. It helps us achieve more. As they say, 'You'll Never Walk Alone'.

Sports psychotherapy is about helping people feel strong enough to build real relationships so that they can thrive. But the profession is in its infancy around the world because many sports clubs still believe that sporting excellence and vulnerability are mutually exclusive. Try – as I have – calming down a football manager whose team has just been beaten in a vital match. His instinct is to blame everyone, from his misfiring centre forward to the referee. The damage he does to himself and to his relationships with the players, other coaches and fans when his emotions are out of control can be huge. In that instance, the role of the sports psychotherapist would be to help him channel his energies into more positive outcomes. Rather than pointing the finger, might he be more vulnerable, accepting his own failings and those of his team, so that he can learn from the mistakes rather than compound them – and so his team, and all individuals in it, can perform at their best.

However, in sport players or coaches who don't reach their potential quickly enough are moved on and replacements sought. The thinking 'We've always done it this way so why change?' still pervades.

In football, for example, I find it inexplicable that a club will pay millions of pounds for a player who was a superstar at his previous club, only for them to be sidelined – rather than helped – when they struggle to reproduce that form at the new club. Few ask 'Why?' and 'What can we do to get the best out of our investment?' Think about how Alexis Sánchez struggled in his two years at Manchester United after a stunning career at Arsenal, or how Fernando Torres could never recreate the same magic after his move to Chelsea from Liverpool.

Football is littered with failed transfers such as these, but few have taken the time or made the effort to examine the personal factors that might be involved in a sudden loss of form. Psychotherapy takes time and makes the effort to examine the internal factors that might be impacting on performance. Imagine being suddenly extracted from your home and work, and thrust into a new job and place to live, away from all your friends and family and everything familiar, and expected to just 'get on with it'. Your performance is bound to be affected.

A club needs the interconnectivity of a group of individuals to perform at its best. To achieve that you need to build strong, positive relationships, founded on authenticity and trust. In rugby, for example, the All Blacks have proved that a positive outlook with empathy and kindness can spread throughout a squad and create a winning formula. They have implemented a strict code of behaviour that engenders respect for every layer of the team, starting with the basic premise 'No dickheads'. No matter how good you are, if you can't/ won't conform to the rules and instead undermine them, then there's no place for you in the team. This sense of the team as a collective is now enshrined within their culture.

Conversely, a selfish, negative attitude can have the opposite effect, destroying the sense of 'team' and instead creating a collection of individuals taking the view 'If he isn't trying why should I?' And this is just as true in individual sports, because you don't become the best athlete, tennis player or jockey all by yourself.

Most days for most people, life ticks along OK. We all

have our plans and ambitions, but then sometimes something comes along and trips us up. As Mike Tyson, the former world champion boxer, once said, 'Everyone has a plan until they get punched in the mouth.' What happens when you get punched in the mouth? 'Keeping your head in the game' means realizing when you need help, because now and then you will. It's vitally important to have somebody in your corner, be that a friend, a partner, a parent, a colleague or even a therapist, because they can help you achieve more. Don't be afraid of being vulnerable, as we all need someone to help us up from the canvas.

Acknowledgements

Before I started, I had no idea how many people's help I would need to write this book. This page is a small thank you to all those I owe a huge debt of gratitude to.

First and foremost, I want to thank my partner, Sue, for all her help in just about every aspect of the planning, creation and editing of this book. Sue's daughter warned her mum that working with me on the project would prove the undoing of our relationship. At times she was frighteningly close to the truth!

I also owe a huge thank you to my agent, Nick Walters of David Luxton Associates, and my editor at Penguin Life, Connor Brown. They have taken me step by step along the journey with patience, wisdom and humour.

Massive thanks to my technical editor, Jim Pye, who read and reread my work to check for technical inaccuracies in the world of psychotherapy. There were a few!

I have lost two important figures who helped breathe life into this book, whose deaths hit me hard during the writing process. While all the sportspeople in the book are fictitious, the character of Tom, my supervisor, is based solely on my own supervisor, Nick Luxmoore, who died suddenly towards the end of 2019. He was a massive champion of this book and his death has left a huge hole in my professional life.

I had a whole group of friends reading the chapters as they were being written and one of them, Mark Wilson, my closest friend, died last summer after a long illness. His revisions and suggestions are very much part of the book.

Thanks too to other readers, including Steve Allen, Karen Stowe and Tim May.

I didn't take up all the suggestions I was offered, including 'I think you should take an online writing course.' Ouch!

Many thanks to Oxford United Football Club for being the first – as far as I know – to allow a psychotherapist to work inside the building. Without the club's encouragement this book would not have been possible. I'd like to single out first-team manager, Karl Robinson, and managing director, Niall McWilliams, who have been so supportive during my time with the club.

Finally, I want to say thank you to you for buying this book. I hope you'll find something in these pages that you can use on your own journey. If that's the case for just one reader, then, as they say in the football world, 'That's a result!'